# JUSTICE
## GONE
# HAYWIRE

# JUSTICE
## GONE
# HAYWIRE

## Denise Noe

Black Lyon Publishing, LLC

**JUSTICE GONE HAYWIRE**

Copyright © 2021 by DENISE NOE

This is a work of non-fiction. All direct quotes are either from
recorded interviews, interviews with individuals by local
media at the time or the recollection of the individuals during
interviews with the author of what was said at the time. When
possible, those interviewed reviewed their recollected quotes for
accuracy.

Our books may be ordered through your local bookstore or by
visiting the publisher:

**www.BlackLyonPublishing.com**

Black Lyon Publishing, LLC
PO Box 567
Baker City, OR 97814

ISBN: 978-1-934912-98-0
Library of Congress Control Number: 2021948680

Published and printed in the United States of America.

**Black Lyon True Crime**

## Dedication

*Dedicated to Shanta Mitchell,*
*for being my friend.*

# CONTENTS

# INTRODUCTION

Winston Churchill famously said, "Democracy is the worst form of government except for all the others that have ever been tried." This wry and witty statement could also be made about the American judicial system. The adversary system that we have in this country usually protects the rights of the suspect while also getting justice for the wronged. This author has no quarrel with it. However, like any legal system, it is made up of human beings and subject to human error. The innocent may sometimes be imprisoned and even executed. Mistakes are made. In addition, as I argue in the case of Jonathan Pollard, a sentence can be passed on a guilty defendant that is so disproportionate to the crime that it constitutes justice gone wrong.

Of course, the first case featured in the collection, that of Henry VIII's famous—or infamous—fifth queen was not done under the American judicial system but that of early modern era England. Does the case of Queen Katherine Howard, executed in the 16th century for treasonous adultery, even belong in this collection? I believe it does due to the fact that her guilt is assumed in the popular imagination even though, as I hope I showed in my article, the case for it is far weaker than generally thought.

No system of justice can ever be perfect just as no human being or group of human beings can ever be free of flaws. There will always be odd coincidences, mistaken identifications, and evidence that gets mislaid or misinterpreted. What's more, human memory is notoriously unreliable and subject to change based on fear, hope, and confusion. These factors play a large role in the cases discussed with that of the fallibility of memory given special attention.

Other factors that lead to miscarriages of justice include legitimate societal concerns—and illegitimate common prejudices. These factors are seen in stark form in these cases.

It is the belief of this author that Tudor era fears that a religiously conservative Queen would impede the "reform" of the new Church of England, perhaps even leading to a reconciliation with Rome, may have led to the railroading of Katherine Howard for an adultery that never occurred. At the same time, the popular archetype of the young woman who marries an older and less attractive male but dallies with a younger paramour helped condemn her literally in her own time and figuratively in the centuries since.

Legitimate concerns about the sexual vulnerabilities of young females and their exploitation by powerful male predators played a role in the cases of Roscoe "Fatty" Arbuckle and Leo Frank. Revulsion at violence against women factored into the persecution of the "Scottsboro Boys." The sense that marriage was threatened by the loosening of traditional sexual morals may have played a role in the cases of both Dr. Sam Sheppard and Alice Crimmins. The attention given to the Jean Harris case was partly because many women identified with the story of a woman wronged by a compulsively promiscuous man as well as the special plight of an aging woman finding herself replaced in her man's life by a younger woman. Jonathan Pollard's case brought public attention to the fact that allies spy on each other and aroused fears about America's security.

Prejudices perverting the course of justice can take varied forms. Anti-Semitism was a clear culprit in the lynching of Leo Frank. I believe this bias may also have played a role in the extreme punishment meted out to Jonathan Pollard. White racism looms over the persecution of "The Scottsboro Boys." This case, as I point out in my article, often seemed to plunge into a duel of prejudices based alternately on race, class, and gender or a combination thereof. Indeed, in order to free black men wrongly accused of raping white women, their supporters played upon prejudices against lower-class white women, especially those whose sexual experience was not confined to matrimony.

Less commonly acknowledged prejudices played a role in some of these cases. Prejudice around weight worked against Roscoe "Fatty" Arbuckle with his public image shifting from the jolly fat man to the obese ogre. Anthony Capozzi's schizophrenia may have been a factor in his taking the rap for crimes committed by another man. Prejudice against sexual adventurousness among females together with a stereotype of glamorous women as cold and unmotherly hovered over the prosecution of Alice Crimmins. Although poor people certainly have it worse than the more advantaged, there is the possibility that resentment against the affluent—or those with an appearance of affluence—can bias the public. This sort of bias can be seen in the case of the affluent Dr. Sam Sheppard and the non-affluent Jean Harris who seemed like a "rich bitch" to many because of her mink collars, job as headmistress of an exclusive girls' school, and associations with the likes of lover/victim Dr. Herman Tarnower.

Concerns around gender roles shadowed both the Alice Crimmins and Jean Harris cases, albeit in different ways. The Crimmins case broke at about the same time that the second wave of the feminist movement was gearing up. Although Alice Crimmins was far from a feminist—her obsession with her appearance and femininity epitomized things feminists worked against—her case aroused fears around the "rebelliousness" of modern women. Jean Harris was seen as a long-suffering and faithful woman victimized by the indiscreet and compulsively promiscuous ways of Dr. Herman Tarnower. Middle-aged women identified with her as an older woman traded in for a younger model.

Many social problems are caused by the gap in years between the time young females become fertile, alluring, and sexually curious and the time (if it comes) when they are prepared to become mothers. Luckily, few teen girls who suspect they might be pregnant fake a rape to cover it up but the case of false accuser Cathleen Crowell Webb and the unfairly convicted Gary Dotson is relevant to this greater issue.

Perhaps the most important thing about the cases collected in this volume is that they remind us of how individuals can find themselves trampled under the weight of justice gone haywire.

# CHAPTER ONE

## Queen Katherine Howard: In her Defense

Of Henry VIII's famous six wives, there is no doubt who possesses the worst reputation: fifth wife Katherine Howard. Anne Boleyn may be seen as the "Temptress" but is known as innocent of the adultery and incest charges trumped up to separate Henry from Anne and Anne's head from the rest of her.

As author Antonia Fraser observes, Katherine Howard is viewed as the "Bad Girl," a 16th Century Miss Hot Pants recklessly enjoying premarital dalliances and even more recklessly committing adultery when a queen's adultery was treason.

Modern people may sympathize with a woman who lived in a culture in which losing her head over a man could mean – well, losing her head. However, that sympathy is tempered by viewing Katherine as a shallow, horny, hedonist.

Historian Karen Lindsey accepts Katherine's guilt but attempts a positive spin, seeing "courage to [Katherine's] reckless affair with Culpeper" because she was "a woman who listened to her body's yearnings." Trying to force a 16th Century Queen into a contemporary feminist, Sex Revolution mold does not quite gel.

Some writers, including this one, question Katherine's guilt.

**A New Church and the Battle for its Soul**

To understand Katherine's tragedy, we must review the link between Henry's marital history and his era's religious conflicts. When the Pope refused to annul Henry's marriage to Katherine of Aragon, Henry founded the Church of England of which he was head so he could annul that marriage, enabling him to wed Anne Boleyn. Except for being headed by Henry instead of the Pope, the new church was as Catholic as the Roman Church.

However, many hoped to "Protestanize" the new church. Anne Boleyn herself was among the "reformists." Holy Roman Empire Ambassador Eustace Chapuys derided her as "more Lutheran than Luther himself."

"Conformists" wanted to preserve Catholic ways in the new church and, at best, hoped to reconcile with Rome.

Henry's marriage to Anne Boleyn typifies the old saying, "Be careful what you wish for, you might get it." The king had pursued Anne for years, emotionally devastating the wife he had once loved, scandalizing the world, and breaking with his church and founding a new one to get her. That he had done so very much that was strenuous and painful to get her meant that when he finally got her, she simply could not be fantastic enough to justify his efforts. To make matters worse, the disappointing birth history with Katherine of Aragon repeated itself when Anne had daughter Elizabeth followed by multiple miscarriages. Tired of Anne, disappointed in her, Henry was all-too-eager to trump up charges of adultery—including incestuous adultery with her brother—to rid himself of her.

Thus, Anne Boleyn's execution on May 19, 1536.

Only a child at the time, Katherine Howard must have been proud when her cousin became queen but dismayed by her death in disgrace. However, the rift between England and Rome that Anne triggered also triggered a rift between the Boleyn and Howard wings of the family. The latter were solidly conformist. In *Katherine Howard: A Tudor Conspiracy*, Joanna Denny writes, "[Katherine] lit candles for her dead parents, ate fish on Fridays and said her prayers by rote in the happy assurance that whatever she did would be forgiven in the confessional."

Henry's marriage to Anne Seymour provided an heir but her death after childbirth led to the search for a wife to birth a "spare." Since Henry was a second son, taking the throne after brother Arthur's death, he knew the importance of an extra.

Reformists tasted triumph when Henry agreed to marry Anne of Cleves who hailed from the Protestant German state of Cleves. They were certain a Protestant Queen would exclude reunion with Rome as well as mean that the English Church would be open to becoming more Protestant in its beliefs and practices. They were undoubtedly crushed when Henry found her so repulsive he could not even consummate their marriage.

After ridiculing Anne as a "great Flanders mare," Henry's eye was caught by one of her ladies-in-waiting: petite, graceful, fair-haired Katherine Howard.

Perhaps her tender age was a strong attraction. Denny argues, "The anonymous Chronicle of Henry VIII reports Katherine was 15 when she first met the King in late 1539, making her year of birth 1524 or 1525." Denny elaborates that the traditional view that Katherine was born in 1520 or 1521 was based on a French Ambassador's "guesswork." Contemporary observers frequently mentioned her "youth" which supports the later date as they would be unlikely to comment on it had she been older than that date suggests. Conformists hoped the religiously conservative Katherine would influence Henry to hold the line against Protestant tendencies and perhaps even bring him back under the Pope.

Henry married Katherine on July 28, 1540.

## A Caring Queen

Graciousness and compassion characterized Katherine's Queenship. The discarded Anne of Cleves visited the newly-weds and knelt before Katherine—who lifted her up. When Anne rose, Henry hugged and kissed his "sister" before they dined. Katherine and Anne danced together. Katherine gifted Anne with two small dogs and a ring.

Katherine took a protective interest in cousin Anne

Boleyn's daughter, seven-year-old Elizabeth, playing with the child and giving her trinkets.

Although Katherine and Mary Tudor shared religious persuasions, there were reports of early tension between them. It had apparently dissipated by May 1541 when Katherine approved Henry's granting permission for Mary to live at court.

In *Men of Power: Court Intrigue in the Life of Catherine Howard*, Elisabeth Wheeler writes that Katherine "sent warm clothing" to elderly Lady Salisbury Margaret Pole, imprisoned for treason for Papist sympathies. However, Katherine could not persuade Henry to pardon Salisbury who was later executed.

Denny writes, "In February [1541] [Katherine] intervened in the case of Sir Edmund Knyvet, who was involved in a quarrel with Thomas Clere." Clere was injured and Knyvet sentenced to have a hand amputated. Henry approved the sentence. Katherine begged him to withdraw that approval. He did—just in time. A terrified Sir Edmund learned of the clemency just before his hand was to be severed.

Sir Thomas Wyatt was another beneficiary of Katherine's kindness. An informer reported Wyatt had made treasonable statements. Thrown into the Tower, a baffled Wyatt said he had no idea "whereby a malicious enemy might take advantage by evil interpretation." Even though he was a reformist, the conformist Queen helped him. Chapuys wrote that Henry and Katherine "passed through London by the Thames [and] the people gave her a splendid reception, and the Tower guns saluted her. From this triumphal march she took occasion to ask the release of Wyatt." Henry pardoned Wyatt. Katherine also successfully persuaded Henry to pardon suspected traitor Sir John Gallop and suspected felon Helen Page.

On November 1, 1541, All Saints Day, Henry ordered churches to offer special prayers of thanksgiving for Katherine, his "jewel of womanhood" and "the good life he led and trusted to lead" with her.

## Ominous Allegations

Only days after this victory, Cranmer left a note with allegations that Katherine had engaged in pre-marital sexual activities in Henry's private pew. Henry turned pale as he read the allegation that Katherine had enjoyed two lovers in her youth. While not treasonous, having occurred before they married, her lack of chastity would be enough for Henry to want out of the marriage. Cranmer's letter stated that courtier John Lascelles had learned of Katherine's youthful indiscretions from his sister Mary Hall, who had lived at Norfolk House with Katherine under the guidance of Katherine's step-grandmother Dowager Duchess of Norfolk Agnes Tilney.

Henry put Cranmer in charge of an investigation. Cranmer soon informed Henry that not only had Katherine enjoyed pre-marital dalliance but she had committed adultery. The last charge was extremely serious as a queen who had sexual intercourse with a man other than the king risked getting pregnant with a child who was unqualified to inherit the throne and, therefore, to put on the throne someone who did not belong there. Thus, adultery by a queen was treason and punishable by death as was committing adultery with her.

Norah Lofts writes in Queens of England that, only days after publicly thanking God for Katherine, Henry "was accepting—in a passion of tears—some far from conclusive evidence of her infidelity." Lofts continues that Henry "wept when told what gossip was saying; yet, although they were still under the same roof, he made no attempt to face his wife with the rumors or to hear what she had to say; he simply hurried away from Hampton Court, leaving everything to Archbishop Cranmer who [was] prejudiced against Catherine on account of her religion."

Indeed, Henry should have suspected at least the possibility of a reformist plot. John Lascelles, who had supposedly first informed Cranmer of Katherine's misdeed, was so strongly reformist that he would be burned to death during Mary Tudor's reign—as would Cranmer.

### "No More the Time to Dance"

Katherine was practicing dance steps in her Hampton Court Palace chambers when a door burst open. Guards told her, "It is no more the time to dance." Then they arrested her and ordered her to stay in the chambers. She asked to see Henry but was denied.

Katherine's alleged "paramours" were Henry Manox and Francis Dereham before marriage; Thomas Culpeper after it.

In 1536, Henry Manox tutored Katherine in music. In 1538, Francis Dereham, employed by Katherine's uncle, Thomas Howard, Duke of Norfolk, to conduct business, frequently visited Dowager Duchess of Norfolk Agnes Tilney's residence. In August 1541, Queen Katherine had appointed Dereham usher to her chamber.

Thomas Culpeper, a Gentleman of the King's Privy Chamber and distant cousin to Katherine, was charged as her adulterous partner. There are reports Culpeper once raped a park-keeper's wife, murdered a villager who attempted a rescue, and was pardoned by Henry for these brutal crimes. However, in Wicked Women of Tudor England, Retha M. Warnicke notes that this story is suspect, being based on "an unverifiable rumor" that a Tudor contemporary named Richard Hilles reported in a letter months after Culpeper's execution.

A series of interrogations were made of Katherine, the other suspects, and various "witnesses."

More than one problem exists with the "confessions" and "evidence" assembled. The "confessions" could be unreliable because possibly extracted under torture; both the confessions and the "evidence" could have been manufactured.

However, even as given, much is susceptible to less sinister interpretations—at least regarding Katherine—than usually placed on them. For example, Cranmer reported Katherine confessing: "At the flattering and fair persuasions of Manox, being but a young girl, I suffered him … to handle and touch the secret parts of my body." This would have been in 1536—when Katherine was 11 or 12. It would not make her a "delinquent" but a molested child. Manox is recorded as telling interrogators that he stroked Katherine's genitals, admitting she was reluctant but claiming she was "content" to permit it. If this did happen, it is more likely she was unable to effectively resist as the era was one in which molested children were often blamed and shamed.

Interrogators claimed Dereham admitted sexual intercourse with Katherine before her marriage but said he and Katherine were "pre-contracted" in marriage. In those days, saying you were married and consummating it through intercourse made you married. Katherine is recorded as saying, "Francis Dereham by many persuasions procured me to his vicious purpose and obtained first to lie upon my bed with his doublet and hose … and finally he lay with me naked and used me in such sort as a man doth his wife many and sundry times." She was 12 or 13, either not yet or just barely a teenager. Cranmer reported Katherine insisted Dereham used "force" and "violence" and she never willingly had sex with him. That Katherine appointed Dereham usher does not mean she could not have been raped by him; the knowledge she was not a virgin meant a potential for blackmail, making her beholden to her rapist.

Cranmer also said Katherine adamantly denied a pre-contract. Historians have been baffled by this denial since it could have annulled her marriage to Henry and saved her life. Some have thought she was too stupid or too upset to realize the escape offered; Denny ascribes her denial to "pride."

Lofts suggests Katherine showed "integrity" in her "refusal to take the easy way out which a previous marital arrangement with Dereham offered." Warnicke observes, "The church required a [marriage] vow be freely given and not coerced." Katherine may not have considered herself pre-contracted if Dereham raped her. Warnicke elaborates, "[Katherine's] denial was consistent with the claim that Dereham forced his attentions upon her."

Indeed, Katherine sounds principled when asserting, "I am innocent of all charges and will never admit to these lies. If there is any ground of truth in these statements, then it is because of childish ignorance and the evil companions with whom I was formerly surrounded. I also seek to state that I am faithful to the King and would never wish harm upon him. I will seek his mercy but not by admitting to these treacherous lies."

Cranmer reported Katherine admitted meeting with Culpeper but insisted Culpeper touched no part of her body other than her hand and that Katherine's Chief of Privy Chamber, Jane Parker, Lady Rochford, had always been present. Katherine also said she had told Jane, "I pray you, bid him desire no more to trouble me or send to me."

Jane contributed to the tragedy suffered by Katherine's cousin, Anne Boleyn. From the strongly Catholic Parker family, Jane probably resented Anne Boleyn's role in England's break with Rome. The Parkers supported Katherine of Aragon and Princess Mary after Anne became Queen. Anne sent Jane from court in 1534. In the trial of Anne, Jane testified that her husband, Anne's brother George Boleyn, had committed incest with his sister, helping ensure their executions.

Although Dereham denied relations with Katherine after she was Queen, interrogators extracted a "recollection" from his friend Robert Davenport that Dereham once remarked, "If the King were dead I am sure I might marry [Katherine]." A recently passed law made it treason to "maliciously wish, will or desire by words or writing" harm or death to the King so that was enough to execute Dereham. Lofts observes that the "recollection" is suspect since interrogators knocked out Davenport's teeth to get it!

Katherine was taken to Syon Abbey and incarcerated in a sparsely furnished room. On November 24, a formal indictment was issued against Katherine for leading "an abominable, base, carnal, voluptuous, and vicious life."

While Culpeper denied sex, he supposedly admitted intending "to do ill with her," also sufficient for execution. Culpeper's room at court was searched. Investigators said they found a letter from Katherine in that room. The letter was taken as proof of treasonous adultery.

Katherine has been damned as an adulteress in many eyes by it.

*Master Culpepper, I heartily recommend me unto you, praying you to send me word how that you do. It was showed me that you was sick, the which thing troubled me very much till such time that I hear from you praying you to send me word how that you do, for I never longed so much for [a] thing as I do to see you and to speak with you, the which I trust shall be shortly now. The which doth comfortly me very much when I think of it, and when I think again that you shall depart from me again it makes my heart to die to think what fortune I have that I cannot be always in your company. It my trust is always in you that you will be as you have promised me, and in that hope I trust upon still, praying you that you will come when my Lady Rochford is here for then I shall be best at leisure to be at your commandment, thanking you for that you have promised me to be good unto that poor fellow my man which is one of the griefs that I do feel to depart from him for then I do know no one that I dare trust to send to you, and therefore I pray you take him to with you that I may sometime hear from you one thing. I pray you to give me a horse for my man for I have much ado to get one and therefore I pray send me one by him in so doing I am as I said afor, and thus I take my leave of your, trusting to see you shortly again and I would you were with me now that you might see what pain I take in writing to you.*

*Yours as long as life endures,*
*Katherine*

*One thing I had forgotten and that is to instruct my man to tarry here with me still for he says whatsomever you bid him he will do it.*

A love letter? Maybe not. Warnicke notes that the beginning, "Master Culpeper," is "quite abrupt" since "Cupeper was a knight and a member of the privy chamber and thus deserved a title." Lady Lisle wrote a 1537 letter to him beginning "Good Master Culpeper." Warnicke writes that Katherine's sympathy with him about a recent illness may have been an attempt to "placate him with politeness." Warnicke reports that phrases such as "at your commandment" were part of the "elaborate contemporary formula of letter-writing." Culpeper had used that exact phrase in a letter to Lady Lisle—and no one has suggested they enjoyed a romance.

The sign-off may not indicate intimacy. Warnicke observes that "Yours" was a standard sign off. In letters to Cromwell, Mary Tudor signed off "Your loving, assured friend during my life" and Elizabeth, Duchess of Norfolk, signed off "By yours most bounden during my life." Neither woman was suspected of intimacy with Cromwell. Warnicke believes the word "endures" indicates tension. Warnicke writes, "The two items on the fearful queen's agenda were that she desperately wanted to speak with Culpeper and learn whether he would keep his promise to her." Warnicke believes Culpeper was blackmailing Katherine with knowledge of her having not been a virgin at her marriage and that he may have been sexually harassing Katherine.

### A Plot To Take Down A Queen

Ten years of research led writer Elisabeth Wheeler to conclude that Katherine was the victim of a plot in which "reformists Cranmer, [Thomas] Audley, and [Charles] Suffolk" sought to bring her down. Wheeler found it "necessary to dismiss the gathered evidence against Catherine and look instead at the interrogators themselves." Wheeler believes that having a devoutly conformist queen was "an unthinkable blow to the reformists." In addition, there was much resentment against the Howard family which many saw as overly ambitious and proud. Commitment to religious reform and dislike of the Howards led powerful men around Henry to plot against Katherine. Wheeler believes reformists need "to get rid of [Katherine] before a male heir would be born."

Wheeler also believes Henry himself was a victim of "a diabolical plot by his inner cabinet to deprive him of his queen and the chance to provide sufficient male heirs for the security of the realm."

It is also possible that, as Wheeler believes, Katherine's interrogators created "a faked and forced confession."

Wheeler also suggests that the supposed "love letter" from Katherine to Culpeper, may have been forged. In Wheeler's judgment, the "first eight words" of that epistle are "written in a different hand, in a small neat script" distinct from the rest.

Men of Power makes a strong case that reformists sought to destroy a possible threat and that neither "confessions" nor "evidence" should be taken seriously.

## Belated Fairness for the Fifth Queen

Unlike Anne Boleyn, Katherine Howard was allowed no public trial. Perhaps the reason for this is that Anne answered the charges so astutely. Thus, Katherine was not allowed the same chance.

It may be that Katherine Howard was the victim of child molestation and rape when young; of sexual harassment and blackmail when queen. It may also be that her supposed partners were also innocent and, like her, victims of a plot to take down a possible threat to the Privy Council reformists. In either case, she was unfairly judged and that unfairness continues to this day.

The general perception of Queen Katherine Howard renders her death a matter given little weight. Someone as giddy, reckless, and utterly irresponsible as she is often considered would be unlikely to accomplish much even had she lived a normal lifespan. Hopefully, this story will lead at least some readers to a more positive view of her character, to see her as compassionate, and to consider the possibility that she was falsely accused. If some readers see her execution as a genuine tragedy, this story has accomplished its purpose.

## Bibliography

"Catherine Howard." http://englishhistory.net/tudor/monarchs/howard.html#BBiography.

"Catherine Howard." http://www.tudorplace.com.ar/about-CatherineHoward.htm.

Denny, Joanna. *Katherine Howard: A Tudor Conspiracy.* Portrait, an imprint of Piatkus Books. Ltd. 2005.

Lindsey, Karen. "Historical Controversies about Katherine Howard." http://www.thetudorswiki.com/page/Katherine+Howard+Controversies.

Lofts, Norah. *Queens of England.* Doubleday & Company, Inc. 1977.

"The Blessed Margaret Pole, Countess of Salisbury, Martyr – 1473?-1541." http://www.ewtn.com/library/MARY/MARG-POLE.htm.

Warnicke, Retha M. *Wicked Women of Tudor England: Queens, Aristocrats, Commoners.* Palgrave MacMillan. 2012.

Wheeler, Elisabeth. *Men of Power: Court Intrigue in the Life of Catherine Howard.* Martin Wheeler. 2009.

# CHAPTER TWO

## Roscoe "Fatty" Arbuckle

Roscoe Conkling "Fatty" Arbuckle would not do comedy in which his weight was used to get a cheap, easy laugh. For example, he refused to be seen stuck in a chair or doorway.

Of course, while his weight inevitably added to the humor he did use, he was too gifted of a comedian to need to provoke laughter simply at his being fat. In the silent film era, he was considered second only to Charlie Chaplin in his talent. Arbuckle was one of nine children. Born on March 24, 1887, in Smith Center, Kansas, he would joke, "Two big things blew Smith Center, Kansas right off the map—my birth and a cyclone. No one has heard of the place since." His weight at birth has been reported as either 14 or 16 pounds. His family moved to California when he was only one year old.

The life of the Arbuckle family was not happy. Roscoe's father, the hard-drinking William Goodrich Arbuckle, named his son after a Republican politician, Roscoe Conkling. Perhaps the name he affixed to the boy was a bad omen since William Goodrich Arbuckle was not a member of the GOP but a Democrat. Dad blamed the boy's birth for his mother's health problems and was also nagged by a sneaking suspicion that this son was not biologically his. He often punished the boy unreasonably. One of the reasons the elder Arbuckle suspected he had not sired the boy was that Roscoe was so heavy while both his parents were slender. Since Roscoe's mother was a devout, pious Christian, the suspicion was probably unfounded. However, religious people have been known to slip and the old saying, "Mama's baby, Daddy's maybe" has much truth in it.

Other children often made fun of little Roscoe's weight, taunting him as "fatty." As a result of being bullied, Roscoe became a shy, tongue-tied child. He was self-conscious about his size but he had a strong appetite for food and coped with emotional trauma through eating. As happens so frequently, this became a vicious circle in which he was emotionally wounded by others' jeer, comforted himself by overeating, which increased both his weight and painful ostracism from others.

However, the boy soon found that his shyness and self-consciousness seemed to magically melt away when he was performing in front of an audience. Roscoe could sing beautifully and was remarkably limber and agile despite his size.

Arbuckle made his stage debut at the age of 8. From then on, the blue-eyed, exuberant youngster saw a lot of the theater. The multitalented young boy worked as a clown, a singer, and in acrobatic acts.

His mother died in 1899 when he was only 12. Shortly after that, the father who had both emotionally rejected him and physically abused him, abandoned the boy. The teenager supported himself by doing odd jobs in a San Jose hotel. He sang while he worked. On one lucky day a professional singer overheard him and was impressed. She suggested he accompany her to an amateur night at a neighborhood theater. This theater was of the type where a long hook would come out to draw a performer who was not doing well off the stage. The humiliation of such a dramatic rejection terrified young Arbuckle but he made up his mind that he was going to perform and do well. He sang a couple of songs and then started entertaining the audience with a variety of jigs, somersaults and pratfalls. The hook came out from the wing and a panicked Arbuckle jumped and somersaulted out of its way until he finally dived into the orchestra pit.

The audience was delighted and he easily won the contest—and the attention of some important people in show business.

In 1904, the young Arbuckle sang for Sid Grauman at the Unique Theater in San Jose. He was what was called an "illustrated singer." As described in David Yallop's The Day the Laughter Stopped, an illustrated singer was one who sang "while gorgeously-colored slides with the lyrics were projected on a screen … thereby 'illustrating' the song."

During 1905, Arbuckle began a tour of the West Coast with the Pantages circuit. In 1906, the performer was in Portland, Oregon when he was hired by a man named Leon Errol to work in the Orpheum Theater. Then Arbuckle began another tour with Errol's company.

Arbuckle performed at the Last Chance Saloon, a watering hole for miners in Butte, Montana. Their resident singer was a popular, buxom blonde named Lilly. She usually opened the show but one day she did not appear, probably because she drank heavily and was on a bender. The miners became raucous when Arbuckle was put onstage in her stead. They gave him the finger and loudly threatened to tear the place apart.

The comedian had a brainstorm. He dashed to Lily's dressing room. The audience was still restive but soon calmed down considerably when Lily's unexpected replacement strolled onto the stage. She was a very large, well-dressed woman. As she sang, the miners were entranced by her lovely, soprano voice. The new singer became an instant hit. The next night and the next the Last Chance Saloon was more packed than ever. But on that night, a semi-sober Lilly walked in and saw the women onstage who had taken her place. She was outraged. She ran onto the stage and tore her wig off Roscoe Arbuckle's head. The comedian in drag pretended to be scared and ran into the chairs and tables as she followed. As Yallop wrote, "The miners, convinced that the whole things was a superbly-rehearsed piece of comedy, howled with laughter as Roscoe, with Lilly in hot pursuit, jumped over tables, swung on lamps, did cartwheels and pratfalls, and finally vanished into the street."

However, the next day Errol's company left Butte. Lilly had too much clout to allow the cross-dresser usurper to rival her.

## Show Biz Success

Arbuckle was back in California in 1909 when he got a part in a movie called Ben's Kid. Unfortunately, young Arbuckle was not proud of this achievement. He was positively embarrassed about it and did not tell anyone he knew about his role. These were days when stage actors were looked on as less than respectable and those in the young film industry were even more suspect. Boardinghouses often had signs warning NO DOGS OR ACTORS ALLOWED.

Arbuckle matured into a strikingly fastidious man. He always kept himself clean and neat. Perhaps this was partly a reaction to his poverty-stricken and sometimes squalid childhood or to the prejudicial "fat slob" stereotype. He also disliked swearing. Although he would be known as Fatty to audiences, he never allowed his friends to call him that. If they slipped, he would remind them, "My name is Roscoe."

1909 was an important year for Roscoe Arbuckle. He married singer Minta Durfee, whom he usually called "Minty." At their wedding reception, guests teased the couple about the wedding night and how Roscoe's fat body would do against Minta's petite one.

That night he was unable to consummate their marriage. "Minty," he said, "I can't." He was not a virgin but had had a single sexual encounter with a showgirl. However, the jeering of his friends left him feeling awkward and embarrassed. The couple slept in the same bed without having sex but hugging each other tight in their love. About a week passed before he felt comfortable enough to engage in sexual relations.

Soon Arbuckle joined up with the Morosco Burbank stock company. He traveled through China and Japan with Ferris Hartman. Minta accompanied him on his travels. Sometimes she saw a side of him she did not like. He took to drinking with the other guys and, like his father before him, booze caused a negative change in his personality. When drunk he was sullen, nasty, and argumentative, although never physically violent. In 1913, he made his last appearance on the stage in Yokahama, Japan.

Upon returning to the states, also in 1913, he went to work at Mack Sennett's studio, Keystone. There he appeared in hundreds of one-reel comedies. Usually he was a policeman with the famous *Keystone Cops*. Henry "Pathé" Lehrman directed most of the pictures in which Arbuckle appeared. Arbuckle became the very first actor in films to take a pie in the face when he made *A Noise from the Deep*. The agile actor threw pies as well and was able to accomplish the remarkable feat of tossing two pies in opposite directions at the same time. Actors Arbuckle worked with included such greats Charlie Chaplin, Mabel Normand, and Fred Sterling.

In 1914, Arbuckle began directing some of the films in which he acted. The next year, he moved from one-reelers to two-reelers and proved that he could sustain his comedy.

Mabel Normand was called "The Queen of Comedy" and "The Female Chaplin." She and Roscoe paired up regularly in such movies as *Mabel, Fatty and the Law, Mabel and Fatty's Wash Day,* and *Mable and Fatty Viewing the World's Fair at San Francisco.* For the last motion picture, the actors and crew traveled to the actual World's Fair that was going on in San Francisco in 1915.

Late in 1916, Arbuckle made a deal with Joseph Schenck. Arbuckle signed a contract giving him $1,000 per day plus 25% of the profits. He also had the last word on the creative end.

That same year saw the comedian face a health crisis. He had a carbuncle on his leg. It was so bad that the doctors thought for a while that they might have to amputate his leg. Luckily, he did not lose a limb but the sickness made the heavy man lose 80 pounds. Given morphine to ease the intense physical pain, he became addicted. But he was able to wean himself off narcotics without the relapse that so often plagues those who are psychologically rather than, as Arbuckle was, just physically dependent upon them.

In 1917, Arbuckle partnered up with Joseph Schenck, Norma Talmadge's husband, to form a film company called

Comique. Arbuckle wanted more creative control over his work and this gave it to him.

He soon hired a young performer named Buster Keaton who would become a leading light in the world of comedy. Roscoe and Keaton would star in 1917 in *The Butcher Boy.*

However, professional glory was marred by personal trauma. He and Minta were having trouble in their marriage. Arbuckle would not give up his Prohibition booze. They separated in 1917. Interestingly, and ironically in view of later events, most familiar with Arbuckle's life believe he was never unfaithful to Minty, even after they separated. Yallop wrote, "Arbuckle may have been the most chaste man in Hollywood."

Continuing to make Comique films, Arbuckle turned out some of the greatest classics of the silent era. They include movies like *Coney Island, Goodnight Nurse!* and *The Garage.* As far as his films went, it seemed like Roscoe "Fatty" Arbuckle could only get better. Eventually, Arbuckle relinquished control of Comique to Keaton and signed with Paramount after being offered a cool $1,000,000 per year.

In 1919, Paramount asked him to move from two-reel films to feature movies. That studio also wanted him to make films at a much faster clip than he was usual and his work suffered as a result. However, movies like *Brewster's Millions* in 1920 and *Gasoline Gus* in 1921 are very worthwhile comedies. Arbuckle was making about six motion pictures per year and at one point working on three different films at one time. He was understandably exhausted and decided to take a three-day vacation in San Francisco with his friend, director Fred Fischbach.

Before the trip, Arbuckle suffered a burn to his backside. There are two different accounts of how he was burned. According to Andy Edmonds in *Frame-Up!* Arbuckle asked a mechanic to take a look at his luxurious Pierce-Arrow. While his car was getting a check-up, Arbuckle sat down on an old crate. "Owwwwww!" he shrieked, jumping up instantly. He had sat down on an acid-soaked rag. In that brief moment, the acid had burned through his pants and caused him second-degree burns.

In David Yallop's *The Day the Laughter Stopped*, "He had backed into a hot stove."

In any case, he was injured. The trip had to be called off, Arbuckle decided. He was in too much pain. He called up Fischbach to tell him that they couldn't take their little vacation as planned. Fischbach exploded. He was looking forward to this trip. Arbuckle had to make it.

"I can't sit very long because of the burns," the comedian told him.

Yes he could if he really wanted to, the director insisted.

Arbuckle decided to try to make it anyway because his buddy wanted the trip so badly. "I'll put some cases of booze from my cellar in the trunk," Arbuckle told Fischbach.

"Don't do that," Fischbach retorted. "You don't want to travel with bootleg booze in your car. In case we get stopped, we'll be clean. Let me take care of everything when we get to 'Frisco. I've got connections."

So Arbuckle, Fischbach, and actor Lowell Sherman got in the entertainer's Pierce-Arrow for the ride to San Francisco. Arbuckle was at the wheel. After driving for several hours, Arbuckle complained about the pain he was in. The group stopped at a store and bought a rubber ring for him to sit on that gave him some relief.

The group rented three adjoining rooms, 1219, 1220, and 1221, at the St. Francis hotel. 1219 was Fischbach and Arbuckle's room; 1220 was the party room; and 1221 was Sherman's room.

There, on Labor Day, September 5, 1921, disaster struck.

## Tragic Virginia

In some accounts, Arbuckle was the host of the party in 1220 of the St. Francis hotel. In others, his roommate, the director Fred Fischbach, was.

One of those present was a young actress named Virginia Rappe. Born Virginia Rapp, she had changed her last name to Rappe because she thought it sounded "more elegant." The name, of course, has an unfortunate and ironic resemblance to the word "rape."

Rappe's background was sad. She had been born out of wedlock at a time when "illegitimate" was a dirty word. Her mother, Mabel Rapp, lived in Chicago but moved to New York when pregnant to hide her "shame" from those closest to her. Mabel died when Virginia was only 11. Then Virginia went to Chicago so her grandmother could take over the raising of her.

She grew into a strikingly lovely young woman with thick dark hair. She also grew up much too fast. The yellow journalism accounts that dogged Arbuckle tended to depict Virginia Rappe as a kind of latter-day Snow White so some modern authors, in their defenses of the comedian, have made her out to be a kind of Venus Flytrap. The truth is probably that her childhood was unstable and lonely and the lack of a father figure in her early years caused the heterosexually oriented girl to crave relationships with men. In those days when contraception was anything but reliable, she suffered the consequences.

It is believed that she had five illegal abortions by the age of 16. She had also suffered bouts of venereal disease. At the age of 17, she gave birth to an out-of-wedlock child. Wisely reasoning that she was not equipped to raise the child herself, she put it into foster care.

Rappe's good looks led to a modeling career in her teens. She soon became well known for her excellent fashion sense. She moved to San Francisco where she worked as an artist's model. There are reports that the slender, shapely young woman sometimes modeled in the nude. She met a dress designer named Robert Moscovitz. The couple began dating, got serious, and became engaged but Moscovitz was killed in a trolley-car accident before they could wed.

Crushed psychologically and financially, Rappe moved to Los Angeles where an aunt of hers was living. She moved in with her Aunt Leora Deltag.

In 1917, Virginian met director Henry "Pathé" Lehrman whom she began dating. She also started getting work in motion pictures. Her parts were small and sometimes uncredited. Perhaps her greatest triumph was being awarded the title "Best Dressed Girl in Pictures" in 1918 and having her photo appear on the cover of several sheet-music scores. The best known of these would be *Let Me Call You Sweetheart.*

The career of Virginia Rappe did not take off like gangbusters and she did not earn a lot of money through it. There were rumors that she dabbled in prostitution to pay her bills.

She was doing well enough, however, that newspapers and movie magazines interviewed her. In one of these interviews she discussed a meeting with Roscoe Arbuckle. She called him "disgusting and crude … vulgar and disrespectful of women."

However, Andy Edmonds, author of *Frame-Up!*, believes that the young actress said this because her boyfriend Lehrman had a long-running feud with Arbuckle. Her negative comments do not accord with those of other women who knew the comedian as a dapper and polite gentleman.

Alcohol seemed to bring out a bizarre side of Virginia Rappe. Journalist Adela Rogers St. Johns said, "The day after Fatty had been indicted … the man who did my cleaning came to me and told me: 'I did Virginia Rappe's cleaning. I see where one side says she was a sweet young girl and Mr. Arbuckle dragged her into the bedroom. Well, once I went in her house to hang up some cleaning and the first thing I knew she'd torn off her dress and was running outdoors yelling, 'Save me, a man attacked me.' … The neighbors told me whenever she got a few drinks she did that."

Lehrman and Rappe apparently had a troubled relationship. They would break up, reconcile and then break up again. The two were also suspected of having venereal disease by Mack Sennett and ordered to leave a Keystone lot because of that. Of course, venereal diseases are not spread through casual contact but apparently Mack Sennett was ignorant and superstitious about them because he had the lot fumigated! Then again, some people have said the couple had lice and that is far more easily spread and can be transmitted through shared towels and sheets.

At any rate, Lehrman starred Rappe in a 1920 motion picture called *A Twilight Baby*. Shortly after that film was made, the couple broke up. Some people close to Rappe believe she was pregnant by Lehrman and seeking an abortion when she headed up to San Francisco on the fateful Labor Day weekend of 1921.

## The "Wild Party"

Sources differ on whether or not Virginia was invited to the party or crashed it along with her manager, Al Semnacher, and a woman accompanying them named Bambina Maude Delmont. Delmont had many run-ins with the police. She had been charged with extortion, bigamy, fraud, and racketeering. In *Frame-Up!*, Edmonds writes that Delmont was "a professional co-respondent: a woman hired to provide compromising pictures to use in divorce cases or for more unscrupulous purposes such as blackmail."

Seeing Rappe and Delmont, Arbuckle is said to have voiced concern. Their bad reputations, he feared, might cause police to raid the party.

Several other people attended the party at one point or another. One was a nightgown salesman named Ira Fortlois who was friends with Fischbach. Actresses Zey Prevon and Alice Blake also showed up.

The party had a lot of catered food and snacks, bootleg booze, and dancing to the music playing on the Victrola. As is usual as such gatherings, there was joking and laughter, flirting and storytelling. At one point, Delmont put on Lowell Sherman's pajamas; at another the two of them went into his room.

Arbuckle decided to leave the party at about 3:00 p.m. to drive a friend of his, Mae Taub, into town. Ironically, Taub was the daughter-in-law of Billy Sunday, a fiery evangelist who strongly supported Prohibition, but she did not seem to mind being in a place where illegal liquor was flowing freely.

The comedian went to his adjoining bedroom to change clothes. Exactly what happened after that would become a matter of fierce dispute.

According to the story Arbuckle gave and to which he

stuck, he entered the bathroom to find poor Rappe lying in a dead faint on the floor. He picked her up and placed her on a bed.

"Water," the sick woman requested in a weak voice.

Arbuckle brought a glass of cold water to her. Thinking she was probably just suffering the ill effects of too much drinking, the comedian left the room to dress himself for his ride.

When he went back to the bedroom, he saw that Virginia had rolled off the bed. She was lying on the floor, moaning and writhing. He helped her back onto the bed, then left for a bucket of ice. The ice would serve a dual purpose, Arbuckle believed: it would calm the woman down if she was really hysterical but it would also show whether or not she was faking. Buster Keaton had told his friend that one can discern a faked fainting or hysterical fit by holding ice against the suspected person's thigh. According to Edmonds' book, Arbuckle placed the ice on Virginia's thigh. Yallop's volume has him putting it directly on her vulva. In either case, it did no good.

Delmont came into the room. She saw Arbuckle placing an ice cube on the sick woman's thigh. The two discussed Virginia's distress. Both thought she was merely drunk.

Then Virginia began tearing at her clothes and screaming. The sounds caused other party-goers, Zey Prevon and Alice Blake, to rush in. Still believing that Virginia was just soused or deliberately making a scene, an aggravated Arbuckle told them, "Shut her up! Get her out of here. She makes too much noise."

Fischbach went into the room, and seeing Arbuckle putting ice on the semiconscious woman, teased him that he was still able to do something raunchy despite the burn on his backside and leg. "Having fun with her?" he asked.

The comedian was in no mood for jokes and snapped at Fischbach.

Suddenly Virginia began screaming. "Stay away from me! I don't want you near me!" she shouted at Arbuckle. Then she turned to Delmont and said words that would damn the entertainer, "What did he do to me, Maudie? Roscoe did this to me."

The bathtub had been filled with cold water as Delmont asked that it be and Virginia was placed in the tub. Time in the water seemed to have a calming effect on the distressed woman. Fischbach and Arbuckle helped her out of it and escorted her to room 1227. Delmont went into the room with them. Arbuckle phone the hotel manager and hotel doctor. The latter was not available but another physician, Dr. Olav Kaarboe, came to the room and took a look at Virginia. His diagnosis was that she was simply drunk.

With Virginia lying in bed, the party continued. There was more drinking and dancing and the sort of flirting and acting silly that usually characterizes parties where alcohol is served.

Later, Arbuckle took off for the delayed trip with Mae Taub. He dropped Taub off at her requested destination. After he returned, the hotel physician, Dr. Arthur Beardslee, arrived to take a look at poor Virginia. He gave her a shot of morphine and Virginia drifted off to sleep for the night.

The next day, Dr. Beardslee again treated Virginia with morphine. He also catheterized her because Delmont told him the sick woman had not urinated in many hours.

Later, Delmont called Dr. Melville Rumwell, a man she knew well enough to call "Rummy." When the doctor arrived, Delmont told him, as she had previously told Beardslee, that Virginia took sick after a drunken Roscoe Arbuckle dragged her into a room and raped her or at least tried to. Rumwell found no evidence of rape but treated the girl for pain and trouble urinating.

Tuesday afternoon, Arbuckle checked out of the hotel.

A couple days later, a feverish Virginia Rappe was finally taken to a hospital. She died there on Friday, September 9, of peritonitis, an acute infection that was, in her case, caused by a ruptured bladder. Why that bladder ruptured would become a matter of great dispute and the most serious importance.

Authorities would allege that Rappe's bladder tore because the overweight comedian sexually assaulted her. Rumors swirled around that he had also raped her with an instrument like a Coca-Cola bottle or a champagne bottle. However, these rumors were undoubtedly false. No such attack was even alleged in court.

The newspapers were filled with headlines about the sexual horror Roscoe supposedly perpetrated against young Rappe. It was Hollywood's first major scandal although it would, of course, by no means be its last.

Newspapers, led by William Randolph Hearst's *San Francisco Examiner,* had a field day. Yellow journalism was at its peak and readers were regaled with stories about Arbuckle's supposedly debauched private life and his alleged cruelty to the deceased Virginia Rappe. Hearst once bragged, to Arbuckle's good friend Buster Keaton, that the *Examiner* had sold more newspapers because of the Arbuckle case than the sinking of the Lusitania.

The comedian was bewildered by his dizzying fall from public grace. "I don't understand it," he complained. "One minute I'm the guy everybody loved, the next I'm the guy everybody loves to hate."

Part of the reason that accusations transfixed the public was that there were genuine reasons to be concerned about the treatment of women in the entertainment industry—as there is to this day. Aspiring actresses were often the victims of sexually predatory men in powerful positions. The "casting couch" was already well-known and rightly abhorred. Indeed, what is known of the life of Virginia Rappe—her multiple abortions, out of wedlock child, and history of STDs—strongly suggests that, like all-too-many young women who sought film careers, she was the victim of sexual exploitation.

While there were good reasons to fear female exploitation by powerful men, it is both ironic and sad that "one of the most chaste men in Hollywood," became a scapegoat for wrongs perpetrated by his far from chaste peers.

In the meantime, San Francisco District Attorney Mathew Brady was conducting repeated interviews with Maude Delmont, his prospective star witness. Every time she talked about the events of that terrible night, her story changed.

When Brady brought the Arbuckle case before a grand jury, he threatened Zey Prevon with prosecution for perjury unless she agreed with a police statement alleging that a dying Virginia Rappe had said, "Roscoe hurt me."

## "Minty, I Swear to God"

Arbuckle was originally arrested for first-degree murder, a crime punishable by the death penalty. Later, the charge was reduced to manslaughter that carried a possible ten-year prison sentence.

Earl Rogers, father of Adela Rogers St. John, predicted that the entertainer would face prejudice because of his size. "Arbuckle's weight will damn him," Rogers prophesied. "He will no longer be the roly-poly, good-natured, funny 350-pound fat man everybody loves. He will become a monster. If he were an ordinary man, his own spotless reputation, his clean pictures would save him. They'll never convict him, but this will ruin him and maybe motion pictures for some time."

The comedian's sexual attack on Virginia Rappe, the prosecution argued, had ruptured the victim's bladder, causing her death. The first trial began on November 14, 1921. The prosecutor was San Francisco District Attorney Mathew Brady, an ambitious, hot-tempered man with a dramatic manner that often came in handy in the courtroom.

Gavin McNab was the lawyer defending Roscoe Arbuckle. Like Brady, he was a native of San Francisco. He was a respected attorney who was often hired by people associated with the motion picture industry.

Presiding over the case was Judge Sylvain Lazarus.

Despite their marital difficulties, Minta Durfee believed her husband innocent of the felonies of which he stood accused.

She had visited him in jail before he was bailed out. "Roscoe," she began, embarrassed but needing his reassurance, "I have only one question to ask you. Please don't get angry but I must know. Were you in any way responsible for Virginia Rappe's death?"

"Minty, I swear to God I never touched that girl like they say I did."

That was good enough for Minta. She appeared regularly in the courtroom to show her support for him.

The prosecution's first witness was a nurse named Grace Halston. She glared at the defendant, obviously convinced of his guilt. She testified that the late Rappe had several bruises on her body and that her organs were torn in a way that suggested force.

McNab got Halston to admit that the ruptured bladder could have been caused by cancer and that the bruises might have been caused by Rappe's heavy jewelry.

Dr. Arthur Beardslee testified that the bladder seemed to be injured from force inflicted from outside of her body. On cross-examination, he admitted that Rappe had said nothing to him indicating she had been assaulted by the accused. Beardslee also said that the sick woman would have benefited from surgery.

The defense attorney zeroed in on this admission. "Then, Dr. Beardslee, let me ask you this," he began. "If you saw evidence that Miss Rappe would benefit from surgery, why was no surgery ordered at that time?"

"I have no answer for that," he said.

"You have no answer," McNab observed. "I wonder if Miss Rappe might be alive today if you had."

Brady called Betty Campbell to the stand. She was a model who had been at the party. She testified that, about an hour after the alleged rape, she had seen Arbuckle relaxed and enjoying himself. Edmonds wrote that, "Brady tried to use this in an attempt to show Arbuckle had neither remorse nor concern for the condition of Virginia Rappe." Under cross-examination, Campbell said the comedian seemed not the least bit intoxicated. Then McNab brought out a true bombshell. Campbell testified that the prosecutor had threatened to get her imprisoned if she didn't testify against Arbuckle.

This understandably sent Brady into a frenzy of objections.

The defense attorney presented the judge with affidavits

from Alice Blake and Zey Prevon backing up the claim of intimidation by the prosecution. Prevon was called to the stand and testified that she had signed the statement saying Rappe had claimed, "He killed me," under duress. Alice Blake made similar assertions from the witness stand.

The prosecution struck a hard blow with the testimony of Jesse Norgard who had worked as a security guard at Lehrman's Culver City studio. The former security guard testified that Arbuckle had once shown up at the studio and offered Norgard cash in exchange for the key to Rappe's dressing room. The comedian supposedly said he wanted it to play a joke on the actress. Norgard said he refused to give out that key.

Oddly, the woman who had originally made the accusation against Arbuckle, the shady Maude Delmont, never appeared in court, something the defense would gleefully point out.

Dr. Edward Heinrich, a criminologist who was especially expert in fingerprints, testified that partial prints of Rappe were found on the inside of the door to 1219 with Arbuckle's superimposed over them. This seemed to indicate that the two had struggled over the door and implied that the actress tried to open it while the comedian slammed it shut.

To rebut this testimony, McNab would put Ignatius McCarthy on the stand. McCarthy had been a federal investigator. He said he could prove the fingerprints were faked. McNab also called to the stand a hotel maid who claimed she had dusted the door several times before it was sealed and examined by the District Attorney.

## The Accused Testifies

On Monday, November 28, the defense called Roscoe Arbuckle to the witness stand. It was a welcome move to Arbuckle. He had heard himself accused of one of the most terrible crimes imaginable and was relieved to able to publicly and emphatically deny it. He walked to the stand looking tired and drawn, with dark circles obvious under his eyes. He was neatly attired in a dark suit and white shirt and his expression appropriately somber. He would be on the stand for a little over four hours.

"Mr. Arbuckle," Gavin McNab began, "where were you on September 5, 1921?"

"At the St. Francis Hotel occupying rooms 1219, 1220, and 1221," the accused entertainer answered.

"Did you see Miss Virginia Rappe on that day?"

"Yes, sir."

"At what time and where did you see her?"

"She came into room 1220 at about 12:00 noon," was Arbuckle's calm reply.

Under the lawyer's questioning, Arbuckle gave names of others at the party. He told how he had planned to take Mae Taub into town and was going into the bathroom to get dressed when he discovered Virginia in pain.

"When I walked into 1219," the witness recalled, "I closed and locked the door, and I went straight to the bathroom and found Miss Rappe on the floor in front of the toilet. She'd been vomiting."

"What did you do?"

"When I opened the door, the door struck her, and I had to slide in this way to get in, to get by her and get hold of her. Then I closed the door and picked her up. When I picked her up … she vomited again. I held her under the waist … and the forehead, to keep her hair back off her face so she could vomit. When she finished, I put the seat down, then I sat her down on it.

"'Can I do anything for you?' I asked her. She said she wanted to lie down. I carried her into 1219 and put her on the bed. I lifted her feet off the floor. I went to the bathroom again and came back in two or three minutes. I found her rolling on the floor between two beds holding her stomach. I tried to pick her up but I couldn't. I immediately went out of 1219 to 1220 and asked Mrs. Delmont and Miss Prevon to come in. I told them Miss Rappe was sick."

He vehemently denied having every put his hand over Rappe's on the door. He also told how a frantic Virginia had torn at her clothes and Arbuckle had helped her off with a dress and Fischbach came into the room. Then he said that Fischbach had taken the sick woman to the bathroom and put her in a tub of cold water. This was done, Arbuckle claimed, in hopes of calming down her apparent hysteria. When Virginia was carried back to the bed, Maude Delmont rubbed her with ice. Arbuckle said he tried to cover Virginia with the bedspread and an infuriated Delmont spoke rudely to him and he in turn barked, "If you don't shut up, I'll throw you out the window."

The witness remained unshaken under an intense cross-examination by Assistant District Attorney Leo Friedman.

"What time did you say Miss Rappe entered your rooms?"

"Around 12:00," Arbuckle said.

"You had know her before?" Friedman asked.

"Uh-huh. About five or six years."

Arbuckle admitted to drinking some Prohibition booze but indicated that he was not drunk. The judge called a recess. Court resumed with a startling exhibit by the prosecution. Virginia Rappe's bladder was brought into the courtroom!

Friedman tried to get Arbuckle to admit he had deliberately followed Virginia. The defendant stuck to his story. The D. A. tried to wring admissions at least of callousness from the witness.

"Did you tell the hotel manager what had caused Miss Rappe's sickness?"

"No," Arbuckle replied. "How should I know what caused her sickness?"

"You didn't tell anybody you found her in the bathroom?" the prosecutor asked incredulously.

"Nobody asked me."

"You didn't tell anyone you found her between the beds?"

"Nobody asked me," Arbuckle repeated. "I'm telling you."

"You never said anything to anybody except that Miss Rappe was sick?"

"Nope."

"Not even the doctor?" Friedman pressed.

"Nope."

When Arbuckle stepped down, most observers thought his testimony had scored strongly for his defense.

Both the prosecutor and the defense put on expert witnesses to discuss the state of Virginia Rappe's bladder. Dr. William Ophuls was called by the prosecution and Dr. G. Rusk by the defense. According to Andy Edmonds, "The experts agreed on four points: that the bladder was ruptured, that there was evidence of chronic inflammation, that there were signs of acute peritonitis, and that the examination failed to reveal any pathological change in the vicinity of the tear preceding the rupture. In short—the rupture was not caused by external force."

The defense was jubilant. They believed it would be an easy victory.

However, prosecutor Friedman still thought the evidence pointed straight at Arbuckle. His summation painted a portrait of the actor as a cold-hearted sort. "This big, kindhearted comedian," he said sarcastically. "Did he say 'Get a doctor for this suffering girl?' No. He said, 'Shut up or I'll throw you out the window.'

"He was not content to stop at throwing her out the window. He attempted to make a sport with her by placing ice on her body. This man then and there proved himself guilty of this offense. This act shows you the mental makeup of Roscoe Arbuckle."

In his summation, McNab dramatically charged that his client was the victim of a vicious persecution. "It was a deliberate conspiracy against Arbuckle!" the indignant McNab thundered. "It was the shame of San Francisco. Perjured wretches tried, from the stand, to deprive this defendant, this stranger within our gates, of his liberty."

The first trial ended on December 4, 1921, when, after 43 hours of deliberation and 22 ballots, the jury was unable to reach a verdict. They were deadlocked 10 to two in favor of acquittal.

One of the holdouts, Helen Hubbard, supposedly told the others that she would never change her mind because she had decided Arbuckle was guilty when she heard that he had been arrested.

The prosecution pressed the case a second time. The defense this time around went after the dead woman in a rather distasteful way, playing on popular prejudice against women who drank and enjoyed a variety of sexual partners.

Two major prosecution witnesses reversed their previous testimony. Zey Prevon testified that she had not heard Rappe accuse Arbuckle of hurting her. Of equal significance was the testimony of prosecution witness Dr. Heinrich who said he believed the overlapping fingerprints on the bedroom door may well have been faked.

The defense decided that the district attorney's case was so weak that they would not dignify it by seeming to take it seriously. They not only did not put their client on the witness stand but also did not make a closing summation! This backfired. Most of the jurors assumed that the failure to put on a strong defense was an implicit admission of guilt. This time the jury voted 10-2 for conviction, precisely the opposite of the first jury.

So the case went to trial a third and final time. This time the defense went all out. Arbuckle again took the stand. He appeared forthright in his denials. The district attorney operated under something of a handicap because one of its major witnesses, Zey Prevon, had left the country.

The jury not only came back with a quick acquittal but, on their own initiative, issued an apology to the accused saying he had been wronged. "Acquittal is not enough for Roscoe Arbuckle," the jury's statement began. "We feel that a great injustice has been done him. We feel also that it was only our plain duty to give him this exoneration, under the evidence, for there was not the slightest proof adduced to connect him in any way with the commission of a crime.

"He was manly throughout the case, and told a straightforward story on the witness stand, which we all believed.

"The happening at the hotel was an unfortunate affair for which Arbuckle, so the evidence shows, was in no way responsible.

"We wish him success, and hope that the American people will take the judgment of 14 men and woman who have sat listening for 31 days to evidence, that Roscoe Arbuckle is entirely innocent and free from all blame."

## How did she Die?

What exactly did happen to Virginia Rappe? There is no doubt that the immediate cause of death was peritonitis caused by a ruptured bladder. Why did the bladder rupture?

One common theory is that Rappe had just undergone an illegal and botched abortion. She is said to have told others at the party, "I need money for an abortion." There are two ways this statement can be interpreted. The first, and most obvious, is that she was pregnant at the time she said it. The second is that she had just had a pregnancy terminated and needed to pay the person who had performed the operation.

Was Rappe pregnant at the time she died? The surprising answer is that we do not know! Several of her organs, including her uterus, were removed after the autopsy and secretly destroyed. The physician believed to be behind the destruction of these parts was Dr. Rumwell, a man reputed to perform abortions. Perhaps he wanted to hide evidence that he had recently performed an illegal procedure.

The writer "Shush" speculates in "What Really Happened to Virginia Rappe?" about the cause of her peritonitis. "Shush" notes that there are three major reasons for peritonitis. One of them, due to dialysis treatments, cannot apply to Rappe. Another, related to cirrhosis of the liver, may since there are some who believe the actress was an alcoholic. However, "Shush" observe, "This leaves out the whole issue of the ruptured bladder" and, "It's hard to believe that Virginia's ruptured bladder played no part in her death."

The third type of peritonitis, secondary peritonitis, "caused by bacteria entering the peritoneum through a hole somewhere in the gastrointestinal tract" fits the case best in the opinion of "Shush." While dying, Rappe had told a nurse that she had been having an abnormal vaginal discharge for about six weeks. This may or may not have been related to a vene-real disease. This infection may have traveled upward into her intestines. The vomiting may have ruptured her already distressed bladder.

Edmonds gives an account in which Arbuckle did contribute to her ruptured bladder but in an innocent manner. At the party, the guests started doing "high kicks" in an effort to see who could kick the highest. Arbuckle re-injured the burn he had recently gotten so he sat down.

According to Edmonds, it was well known among Arbuckle's acquaintances that he was ticklish and they would often tickle his ribs, causing him to double over and jerk his knee up. At the party, Rappe (who may or may not have known this about the comedian) got Arbuckle up off the sofa then impulsively tickled him. His knee automatically shot up and jabbed the actress' stomach. She shrieked in sudden pain and fled to the bathroom.

The author notes that, if this story is true, it explains Rappe's alleged remarks, "What did he do to me?" and "He did this to me," but without imputing any criminal action to Arbuckle.

### "A Broken Heart"

At the time of Arbuckle's acquittal, the 35-year-old actor owed $700,000 to his attorneys. He had lost his house and his cars. The acquittal, even accompanied by the extraordinary statement from the jury, did not mean that Arbuckle could resume his career.

The comedian had broken a law on the way to the infamous party: he had brought liquor to it. In 1922, he pled guilty to violating the Volstead Act and paid a $500 fine.

Roscoe "Fatty" Arbuckle had come to represent everything that was supposedly wrong with Hollywood. His very name conjured up the worst type of sexually predatory male, leading to his being the first person to be blacklisted from films. The films in which he starred had been withdrawn from circulation because of his, however undeservedly, sullied reputation. The major force behind this blacklisting was Will Hays.

Formerly U.S. postmaster general, Hays is best remembered for an organization dedicated to sanitizing the motion picture industry. It was called the Motion Picture Producers and Distributors of America (MPPDA). Hays and his organization were courted because Hollywood feared that public outrage would lead to government censorship. Movie producers decided to head that threat off at the pass by agreeing to rules of self-censorship which Hays helped form

On April 18, 1922, Hays issued a statement saying, "After consulting at length with Mr. Nicholas Schenck, representing Mr. Joseph Schenck, the producers, and Mr. Adolph Zukor and Mr. Jessy Lasky of the Famous Players-Lasky Corporation, the distributors, I will state that at my request they have cancelled all showings and all bookings of the Arbuckle films. They do this that the whole matter may have the consideration that its importance warrants, and the action is taken notwithstanding the fact that they had nearly 10,000 contracts in force for the Arbuckle pictures." Hays would officially lift this ban on December 20 of that same year but Arbuckle would not be able to find work in front of a camera for a decade.

He was able to obtain work behind the camera as a director when working under the pseudonym "William B. Goodrich." The name he picked showed that the trauma he had suffered had not erased his sense of humor. Perhaps it also showed that he had finally forgiven his father for parental maltreatment.

As Goodrich, Arbuckle directed a 1927 Eddie Cantor film called *Special Delivery* and a short starring Louise Brooks called *Windy Riley Goes Hollywood* in 1931.

However, Arbuckle was still depressed. Perhaps he needed to perform before real audiences, to have people see him as the jolly fat man he had always played and not the man suspected of a dirty and disgusting crime. For awhile, he returned to the stage. He made a tour on the old Vaudeville circuit. There he found affectionate crowds laughing and applauding at his old antics. Having the public accept him once again was wonderfully gratifying.

He met lovely, dimpled Doris Deane and the two fell in love. Minta divorced him in 1925 and four months later he wed Doris Deane. However, the marriage was not successful. He was still depressed because of his travails and, as he had before, sought comfort in alcohol. They divorced three years after getting married.

Apparently believing that the scandal had finally died down, Warner-Vitaphone hired Arbuckle to work onscreen in the early 1930s. He made a series of two-reelers. One of them, *Buzzin' Around*, showed that he still had a special gift for light-hearted slapstick. Audiences flocked to these delightfully funny movies, showing that there were many who remained his fans and that he could make new ones as well.

Meanwhile, he also found a new love, pretty dark-eyed actress Addie McPhail. The couple was married in June, 1932. It seemed like things were finally looking up for Arbuckle. He was making movies that people loved and enjoying a good marriage.

Warner Brothers offered Arbuckle a feature film contract. He eagerly accepted but never got a chance to fulfill its terms. He and his wife Addie went out to dinner for a double celebration—the contract and their first wedding anniversary.

At the age of 46, he died in his sleep, shortly after he and his wife returned from their night on the town. The cause of death was medically heart disease. His close friend Buster Keaton said, "He died of a broken heart."

However, it should be remembered that he had made a successful comeback. He was also happily married. Thus, it is realistic to believe that, for all his bad luck, including dying at a young age, Roscoe Arbuckle died a happy man. He certainly deserved to.

Sadly, Arbuckle is often remembered today as "the man who raped a girl with a Coke bottle" or "the man who tried to rape an actress and killed her." He was neither of these things. Sometimes people recall him, correctly, as falsely accused of a murder. It would be most appropriate if he were remembered as a genius of comedy, the big, agile man whose talent for pratfalls, somersaults, and extraordinary pie throwing brought joy to audiences of all ages. Those smart enough and lucky enough to see his films will know him as a brilliant comedian. Roscoe Arbuckle loved to make people laugh and he was very good at it. Several decades ago, on a horrible day, the laughter stopped. It is long overdue for it to start again.

## Bibliography

http://silent-movies.com/Arbucklemania/Scandal.htm.

http://us.imdb.com/Bio?Arbuckle,+Roscoe+%27Fatty$27.

http://us.imdb.com/Bio?Rappe,+Virginia

Edmonds, Andy. *Frame-Up!* William Morrow and Company, Inc. New York, NY, 1991.

Yallop, David. *The Day the Laughter Stopped*. St. Martin's Press, New York, NY, 1976.

A&E Home Video. *Biography, Fatty Arbuckle, Betrayed by Hollywood.*

# CHAPTER THREE

## The Murder of Mary Phagan and Lynching of Leo Frank

At approximately 3 a.m. on Sunday, April 27, 1913, the night watchman of the National Pencil Company in Atlanta discovered a girl's brutally battered body in the factory's basement. Covered with sawdust, her skull was caked with dried blood, her eyes were bruised, her face slashed and some of her fingers out of joint. A piece of rope, along with a strip taken from her own underpants, encircled her neck. She was soon identified as 13-year-old Mary Phagan, the child of a working-class family. She had been employed at the factory putting metal tips on pencils. She had recently been laid off because the factory had run out of the metal required for her job. On Saturday, April 26, 1913, Confederate Memorial Day in Atlanta, she planned to see the parade but first wanted to stop off at the factory to collect $1.20 in wages owed her.

The killing captured the next day's headlines and news about it would appear on the front pages of Atlanta newspapers for more than a year afterward. Much of Atlanta suffered a paroxysm of grief over this murder. About 10,000 people showed up at the morgue and over 1,000 attended her funeral. Those grieving over this stranger were nicknamed "Mary's People" while she became known as "the little factory girl."

The crime touched an exposed nerve because it symbolized the vulnerability of young women during a time when the South was transitioning from a rural to an urban economy. During the first two decades of the 20th century many ruined farmers migrated to the city where they, their wives, and often their children, got jobs in factories. When on farms, young women could be closely watched. Families were typically large and often extended, consisting not only of a mom and dad plus children but of grandparents, aunts, uncles, and others.

These systems often worked to protect young females from the sexual abuse and sexual exploitation as well as the out-of-wedlock pregnancies that could result. The system was far from perfect as sexual abuse can take place within families but there was a popular sense that it usually protected females as they grew into womanhood from abuse.

The transition to an urban environment meant that young females could not be as closely watched by their families. It also meant that they were often in contact with unrelated males. What's more, as young women took to working for low wages in factories, they were often under the supervision and authority of more powerful males, a situation that was ripe for exploitation by those without a working moral compass.

In death, Mary Phagan became the sister and daughter of many Georgians, both male and female, because her killing symbolized the deepest fears they had about the sexual vulnerability of their own female relatives and of young women generally in the changing conditions. Public outcry meant the police were under tremendous pressure to solve this homicide. Atlanta's mayor warned the police: "Find this murderer fast, or be fired!"

Two semi-literate notes were found beside her corpse. One read: "Mam that negro hire down here did this i went to make water and he push me down that hole a long tall negro black that hoo it wase long sleam tall negro I wright while play with me." The other read: "he said he wood love me land down play like the night witch did it but that long tall black negro did buy his slef."

The notes appeared to point to the night watchman who

had found her body, an African-American named Newt Lee who was tall, slim and dark-skinned. "Night witch" could be a misspelling of "night watch." Lee was arrested. Police held him while arresting others. The "hole" referred to seemed to be the factory chute.

But police attention soon focused on another suspect: factory superintendent, Leo Frank, the last person known to have seen Mary alive. Leo Frank, at age 24, had left Brooklyn in 1908 for Atlanta to become superintendent of the National Pencil Company's factory. He wed Lucille Selig in 1910. A pretty but heavyset young woman, she had artistic inclinations and a mischievous side. According to Steve Oney in *And the Dead Shall Rise*, she was initially attracted to Leo "because I liked to make him blush." The couple did not have children.

Frank was elected president of the Atlanta chapter of B'nai B'rith, a Jewish fraternal organization, in 1913. Albert Lindemann in *The Jew Accused* wrote that Frank "appointed a committee … to investigate the complaints against Jewish caricatures that are becoming so frequent on the local stage."

Four hours after the discovery of Mary's body, police visited Frank at his home. A nervous Frank initially denied knowing Mary, although he soon recalled a girl who had come for her wages.

Police took Frank to the place where the body had been discovered. The group got into the elevator and descended to the basement. As Steve Oney wrote in his book about the murder: "The instant the lift hit bottom, a powerful stench wafted up from beneath the men" as the lift smashed human feces. The significance of the feces would not be realized until much later.

On Tuesday, April 29, police arrested Frank. Lindemann has pointed out that the police first suspected Frank for "a number of perfectly legitimate reasons having nothing to do with his Jewishness. First, he was one of the few in the factory on the day … of the murder. Since it was never seriously questioned that the murder took place in the factory, he automatically became one of a few natural suspects." There was physical evidence pointing to Frank. Spots that looked like blood were found in the metal workroom across from his office. Hairs were found around the lathe and witnesses said the hairs looked like Mary Phagan's hair. However, these apparent links did not stand up to scrutiny. At Frank's trial, a detective testified that it was uncertain that the stains were blood. It would not come out until after the trial, but a biologist found that the hairs were not Mary's.

## The Frame-Up

On Wednesday, April 30, 1913, a Coroner's Jury inquest convened and the frame-up of Leo Frank commenced. Erroneous evidence given here and widely reported painted Frank as a menace to young women. An acquaintance of Mary's named George Epps testified that he had ridden into town with her on the last day of her life. Bruce L. Jordan wrote in *Murder in the Peach State*, "Epps claimed that he had been told that day by Mary that she was afraid of her boss, Leo Frank, because he was too familiar with her and made advances towards her."

However, as Jordan further wrote, "Epps had been interviewed by an *Atlanta Georgian* reporter a few days earlier and had said only that he sometimes rode to town with her. During that interview Epps said nothing of having ridden to town with her the day she was killed."

After the Coroner's Jury's inquest, more bogus evidence damning Frank surfaced. A police officer claimed to have found Frank in a wooded area with a girl and that Frank had admitted taking her there for "immoral purposes." This same police officer would later admit that he had made a mistaken identification, but this information did not appear on the front pages of the newspapers.

"On May 23, the Atlanta police released an affidavit from Mrs. Nina Formby, the proprietor of a 'rooming house' in Atlanta, disclosing that on the day of the murder Frank had telephoned her repeatedly and had attempted to secure a room for himself and a young girl," Leonard Dinnerstein wrote in *The Leo Frank Case*. Her maid disputed Mrs. Formby's story about Frank making a call to her rooming house.

Quoting Dinnerstein, "In the middle of June the maid …
said that the detectives had been pestering her on numerous
occasions to make an affidavit supporting Mrs. Formby's contention that Frank had phoned several times for a room on the
evening of the murder. The maid refused because she claimed
that there had been no such call that evening, and if there had
been she certainly would have answered the phone."

The most damaging evidence against Frank came from
27-year-old Jim Conley, the janitor at the pencil factory, a
heavy drinker with a criminal record. According to Bruce L.
Jordan's *Murder in the Peach State*, Conley had "several previous arrests for theft and disorderly conduct."

Author Steve Oney wrote that Conley "had served two
sentences on the chain gang. Three months before the Phagan
killing, Jim had fired a shot at Lorena Jones [his common-law
wife]." He missed but grazed another woman and served a jail
term. Conley, a short, stocky, light-skinned African-American,
had been arrested in connection with the Phagan murder on
May 1 after a factory foreman told police he had seen Conley trying to wash what looked like bloodstains from a shirt.
According to Oney, Conley told police "he'd just been trying
to rinse away some rust marks because he had nothing else
to wear to the coroner's inquest." Authorities believed—despite being in possession of two semi-literate notes left near
Phagan's corpse that Frank could not have possibly written or
even dictated—that Conley could not be the killer because he
had told them he was illiterate.

Atlanta's Solicitor-General Hugh Dorsey took charge of
the case. Three days after Conley's arrest, Frank was indicted
for murder.

On May 16, they found out Conley was semi-literate. Exactly how they discovered this was disputed. Frank always
claimed he was the source of this finding. Oney wrote that, "in
the report the agents submitted to both defense counsel and
police, they failed to mention Frank's contribution." Rather,
they said assistant superintendents and the day watchman of
the factory were the sources for this information. They discovered that Conley had written notes to a firm from which he

was buying a watch on installment and confronted him with his own signature.

Police insisted Conley write what they dictated: the Phagan notes. What Conley wrote was almost identical to the originals. The janitor then admitted he wrote the originals but claimed they had also been dictated to him—by Leo Frank. As it happened, Conley would tell three different stories of the murder—all three pinning the murder on Frank. In the first, as Jordan wrote, Conley said, "He had been summoned to Leo Frank's office the day before the murder and ordered to write them. Conley claimed in this first affidavit that while writing the note for his boss, Frank mumbled what Conley believed to be, 'Why should I hang? I've got wealthy people in Brooklyn.' Conley also initially claimed that he was not even in the factory on the day of the murder."

This story meant that Frank had plotted the murder at least a day in advance. Police found this unbelievable because they did not think it had been premeditated.

Pressed, Conley changed his story, admitting he had been at the factory and had written the notes on the day of the killing, but he still denied knowing anything else.

On their third try, the police pulled from Conley the story they wanted. Conley claimed that Frank had summoned him to his office. He stated that the superintendent told him that he had let a girl fall against a machine in the metal room and wanted him to bring her out of the room. Conley said he went into it and found the girl dead. He said he reported this to Frank who asked him to help carry the body to the elevator. Conley said the two of them together took the corpse to the basement and left her in the corner. Afterwards, the pair returned to Frank's office where Frank dictated and Conley penned the notes.

Given the South's history of anti-black prejudice, why was Conley's word accepted instead of Frank's? After all, Frank was a successful businessman with no criminal record. Part of the explanation lies, as Dinnerstein noted, in the "alien" image Frank projected "as a Northerner, an industrialist, and a Jew." Dinnerstein quotes a pastor saying, "When … the police arrested a Jew, and a Yankee Jew at that, all of the inborn prejudice against Jews rose up in a feeling of satisfaction."

Conley understood racist ideology and manipulated it. He explained his complicity by saying, "I was willing to do anything to help Mr. Frank because he was a white man and my superintendent." Adopting this Uncle Tom persona won over investigators. In essences, Conley told a story that was vivid with detail that supported the investigators' preconceived notions regarding Frank's guilt.

## The Trial

The trial of Leo Frank for the murder of Mary Phagan started on July 28, 1913. Conley was charged as an accessory to the crime. Luther Rosser and Reuben Arnold, two respected Georgia attorney, represented him. Frank Hooper assisted Solicitor Dorsey with the prosecution. Judge Leonard S. Roan presided. Spectators packed the courtroom and a throng gathered outside it. The temper of that crowd was so anti-Frank that the police had many officers guarding the courtroom throughout the trial. Lucile Frank sat close behind her husband each day of the trial. She was unwavering in her belief in his innocence and integrity. To the press she said, "He ever has been just the plain, more or less studious and serious minded Leo, gentle and thoughtful, sincere and true."

The state put on witnesses who said Mary's hairs were on a lathe in the second-floor workroom across from Frank's office. They put on doctors who testified that she died between noon and 12:15 p.m.

Employee Monteen Stover took the stand to discredit Frank's story that he had not left his office between noon and 12:30 p.m. and that he had handed the money due Mary to her sometime between 12:05 p.m. and 12:10 p.m. Stover said she had arrived at 12:05 p.m. and not seen Frank in his office.

Detective Starnes testified that he saw red stains in the workroom but acknowledged on cross-examination that he could not know if they were blood.

Conley was the prosecution's star witness. Both Dinnerstein and Oney record that he testified that Frank had told him he was expecting a young lady to come to his office for a "chat." Conley also told the court that he regularly "watched out" for Frank when ladies visited him. According to his story, when Frank stamped his foot Conley would lock the front door, then unlock it after hearing Frank whistle.

On this day, Conley claimed to have seen Mary go upstairs. He also said he heard footsteps going in the direction of the workroom and heard a scream. He said that after that scream, he saw Stover go to the second floor. He recalled the signal of the stomping foot and locking the front door, hearing the whistle, then unlocking the door and trekking up to Frank's office.

Conley said that when he got to Frank's office that Frank was "shivering and trembling and rubbing his hands." In those hands, Conley said, Frank held a piece of rope. Conley testified that Frank asked him if he had seen "that little girl who passed here just a while ago?" Conley said he answered that he had seen "one come along there and she came back again, and then I saw another one come along there and she hasn't been back down." Conley quoted Frank as confiding, "I wanted to be with the little girl, and she refused me, and I struck her and I guess I struck her too hard and she fell and hit her head against something."

Conley further claimed Frank told him to go to the workroom and see how she was. He found her dead, and reported that back to Frank. Conley then described how the two of them together took Mary's body onto the elevator, then left it in the basement. They returned to Frank's office, where Frank dictated the notes found next to Mary's body. Rosser and Arnold cross-examined him for three days but were unable to shake him on anything substantive. They did draw a disclosure—which they failed to pursue—that could have proved vital to Frank's defense.

Under cross-examination, Conley testified that he had defecated at the bottom of the elevator shaft on the morning of the murder. Later, others examining the facts in this case would see this admission as key to the real murderer. Conley had been well prepped for cross-examination by his own lawyer, William Smith. As Oney wrote, "Smith, a fair mimic, gave [Conley] a taste of … Rosser's corrosive manner, preparing him for the inevitable courtroom encounter." Smith said he hoped "to render Conley impervious to cross-examination" and he had.

The defense put on witnesses to show that Frank simply did not have the time to do all the things Conley said he had done. Conley testified that Mary Phagan had been in the pencil factory prior to Monteen Stover's arrival. Stover said she had been outside Frank's office from 12:05 to 12:10 p.m. However, both the motorman and conductor of the trolley Phagan took claimed she left the car at 12:10 p.m.

Defense doctors disputed the time at which their prosecution counterparts had pinpointed her death.

Frank took the stand in his own defense. He testified he left the factory to go home for lunch at 1 p.m. Several defense witnesses took the stand to say they had seen him between 1 p.m. and 1:30 p.m., contradicting Conley's assertion that the two of them had been in the factory at that time.

To murder the child, transport her body to the basement, return to the office and write the murder notes would have taken at least half an hour according to Conley, other witnesses, and common sense. Yet all of Frank's time during the supposed period when he was about his dirty work was accounted for save a period of approximately 18 minutes between 12:01 and 12:20 p.m.

*The Atlanta Constitution* observed that the "chain of testimony, forged with a number of links, has established a seemingly unbreakable corroboration of Frank's account of his whereabouts." Frank testified that Monteen Stover may have missed seeing him at his desk when she arrived because "it is impossible for me to see out into the outer hall when the safe door is open, as it was that morning, and not only is it impossible for me to see out, but it is impossible for people to see in and see me there." He also said he might have been temporarily out of his office for a trip to the restroom. He derided Conley's story as a "tissue of lies."

The defense called a number of character witnesses, several of them females who worked at the pencil factory. Each testified that Frank's conduct had been unimpeachable. The defense also called witnesses who claimed Conley had a reputation for lying.

Lawyers for both sides rested after four weeks of testimony. In his first closing argument, Dorsey called Frank a "Dr. Jekyll and Mr. Hyde," appearing to be a decent man to friends and family while cruelly indulging his sexual appetites at the expense of young women.

In his closing, defense attorney Arnold brought up the issue of anti-Semitism, saying, "If Frank hadn't been a Jew there would never had been any prosecution against him."

Dorsey objected on his second summation as saying that, "the word Jew never escaped our lips."

Outside the jury's presence, Judge Roan summoned Frank's attorneys to the bench. Fearing violence if Frank was acquitted, the judge recommended that neither Frank nor his lawyers attend the verdict's announcement. Without consulting Frank, the lawyers agreed to follow this recommendation.

The jury convicted Frank of first-degree murder. The mood in Atlanta was one of jubilation. Jordan wrote, "When Solicitor Dorsey exited the courthouse and reached the sidewalk, he was physically lifted into the air by the cheering crowd and passed across the street to his office with tears rolling down his cheeks, his hat raised over his head, his feet never touching the ground until he reached his office.

Frank was in his jail cell when he received the news. Shocked, he exclaimed, "My God! Even the jury was influenced by mob law."

The next day Judge Roan sentenced Frank to hang. Jim Conley later pled guilty to being an accessory after the fact and was sentenced to serve one year on a chain gang.

### The Case Becomes a Cause

Frank's attorneys announced that they would appeal. Little known outside the South prior to Frank's conviction, the case gained notoriety in the North as investigators turned up evidence casting doubt on the verdict.

*The Atlanta Journal* revealed that, as Jordan recorded, "the state biologist had issued a report to Solicitor Dorsey shortly after Mary Phagan's murder. After having examined with a microscope the hair found on a lathe in the metal room, the biologist concluded in his report that the hair was not Mary Phagan's." *The Journal* asked Dorsey why he withheld the report from the jury and he replied that he relied on other witnesses who believed the hair was hers.

Adding to doubts were prosecution witnesses' recantations. According to Steve Oney in *And the Dead Shall Rise*, Albert McKnight, husband of the Frank family's cook, signed an affidavit saying "he had concocted his tale regarding Frank's failure to eat lunch the day of the crime and subsequent hasty departure from home." McKnight claimed he had made up this story, Oney wrote, "at the behest of his employers at Beck & Gregg Hardware—who like so many others had been angling for the reward offered in the slaying's aftermath." Nina Formby contacted *The New York Times* to claim that she had made up the story of Frank's wanting to rent a room under police pressure. Finally, George Epps claimed police had pressured him into his statement about Mary's fear of Frank.

The hair evidence and the raft of recantations led *The Atlanta Journal* to run an editorial calling for a new trial.

To add to the confusion, McKnight, Formby and Epps all soon recanted their recantations. Without explaining why they had made the first recantations, they each insisted their testimony against Frank had been accurate.

Frank's defenders found ammunition in a fresh examination of the notes. Dinnerstein recorded that attorney Henry Alexander "showed that these notes were written on the carbons of old order pads which had been used previously by a former factory official. The dateline read 190—," indicating that the forms must have been at least four years-old. The official who signed the orders left the employ of the factory in 1912, and all his office records, including pads, had been removed to the basement, near where Mary Phagan's body had been found.

Alexander concluded that this proved that Conley could not have written the notes on a pad which Frank had given him in his office.

Alexander also believed that a phrase in one of the notes pointed to their author. That phrase was "night witch," previously assumed by investigators to be a misspelling of "night watch." Alexander believed it meant exactly what it said because the "night witch" was a character in Southern African-American folk belief, a witch who strangled children to death. Alexander believed it improbable that Frank, a Northern Jew, would be familiar with this belief and certain that Conley would be.

Judge Roan rejected Frank's first appeal. However, he wrote, "I have thought about this case more than any other I have tried. I am not certain of the man's guilt. With all the thought I have put on this case, I am not thoroughly convinced that Frank is guilty or innocent. The jury was convinced … I feel it is my duty to order that the motion for a new trial be overruled."

A month and a half later, Frank's attorneys went before the Georgia Supreme Court. They argued that the prejudicial atmosphere precluded a fair trial. The court rejected their appeal.

Frank got a new defense team, made up of Herbert and Leonard Haas (brothers), Henry Alexander and the firm of Tye, Peeples, and Jordan. They made errors attributed to Frank's trial attorneys, Rosser and Arnold, the basis of an appeal. In Jordan's words, they claimed that "Rosser and Arnold did not have the right to waive Frank's presence in the courtroom when the jury returned their verdict."

U.S. Supreme Court Justice Oliver Wendall Holmes denied the appeal but added that there was doubt about the fairness of Frank's trial because of "the presence of a hostile demonstration and seemingly dangerous crowd, thought by the presiding judge to be ready for violence unless a verdict of guilty was rendered."

According to Jordan, "In February of 1915, Frank's attorneys were given one more chance to be heard by the U. S. Supreme Court, this time petitioning for a writ of habeas corpus." It was denied.

Frank's supporters believed his only chance was a commutation. They received unexpected support in that effort from Conley's attorney. Smith, Conley's attorney, announced on October 2, 1914, that he believed his client killed Mary Phagan. Smith claimed he did not act unethically in implicating his own client since Conley, convicted as an accessory, could not be tried again because of the constitutional protection against double jeopardy. Smith added that he felt compelled to speak out because the life of an innocent man was in danger.

While Frank garnered support, his case also became a cause that lined prominent people up against him. One of the most notable of these was Tom Watson, who had started his career as a Populist with relatively liberal racial views. Unfortunately, by the time of the Frank affair, he had curdled into an extremist frequently denouncing African-Americans and Roman Catholics. Still seen as a champion by poor white Protestants, he published a weekly, *The Jeffersonian*, and a monthly, *Watson's Magazine*.

In *The Jeffersonian*, Watson ran a lengthy editorial called "The Frank Case: When and Where Shall Rich Criminals Be Tried?" He also posed the question: "Does a Jew expect extraordinary favors and immunities because of his race?"

Frank's supporters looked to Governor John Slaton for a commutation. Slaton made a painstaking study of the evidence. He was under a great deal of tension since, as Dinnerstein wrote, "the governor was bombarded with pleas for commutation or demands that the prisoner hang. More than a thousand of the petitioners threatened to kill Slaton, and his wife, if he let Frank live."

Early on the morning of June 21, he told his wife that he had decided to commute Frank's sentence to life in prison. He admitted he feared for his life. According to Jordan, his wife told him, "I would rather be the widow of a brave and honorable man than the wife of a coward."

Knowing the decision could provoke violence, Slaton directed officials to transport Frank from Atlanta's Fulton County jail to the state prison at Milledgeville over 100 miles away.

Then Slaton made his decision public. In it he said he had grave doubts about Frank's guilt. One factor in his decision was the probability that Mary had been shoved down the chute rather than transported in the elevator as Conley asserted. Here Slaton referred to a "disagreeable" matter, that of the feces at the bottom of the elevator shaft.

The mystery in the case is the question of how Mary Phagan's body got into the basement … Conley testified that on the morning of April 26 he went down into the basement to relieve his bowels and utilized the elevator shaft for the purpose.

On the morning of April 27 at 3 o'clock when the detectives came down into the basement by way of the ladder, they inspected the premises, including the shaft, and they found there human excrement in natural condition.

Subsequently, when they used the elevator, which everybody, including Conley, who had run the elevator for one and a half years admits only stops by hitting the ground in the basement, the elevator struck the excrement and mashed it, thus demonstrating that the elevator had not been used since Conley had been there."

The Governor noted other evidence tending to point toward Conley's guilt rather than Frank's including, as Jordan recorded, "the fact that the notes were written on pads normally kept in the basement and not in Leo Frank's office.

The Governor was applauded by some newspapers and burned in effigy by those outraged. In Marietta, a town outside Atlanta, the effigy bore a sign reading "John M. Slaton, King of the Jews and Georgia's Traitor Forever." In *The Jeffersonian*, Tom Watson blasted the decision, writing, "… let no man reproach the South with Lynch law: Let him remember the unendurable provocation: and let him say whether Lynch law is not better than no law at all."

## The Lynching

"Less than two weeks after Slaton had commuted Leo Frank's sentence state newspapers prominently featured the somber pilgrimage of saddened Georgians to the unveiling of Mary Phagan's monument ... A group of 150 men, who called themselves the Knights of Mary Phagan, then met secretly near her grave, and pledged to avenge the little girl's death," Dinnerstein wrote. On the night of July 18, 1915, a prisoner named William Creen slashed the sleeping Frank's throat. Two other prisoners, both doctors, managed to clamp the jugular vein. Frank was taken to the prison hospital and his wound stitched. According to Dinnerstein, when Frank was conscious he said, "I am going to live. I must live. I must vindicate myself."

One month later, on Aug. 16, a mob of about 25 men stormed the Milledgeville prison. They overpowered the two guards on duty, then went to the hospital room where Frank was recovering. The intruders handcuffed Frank and ushered him into the back seat of a waiting car with two men on either side of him. The kidnappers tried to persuade Frank to confess, even offering to spare his life if he did so. The prisoner adamantly denied the crime. According to Dinnerstein, "He sounded so sincere that two of his listeners thought that perhaps he really had not murdered Mary Phagan, and that he should be returned to the prison farm."

The doubters were overruled. When they got to a wooded area on the outskirts of Marietta, they led Frank to an oak tree. Jordan wrote, "Frank was asked if he wanted to make a statement. He said no. He removed his wedding ring from his finger, handed it to one of his abductors and asked that it be given to a newspaperman who would forward the ring to his wife. The request was granted, and the ring eventually was returned to Mrs. Frank."

A rope was wrapped around his neck, then flung over and attached to a sturdy limb of the tree. Frank was forced to stand on a table and the table was kicked out from under him.

## The Rule of Lynch Law

Lynching was common in the American West before formal

legal institutions became established. As *The Columbia Encyclopedia* noted, "Pioneers formed vigilance committees to repress crimes."

The South was the other major area for lynch law. Lynching was not always associated with racism but the very word would eventually conjure up the image of an accused African-American strung up by an angry, white Southern mob. According to the *Encyclopedia Americana*, "The antebellum South was known as the land of lynching before prejudice against black people became a major factor. Of the more than 300 persons hanged or burned by mobs between 1840 and 1860, fewer than 10% were black." However, protecting the slave system was often at issue as mobs set upon white abolitionists for aiding escaping black slaves.

After the defeat of the South in the Civil War, lynching focused more heavily on black victims. "There are 2805 [documented] victims of lynch mobs killed between 1882 and 1930 in 10 southern states, according to Stewart E. Tolnay and E.M. Beck, *A Festival of Violence: An Analysis of Southern Lynchings, 1882-1930.* "Although mobs murdered almost 300 white men and women, the vast majority—almost 2,500—of lynch victims were African-American. Of these black victims, 94 percent died in the hands of white lynch mobs. The scale of this carnage means that, on the average, a black man, woman, or child was murdered nearly once a week, every week, between 1882 and 1930 by a hate-driven white mob."

As *The Columbia Encyclopedia* noted, lynching was used "to intimidate blacks into political, social, and economic submission." Contrary to white supremacist myth and widespread perception, most lynched blacks had not been accused of raping or attempting to rape a white woman; that allegation was at issue in only one-quarter of cases in which black men were lynched. Blacks were lynched for a variety of offenses ranging from common crimes to actions that were "crimes" only according to white supremacist ideology such as "insulting" a white person or registering to vote.

The Leo Frank case was also exceptional, perhaps even unique, in that the victim was a white man lynched for a crime almost certainly committed by a black. However, as to Robert L. Zangrando's segment of "About Lynching," people who were lynched included "Native Americans, Latinos, Jews, Asian immigrants, and European newcomers." Lynching targets were also "labor union organizers, political radicals, critics of America's role in World War I, and civil rights advocates."

An anti-lynching movement had started almost a quarter of a century before a mob took Leo Frank to a tree in Marietta. Its primary leader was African-American journalist Ida B. Wells-Barnett. She published a series of newspaper columns decrying the injustice of lynching and, in 1892, an influential pamphlet called *Southern Horrors: Lynch Law in All Its Phases.* Groups like the National Association for the Advancement of Colored People worked to fight lynching through both education and legal action.

In the 1920s and 1930s, many white women, offended by the defense of lynching as necessary to "protect" them, became prominent in the anti-lynching movement. According to Dickson D. Bruce, Jr. in "Antilynching Campaign," they "worked to create a climate of opinion among white southerners that would lead to lynching's demise." The practice began to die off in the 1940s.

## Aftermath

Much of the Georgia public believed justice had been served by Frank's lynching. The local Marietta newspaper proclaimed: 'We regard the hanging of Leo M. Frank in Cobb County as an act of law abiding citizens.'" No one was ever charged with a crime in connection with the lynching. Dinnerstein quoted the Greensboro, Ga., *Herald-Journal* as saying that "the lynchers could confess, publish their confession in the Atlanta papers, and they would never be molested." While Tom Watson and many other prominent Georgians praised the lynching, there were also voices raised in condemnation. *The Atlanta Constitution* called it "Georgia's Shame!" and wrote, "No word in the language is too strong to apply to the deliberate and carefully conspired deed of the mob."

Gov. Slaton never held another elected public office. By contrast, Hugh Dorsey was elected Georgia's governor in 1916—riding the coattails of his prosecution of Leo Frank. It did not hurt him that he had Tom Watson's endorsement. Dorsey was re-elected in 1918. During that term, he broke ranks with Watson by criticizing Georgia's treatment of African-Americans. The two of them ran against each other for a U. S. Senate seat. Watson won by a wide margin and died in office in 1922.

Lucile Frank lived for several more decades but never remarried. In 1916, she left Atlanta for Tennessee when a brother-in-law offered her a job in a women's clothing shop. In the 1920s, she returned to Atlanta where she worked at the glove counter managed by her brother-in-law at a J.P. Allen clothing store. Although she outwardly functioned normally, those close to her believed she never stopped mourning Leo.

An internist who treated her, Dr. James Kauffman, said, "She somatized [made physical] her complaints. She had chest pains, headaches. When I think of her, I think of depression. Leo may have been killed but she served a life sentence." She signed her name "Mrs. Leo Frank" until her death in 1957. Among her affects were the wedding ring a doomed Leo had asked to be returned to her and letters Lucile had written to her husband—several of them penned after his death.

After serving a year on a chain gang for his confessed crime of accessory after the fact for helping to move Mary Phagan's body, Jim Conley was released. He had more scrapes with the law for offenses ranging from public intoxication to burglary and died in 1962.

B'nai B'rith established the Anti-Defamation League shortly after Frank's trial. Frank's trial was one of the factors leading to the formation of this organization but by no means the sole cause.

After Frank's death, the Knights of Mary Phagan served as the launching pad for the resurrected Knights of the Ku Klux Klan, an organization that had been dormant since its Reconstruction heyday. According to "The Leo Frank Case" compiled by Charles Pou, "It must be noted that the Phagan family has not condoned Klan activity, especially in regards to Mary. In fact the family expressly forbade a Klan request to hold a ceremony at Mary Phagan's gravesite."

Pou recorded that on March 11, 1986, "the Georgia Board of Pardons and Paroles finally issued a posthumous pardon to Leo Frank, based on the state's failure to protect him while in custody; it did not officially absolve him of the crime."

On the 80th anniversary of Frank's lynching, Rabbi Steven Lebow had a plaque placed on an office building at the site where Frank was killed. That plaque states: *Wrongly accused. Falsely convicted. Wantonly murdered.*

Over a century after her death, people have not forgotten "the little factory girl" who went to pick up her pay and never returned home. Her grave in the Marietta City Cemetery continues to be visited and some people even leave gifts of toys and model angels.

# CHAPTER FOUR
## The Scottsboro Boys

Few cases in the annals of American justice have had as far-reaching effects as the "Scottsboro Boys." Through years of trials, convictions, appeals winding all the way up to the United States Supreme Court, and re-trials, the Scottsboro Boys case exposed the way sexual and racial tensions met and exploded in the Jim Crow South. It sent shock waves through the American psyche that reverberate to this day. Scottsboro helped fan the fires of the nascent civil rights movement. It also heightened conflict between that movement and other branches of the American left. While nine innocent youths grew to adulthood in the purgatory of prison, many people rose up to protest the injustice they had suffered and, in the process, move against the racism that made that injustice possible and perhaps inevitable.

The case of the Scottsboro Boys often seemed like one of dueling prejudices. Entrenched racism against blacks, anti-Semitism, the Madonna/Whore dichotomy, and regional stereotypes would all be on full display as the Scottsboro Boys grabbed headlines for well over a decade. It is a story of cowardice and heroism, of lies and manipulation, of fear and hatred, of caring and commitment, a story in which every facet of the human personality is seen in all its embarrassing weakness and glorious strength.

## A Fuss on a Train

"The next time you want by, just tell me you want by and I let you by," an irritated Haywood Patterson, 19, said to the white youth who had for the second time stepped on Patterson's hand. The black teenager hung onto the side of a freight train and the white teen was walking across the top of the cars. The white youth responded with a racial epithet.

It was March 25, 1931, in the midst of the Great Depression and Patterson, like the white boy with whom he quarreled, was doing what many impoverished people, blacks and whites, usually men but sometimes women, did on freight trains: hitching a ride to get from one place to another for free. It was illegal to "hobo" on these trains but even train workers tended to look the other way during this desperate period. Patterson was accompanied by three close friends who, like himself, were from Chattanooga, Tennessee, and sought work in Memphis, Alabama. They were Eugene Williams, 13, and brothers Andrew and Leroy "Roy" Wright who were 19 and 13 respectively.

Patterson and the white boy exchanged insults and the latter shouted, "All you black bastards better get off!"

Racist protocol of the period dictated that blacks submit to whites but Patterson would not take guff from anyone. "We got as much right here as you!" he replied.

The train slowed at a steep grade. The white boy and his friends jumped off the train. They grabbed rocks and tossed them at the four black youths hanging off the sides of the cars. Patterson, Williams and the two Wrights took cover inside a freight car. The train stopped at Stevenson, Alabama, where Patterson and his buddies went off. They met up with some other black youths who planned to hop aboard the train. These black youths agreed to help Patterson and his friends if the whites confronted them again.

The white youths clambered back aboard the train, the blacks returned to it as well and the fight resumed. Soon the blacks got the best of it and began chasing the whites off the train.

By the time only one white, Orville Gilley, was left, the train had picked up speed and it was likely he would be severely injured if not killed from going off it. In Patterson's words, the blacks "took pity on him" and pulled him back into a car as he hung from a side.

The bloodied whites made their way to the Stevenson train station. They reported that a group of blacks had picked a fight with them and that they wanted to press charges against their attackers. The stationmaster got on the phone to alert authorities in the next Alabama town, Scottsboro. Those on the other end of the line said that the train had passed through a few minutes before and that its next stop was Paint Rock, Alabama.

## Posse at Paint Rock

Alabama Jackson County Sheriff M. L. Wann telephoned Deputy Sheriff Charlie Latham and told Latham to "capture every Negro on the train and bring them to Scottsboro." Latham deputized men who lined up along the Paint Rock train station. The train stopped and the recently deputized posse went on board to search the freight cars.

The posse found nine black youths, a young white man named Orville Gilley, and, much to their surprise, two young white women decked out in men's caps and wearing overalls covering their dresses. The women were close friends Victoria Price, 21, and Ruby Bates, 17, who were returning home to Huntsville, Alabama. They had ridden to Chattanooga in search of mill work but failed to find it.

There are differing reports as to exactly when and under what circumstances an accusation of rape was made. It seems most likely that, as one of the reports recorded in *Stories of Scottsboro* states, a deputy asked the women "if the Negroes had bothered them." Bates and Price knew that racist ideology held that black men would rape white women at the first opportunity and that the officers questioning them believed the arrested men had enjoyed such an opportunity. They probably also feared that they themselves might be arrested for illegally riding the train.

The women gave the answer that they probably believed was expected: "Yes."

The blacks were taken to jail, initially under the impression that they were being charged for the brawl. In addition to Patterson, Williams, and the Wrights, were five others, all strangers to the four friends and to each other.

Charlie Weems at 20 was the only one out of his teens. Clarence Norris and Ozie Powell were older teenagers. There were also two youths who had taken no part in the brawl. They were Olen Montgomery, blind in his left eye and possessing partial vision in his right, and Willie Roberson, afflicted with advanced syphilis and gonorrhea. Roberson's illnesses led to severe swelling in his genital area and needing a cane to walk.

When the group arrived in Scottsboro, Sheriff Wann sent Ruby Bates and Victoria Price for a medical examination.

The rape accusations led a mob to assemble in front of the jail. Sabrina Crewe and Michael V. Uschan write in The Scottsboro Case, "some 500 angry white people gathered around the jail in Scottsboro."

The accused, who would become known as the "Scottsboro Boys," were not the only ones behind bars for the alleged rapes. As James R. Acker reports in *Scottsboro and Its Legacy: The Cases That Challenged American Legal and Social Justice,* "Price, Bates, and the several white boys who had been on the train and had fought with the blacks, were all held in the Scottsboro jail as material witnesses."

## White Women in the South: Delicate Ideal vs. Grubby Reality

The South had a famously chivalrous ideal of white women as pure, delicate, and genteel. However, the reality lived by many Southern white women was far removed from that ideal. James Goodman in *Stories of Scottsboro* notes that Ruby Bates and Victoria Price "lived with their mothers in unpainted shacks in the worst sections of town."

Ruby Bates's mother, Emma, had picked cotton and taken in laundry. Ruby's hard-drinking, violence-prone father also picked cotton. Emma fled more than once from her husband. She worked for awhile in a Huntsville mill but was unemployed and widowed by 1931. Ruby was her sole support.

Victoria Price's mother had worked in a mill until left disabled by a fall. Like Ruby, Victoria was the sole support of both herself and her mother.

Bates and Price were what most Southerners reviled as "white trash"—until they accused blacks of raping them. In their alleged violation, they became martyrs to many whites. Price would come to relish her new role.

Sadly, the lies were soon supported by one of the accused. As Carter wrote, "Roy Wright—when accused by Orville Gilley in the presence of newsmen—began insisting that he and his three friends were innocent; the other five had assaulted the girls."

## A Dodderer and a Drunk for the Defense

Most local attorneys did not want to be associated with blacks accused of raping white women. Lawyer Milo C. Moody agreed to represent the Scottsboro Boys, perhaps because the 69-year-old no longer had much business. Carter quotes an observer describing Moody as "doddering."

In Chattanooga a leading black physician, Dr. P. A. Stephens, summoned a group called the Interdenominational Colored Ministers' Alliance and they raised $50.08 for the defense. Even in 1931, it was a small sum for an attorney's retainer but Dr. Stephens and the Alliance found a taker in attorney Stephen R. Roddy. Like Moody, Roddy's skills were modest. Drinking often hampered what skills he had. Retainer in hand, he headed for Scottsboro.

Trials of all nine defendants began April 6, 1931.

Judge Alfred E. Hawkins presided. Circuit Solicitor H. G. Bailey prosecuted.

For reasons not clarified at the time, Bailey moved to have the trials separated as follows: Clarence Norris and Charlie Weems tried first; Haywood Patterson tried second; Olen Montgomery, Ozie Powell, Willie Roberson, Andy Wright and

Eugene Williams fourth; Roy Wright tried last.Hawkins granted this motion and the trial of Norris and Weems started that same day.

Alabama law at the time limited jury service to a county's "male citizens" between the ages of 21 and 65. It did not state that jurors had to be white but the entire jury pool was white. Victoria Price gave her testimony in a straightforward but flamboyant manner. Acker records, "She testified that she and Ruby Bates had traveled from their hometown of Huntsville, Alabama to Chattanooga on Tuesday, March 24. They spent the night with Mrs. Callie Brochie, a friend of [Victoria's] who lived in Chattanooga on Seventh Street. When their search for a mill job proved unfruitful, the two women hopped a freight train to return home shortly before noon on the 25th." She described a fight breaking out between black and white youths on the train and the whites, except for Gilley, being tossed off.

### "Are You Going to Put out?"

Then she got to Clarence Norris. Price said he had demanded, "Are you going to put out?"

She testified she replied, "No, sir, I am not." Then six of the defendants overpowered her. For what seemed like hours, she elaborated, six men—Weems, Norris, the Wrights, Patterson, and Montgomery—raped her.

In an attempt to appeal to the common sentiments of the day against women with non-marital sexual experience, Roddy tried to cast doubt on Price's testimony on cross-examination by showing she had been promiscuous. Bailey objected and Judge Hawkins sustained.

Bailey called Dr. R. R. Bridges, one of the physicians who had examined Price and Bates within an hour and a half after the alleged attacks, to the stand. Bridges testified that he had found only a few small bruises and scratches on her. "She was not lacerated at all," he said. "She was not bloody, neither was the other girl."

Bridges said he had found semen in Price's vagina but that the spermatozoa in it was "non-motile," meaning it was no longer alive. The significance of this would not be clarified in this trial. In answer to a question from Bailey, Bridges said it was "possible" that Price and Bates had been raped.

Dr. Marvin Lynch testified that there had been a fair amount of semen in Bates's vagina but a very small amount in Price's. He testified that, "the vagina was in good condition on both of the girls. There was nothing to indicate any violence about the vagina."

Although neither Weems nor Norris was charged with raping Ruby Bates, the prosecution wanted her to corroborate Price's story.

On the witness stand, Bates's demeanor contrasted sharply with that of Price. Bates appeared nervous and often hesitated before replying to questions. Bates supported her friend's testimony in basics. Acker reports, "She confirmed Price's testimony that the two young women had spent the previous night at Mrs. Brochie's house on Seventh Street in Chattanooga and had sought jobs in a mill."

The defense called Charlie Weems to the stand. The youth appeared sure of his answers as Roddy questioned him. Weems recalled how Patterson had claimed some white boys had started a fight and Weems agreed to help the blacks.

Then Bailey cross-examined Weems. Carter writes, "In rapid succession, [Bailey] fired question after question ... But Weems held his ground."

Roddy and Moody put Clarence Norris on the stand. Carter describes Norris as "fidgeting" as he testified.

Bailey cross-examined and Norris appeared to panic. To the horror of defense counsels, Norris testified that "every one of them have something to do with those girls after they put the white boys off the train." Norris described a gang rape but claimed he alone was innocent.

A flustered Roddy requested a recess. Judge Hawkins granted it.

Roddy offered to plead not only Norris but Weems as well guilty in exchange for a sentence of life imprisonment instead of death. Bailey refused the offer.

Under re-direct-examination, Roddy tried to undo the

damage. He showed that Norris claimed to not know whether Price and Bates had worn dresses or overalls. Roddy drew forth the admission that he had recently claimed he had seen no rape but Norris stuck to his new story claiming that not only Weems but all the others accused had raped the women while insisting: "I did not."

After a brief but dramatic trial, the defense rested in despair.

As the jury retired to deliberate the fates of Norris and Weems, the trial of Haywood Patterson began before an all male, white jury. Price was as confident as she had been at the previous proceeding. Ruby Bates was again nervous and hesitant.

As Bates left the stand, the bailiff informed Hawkins that the Norris and Weems jury had reached a verdict. The Patterson jury was escorted into the jury room.

The foreman of the Norris and Weems jury announced, "We find the defendants guilty of rape and fix their sentence at death."

"The announcement spawned a raucous celebration in the courtroom that quickly spilled into the street," according to Acker.

At Patterson's trial, Dr. Bridges gave essentially the same testimony he had at the previous trial. The prosecution did not call Dr. Lynch.

The defense called Patterson to the stand. Patterson recalled how he and his friends had hopped the freight train to Memphis in hopes of finding work.

Under cross-examination, Patterson appeared to fall apart. Like Norris, Patterson apparently panicked and thought he could save himself by implicating others. He testified he had seen five of the defendants rape Price but he and his three friends had not. Within minutes, he contradicted himself by saying he had never even seen the females while he was on the train. "I did not see the girls in there," he insisted. "I did not see any girls in there until we got to Paint Rock."

Roddy called 13-year-old Roy Wright to the stand. He described the fight and how the whites were forced off the train except for Orville Gilley.

Then Roy Wright, like Norris before him, dropped a bomb on the defense. He testified to seeing the accused—save for himself, his brother Andy, and his friends Williams and Patterson—"Down there with the girls and all had intercourse with them."

Roddy and Moody did not make a summation. The prosecution made a brief one, the judge instructed the jury on the law, and Patterson's case went to the jury.

### Five on Trial

As a jury pondered Patterson's fate, Ozie Powell, Willie Roberson, Andy Wright, Eugene Williams, and Olen Montgomery went on trial, once again before an all-white, all-male jury.

"It was easy to see why the solicitor had postponed these cases until last, as they presented a number of problems," Carter wrote in his book. "In the first place, each defendant so far had told a relatively plausible story and had held to it through cross-examination. Norris, Weems, and Patterson had all been positively identified by Victoria Price, the state's star witness. In this trial, however, it was up to Ruby Bates to point out at least three of the defendants."

Additionally, Roberson's advanced venereal diseases had left his genitals painfully swollen and Montgomery had limited vision. Both conditions would make it difficult to rape.

Price testified that the first man "to put his hands on me" was the man "with the sleepy eyes, Olen Montgomery." Montgomery had raped her while Williams held an open knife above her and Roberson held her legs open. Others ran excitedly about shouting, "Pour it to her! Pour it to her!" Price firmly stated that Montgomery, Andy Wright, and Williams had raped her and that she had seen Powell and Roberson rape Bates.

Word came that Patterson's jury had reached a verdict after deliberating for only 25 minutes. Judge Hawkins ordered the jury for the present trial out of the courtroom. The Patterson jurors trooped in. The verdict was read: Patterson was guilty and sentenced to death. The trial of Powell, Roberson, Andy Wright, Williams, and Montgomery resumed, with the state calling Bates to the stand. As usual, she was shaky. However, she did testify that she and Price had been to Chattanooga in search of work and spent the night at Mrs. Brochie's establishment. When talking about the alleged events on the train, Bates testified that the defendants, armed with both knives and guns, had barged into the gondola in which she and Price were riding.

Dr. Bridges went through the same evidence he had given in the two previous trials. Bridges testified that Roberson's sex organ had been "very sore" so that intercourse would inevitably be "attended with some pain" but speculated it would still be "possible."

The defense called Roberson to the stand. He testified he had been on the freight train to seek help for his illnesses in Memphis. Acker reports that Roberson testified to getting into an empty boxcar toward the end of the train. He said he had not even known about the fight and could not have committed rape. Acker quotes Roberson as testifying, "There was something the matter with my privates down there; it was sore and swelled up ... I am not able to have sexual intercourse."

Andy Wright testified to the fight but claimed innocence even of that. Carter describes Bailey's cross-examination as "brief and fiery." Bailey asked, "Did you not tell her after the rape, 'Yes, you will have a baby after this?'"

Andy Wright replied, "I did not have any such talk as that; I swear that I was not in that car where the women were." Regardless of Andy Wright's denials, the scenario Bailey suggested had to have a powerful emotional impact on the jurors. It brought up the universal specter of the horror of rape being extended by the victim's pregnancy and, equally horrifying to a jury of the time period, the specter of a white woman giving birth to a black baby.

Montgomery testified, "If I had seen them, I would not have known whether they were men or women."

For the first time in any of the Scottsboro Boys trials, Orville Gilley testified. "I saw those five in the car," Gilley stated.

"I saw every one of those five in the gondola." He was asked if Price and Bates were there as well and he replied, "Yes, sir." Acker writes that Gilley "offered nothing to confirm that the women had been raped and he was asked no questions on cross-examination."

After a trial lasting one day, the case went to the jury.

One defendant had yet to be tried: Roy Wright. He was 13 and, as Carter reports, "Under Alabama law he could be tried only in a juvenile court unless the state brought waiver proceedings."

On April 9, 1931, the jury for the other five announced its verdict: guilty. It recommended death for each.

Despite the prosecution having asked for only life imprisonment for the 13-year-old Roy Wright, seven of his jurors wanted to sentence him to death. After being told the jury was deadlocked, Judge Hawkins declared a mistrial.

Later that same afternoon, Judge Hawkins, with tears in his eyes, sentenced the other eight defendants to die.

Letters poured into Governor Miller's office asking for mercy and the Alabama Interracial Commission met in Birmingham to pass a resolution demanding a "careful review of these cases in the courts."

## Peculiar Political Tug of War

Perhaps the most important communications received by both Judge Hawkins and Alabama Governor Miller were telegrams demanding a "stay of execution and opportunity to investigate and prepare for a new trial" that were signed by the International Labor Defense (ILD), the legal arm of the Communist Party, U. S. A. Its chief lawyer was Joseph Brodsky.

The case also attracted the attention of the National Association for the Advancement of Colored People. The organization was then headed by Executive Secretary Walter White who, like other NAACP officials, was alarmed by the communist entrance into the case. Acker writes, "The NAACP accused the ILD of exploiting the case for propaganda purposes and being willing to make martyrs of the Boys to advance its political agenda."

The ILD recruited respected attorney George W. Chamlee Sr. to take over the case.

Soon Brodsky headed to the Birmingham jail where he spoke with the Scottsboro Boys. Brodsky told them that the ILD wanted to do everything possible to save them. Then he asked them to sign an affidavit giving the ILD control of their cases. Impressed by the man's apparent sincerity and absence of racial prejudice, Andy Wright signed and the others, who were unable to write their own names, placed their marks on the document.

Upon learning of this agreement, Walter White sent word to Dr. P. A. Stephens, a member of the Chattanooga Negro Ministers' Alliance, telling him that the Chattanooga Negro Ministers' Alliance must be made aware of the communist philosophy of the ILD and that the Boys must be persuaded to cut the connection. Stephens convened a meeting of the alliance in which he informed them of the nature of the ILD and then contacted Roddy.

Roddy drove to the Birmingham jail for a chat with the Boys. Roddy told them that the ILD could do them more harm than good and they signed a statement Roddy had prepared telling the ILD to leave the case.

Acker writes that there were "months of wrangling and altering allegiances" that left the Boys "bewildered." He continues, "After a last-ditch effort, negotiations broke down … the NAACP bowed out of the case."

## ILD: No fair trial

The ILD attorneys went before the Alabama Supreme Court on January 21, 1932. Brodsky argued that the juries were not composed of "peers" of the defendants since blacks had been excluded. Brodsky also argued that biased newspaper accounts together with the presence of crowds obviously hostile to the defendants had made a fair trial impossible. Finally, Brodsky told the court that Roy Wright should have been tried in a juvenile court because of his age.

Chamlee argued that defense counsel had been inadequate.

Alabama Attorney General Thomas G. Knight Jr. argued for the state. It would seem that he had an advantage in arguing before the Alabama Supreme Court because one of the sitting justices on it was his father, Justice Thomas Knight Sr.

"Why should we assume that the gathering of a curious mob would have influenced the jurors and judge of the trial court?" Knight asked.

The Alabama Supreme Court upheld the convictions of all defendants except Eugene Williams, who was granted a new trial because he was a juvenile when first tried and should have been tried in a juvenile court. (Instead of getting a new trial, Williams was left to languish in jail for six years before being released in 1937.)

Justice Thomas Knight Sr. wrote of the argument that the Scottsboro Boys had not been denied a fair trial because blacks were excluded from the state's juries: "The State of Alabama has the right, within constitutional limitations, to fix the qualifications for jurors."

After this defeat, the ILD engaged Walter Pollak, a lawyer known for his acumen in constitutional law. On May 27, 1932, Pollak presented preliminary arguments to the United States Supreme Court and the highest court in the land agreed to review the Scottsboro Boys case.

Pollak made the same arguments before the U.S. Supreme Court that Brodsky and Chamlee had previously made before the Alabama Supreme Court.

On November 7, 1932, the U.S. Supreme Court overturned all Scottsboro convictions, without addressing the exclusion of blacks from juries. It made its decision solely on the grounds that the defendants had been denied adequate counsel. The ruling stated that the "due process" clause of the 14th Amendment meant that inadequate counsel rendered a trial unfair.

To continue fighting the good fight, the ILD approached Samuel Leibowitz, a New York City attorney who was widely considered one of the top legal talents in the country, second only to Clarence Darrow in reputation. The ILD told this usually expensive lawyer that it would not be able to pay him any fee at all and asked him to take the case for humanitarian reasons. Leibowitz agreed to defend the Scottsboro Boys without payment because, he said, the case "touches no controversial theory of economy or government, but the basic rights of man."

On March 13, 1933, Leibowitz arrived in Alabama and took over leadership of the case.

Knight encountered a worry as he prepared for trial: the Huntsville police could not find Ruby Bates. Her mother said Ruby left the family home on February 27, 1933. While Bates was a much weaker witness than Price, the prosecution still regarded Bates's testimony as vital. However, that testimony had been thrown into question by events earlier in the year.

As Carter reports, "On January 5, 1932, Huntsville police had arrested Miron Pearlman ... on a routine charge of drunkenness. When they searched the ex-prize fighter, however, they found a letter which caused consternation from Scottsboro to Montgomery." It was a letter written by Ruby Bates to a boyfriend. Bates wrote, in part, "... is a goddam lie about those negros jassing me ..."

Pearlman told police that Chamlee had paid Pearlman to get Bates drunk and talk her into writing a letter claiming she had not been raped. Police found Bates. She signed an affidavit disavowing the letter: "I was so drunk that I did not know what I was doing."

The new trial of Haywood Patterson opened March 27, 1932, with Judge James E. Horton Jr. presiding.

For the fifth time, Price dramatically told her story of rapes. She identified Patterson as one of those who had attacked her.

In preparation for his cross-examination of Price, Leibowitz had asked the Lionel Corporation to build a replica of the train. The attorney asked Price if the replica resembled the fateful train.

Price replied, "That is not the train I was on. It was bigger, lots bigger. That is a toy."

In answer to a question from Leibowitz, Price stated she was bleeding from her vagina after the rapes.

Leibowitz returned to her previous statement that she had stayed at the boardinghouse of Callie Brochie the night before being on the train. He questioned her closely about exactly where that establishment was located. Was it two miles from the train yard? "No sir, I wouldn't say two miles," she answered.

When Leibowitz remarked that she was "a little bit of an actress," Price retorted, "You're a pretty good actor yourself."

## A Man Named Lester Carter

Leibowitz questioned her on her activities on the day prior to the incident.

"Do you know a man by the name of Lester Carter?" Leibowitz inquired.

She said she knew that he was thrown off the train but had not known him prior to that.

Leibowitz's manner showed that he considered this of crucial import. He said, "Mrs. Price I … want to ask you that question again and give you an opportunity to change your answer if you want to. Did you know Lester Carter before that day, yes or no?"

For the first time, Price appeared anxious. "Before in Scottsboro—he—was on the train."

Leibowitz pressed, "Before this day on the train did you know Lester Carter?"

"I never did know him," she replied.

Leibowitz then turned to the subject of Jack Tiller. In 1931, Victoria Price had been convicted in Huntsville, Alabama of fornication and adultery with the married Tiller. Both had been fined and sentenced to a short stint in jail. Leibowitz asked, "Did you have intercourse with Tiller a short time before you left Huntsville?"

Price denied it.

Leibowitz queried her about the woman who owned the boardinghouse where she had claimed to stay the night previous to getting on the train. The lawyer said, "The name of Mrs. Callie you apply to this boarding house lady is the name of a boarding house lady used by Octavus Roy Cohen in the Saturday Evening Post series—"Sis Callie," isn't that where you got the name?" Knight instantly objected and Judge Horton sustained the objection.

Dr. R. R. Bridges again took the stand. Knight questioned him and he repeated his previous testimony about finding semen in Price's vagina. Leibowitz then asked him about Price and Bates's physical condition. The physician testified that neither woman had dilated pupils and each had normal pulse and respiration—readings unlikely just an hour and a half after suffering gang rape. Dr. Bridges also testified that the sperm in the women were non-motile and that sperm usually remains motile in the vagina from 12 to 48 hours after being deposited in the vagina—thus making it unlikely, if not impossible, that the semen in the women was the result of intercourse less than two hours prior to the examination. He also said there was no bleeding from Price's vagina.

The second physician to examine Price and Bates after the alleged rapes, Dr. Marvin Lynch, was scheduled to take the stand, but before calling him, Knight asked for a recess to confer with Judge Horton. The recess was granted and Horton, Knight, and Lynch met in another room in the courthouse.

Carter writes, "When Knight and the other lawyers for the state returned to the courtroom, however, the doctor asked Horton if they could meet privately." They did. Carter continues, "The young doctor, who appeared unnerved and agitated, went straight to the point. Contrary to Knight's statement, said Lynch, his testimony would not be a repetition of Dr. Bridge's, because he did not believe the girls had been raped."

Horton exclaimed, "My God, doctor, is this whole thing a horrible mistake?"

The judge urged Dr. Lynch to testify but the doctor cowered and said, "If I testified for those boys I'd never be able to go back into Jackson County." Horton excused him.

When Leibowitz began the defense portion of the trial, he led off with a witness who would contradict Price's testimony about having spent the evening before the train ride in a boardinghouse.

Dallas Ramsey, who lived near the Chattanooga railroad yards, testified that on the morning of the alleged rapes, he strolled through a wooded area near his home and saw two women. Later that same morning, Ramsey claimed to have seen the two women and a man board a freight train. Leibowitz indicated Price and asked if this was one of the women Ramsey had seen. "Yes sir, I recognize her," the witness replied.

Chattanooga gynecologist Dr. Edward A. Reisman testified. "To my mind it would be quite inconceivable that six men should have intercourse with one woman and not leave telltale traces of their presence in considerable quantities in the vagina."

Then Leibowitz gave an explanation for the small amount of semen that had been found in Price by calling Lester Carter to testify. Carter told the jury that he had been in the Huntsville County Jail for vagrancy in January 1931, where he met Price and Tiller who were serving time for adultery.

After Carter's release, Price arranged a date between Carter and Bates. On the evening of March 23, 1931, the four met up together. In a wooded area known as a "hobo jungle," Carter claimed, "I had intercourse with Ruby Bates and Jack Tiller had intercourse with Victoria Price."

Carter testified that he rode a rail headed to Chattanooga as did Bates and Price. The three encountered a man who said his name was "Carolina Slim" but whose real name was Orville Gilley. Now a group of four, they found their way to a hobo jungle where Carter again enjoyed sexual intercourse with Bates. He did not know for sure what, if anything, Price and Gilley might have done.

Just as the defense rested, Leibowitz received a surprise that would result in a genuine shock for the rest of the people assembled in the courtroom.

**Ruby Bates, Witness for the Defense**

A messenger handed Leibowitz a note. Upon reading it, Leibowitz approached Judge Horton. The defense attorney requested a recess that was granted.

When the court reconvened, Leibowitz called Bates to the stand. Bates appeared nervous, as she had in her prior courtroom appearances. This time, though, she was better dressed than she had been in those appearances.

Leibowitz got right to the point. On the evening of March 23, 1931, he asked, "Did you have intercourse with Lester Carter?"

"I certainly did," Bates replied, her answer forthright but her demeanor subdued.

Did Price have sex with Jack Tiller in Bates's presence? "She certainly did," Bates testified.

Leibowitz asked if rape had taken place on the freight train. Bates replied that she had not been raped and that she did not believe Price had been either and that the two of them had been together throughout the train ride.

Bates related how she had left Huntsville for Montgomery after that fateful train ride. She hitched a ride to New York. Her conscience gnawed at her because of the lies she had told. She heard of a famous Christian minister who resided in New York named Dr. Harry Emerson Fosdick. Bates mispronounced his name as "Fostick." She arranged a visit with him and he urged her to return to Alabama and tell the truth.

Knight began cross-examination by taking note of the witness's obviously improved wardrobe. "Where did you get that coat?" the prosecutor asked.

Bates mumbled, "I bought it."

He demanded to know where she got the money to buy it and she answered, "I don't know."

"You don't know?" Knight mocked. "Where did you get that hat? Who was the beneficent donor?"

The judge asked her more gently, "Do you know?"

Bates said, "Dr. Fostick of New York."

Wade Wright gave the summation for the prosecution. He urged the jury to "show them that Alabama justice cannot be bought and sold with Jew money from New York!"

Leibowitz leapt to his feet. "I move for a mistrial," he said. "I submit that a conviction in this case won't be worth a pinch of snuff in view of what this man just said."

Judge Horton rebuked Wright for what the jurist characterized as an "improper" remark but denied the motion for a mistrial.

In the defense summation, Leibowitz pointed out how evasive Price had often seemed. He discussed the testimony of Dr. Bridges and Dr. Reisman and insisted that their statements indicated it was physically impossible for Price and Bates to have been raped. He said that Carter's testimony easily explained the small amount of semen found in the vaginas of the two alleged victims and urged the jury to accept Bates's recantation.

Leibowitz tried to undercut the appeal to anti-Semitism that Wright had made with his "Jew money" comment. "I'm not getting a fee in this case and I'm not getting a penny toward expenses," he said.

The trial had lasted two weeks. Carter describes the case as going "to the jury just before 1 p.m." on a Saturday and the jury sending word at 10 a.m. on Sunday that they had reached a verdict. They found Patterson guilty and sentenced him to die.

Leibowitz was understandably upset. In an interview with a reporter he lashed out in a manner guaranteed to arouse the resentment of Southerners in general. The perplexed reporter asked him how the jury could have come to the decision it did and Leibowitz replied, "If you ever saw those creatures, those bigots whose mouths are slits in their faces, whose eyes pop out like a frog's, whose chins drip tobacco juice, bewhiskered and filthy, you would not ask how they could do it."

Offense to this comment was widespread throughout the South with the *Montgomery Advertiser* representative of many publications in deriding the attorney as the "voice of bigotry."

When court convened on April 18, Judge Horton criticized Leibowitz's statement as a "millstone around the necks of the defendants." He cited it in postponing the trials of the other Scottsboro Boys until there was time for the offense caused by it to subside.

## Female Stereotypes

Judge Horton reconvened court on June 22, 1933, for what was expected to be Patterson's formal sentencing. He discussed the major points of Price's story and pointed out that if she were telling the truth, there should have been independent corroboration for many parts of it. For example, an hour and a half after a rape by six men, one would expect to find large quantities of semen in the vagina and that the sperm would be motile. Price had also testified that her vagina was bleeding after the attack.

Yet doctors had found only a small amount of semen and non-motile sperm. They had found no vaginal bleeding. Thus, Judge Horton concluded, "this woman was not forced into intercourse with all of these Negroes upon that train, but that her condition was clearly due to the intercourse that she had had on the nights previous to this time."

Unfortunately, Judge Horton did not rest his conclusions simply on the absence of physical evidence to support the rape allegations. In a case rife with dueling prejudices, he buttressed his decision with the ancient Madonna/Whore dichotomy. He said, "History, sacred and profane, and the common experience of mankind teach us that women of the character shown in this case are prone for selfish reasons to make false accusations both of rape and of insult upon the slightest provocation or even without provocation for ulterior purposes."

The judge vacated the jury's verdict and ordered a new trial for Haywood Patterson.

While Horton can be faulted for his stereotyping of uneducated, lower-class women, he showed himself to be a judge willing to put principle ahead of his own career. This unpopular decision would doom him to defeat when he ran for reelection the next year in 1934.

After Horton vacated Patterson's verdict, state officials put the Scottsboro cases under the jurisdiction of Judge William Washington Callahan.

In November 1933, Haywood Patterson went on trial yet again.

## Judge "Speedy" Callahan

In Judge Callahan's conduct of the trial, he often appeared decidedly unsympathetic to the defense. Callahan had long been a well-respected jurist but he was also one who had, as Carter notes, "Very fixed ideas about how trials should be conducted." Carter elaborates that Callahan had told friends he wanted to "debunk the Scottsboro case" because he felt that it had simply been over-publicized and received more attention than it deserved.

He made it clear that he wanted the trial to progress at a smart pace. Before the trial proper, as Leibowitz questioned prospective jurors, the judge told him to "hurry it along" and sometimes cut his questioning short with "that's enough on that."

An all-white, all-male jury was seated and the prosecution brought Victoria Price to the stand to once again tell her story, which she did with her usual aplomb.

On cross-examination, Leibowitz tried to lay the foundations for the contention that semen in Price's vagina had been from previous voluntary intercourse. Leibowitz queried Price as to who she had been with on the train to and from Chattanooga.

An irritated Callahan sternly warned Leibowitz, "I can't allow the time of the court wasted on matters so immaterial. You mustn't ask that question again."

With much of the defense case effectively gutted, Leibowitz valiantly pushed forward to try to trap Price in contradictions.

As Carter reports, "At Scottsboro and before Judge Horton she insisted Norris had tried to hurl her from the train; now she was first certain and then 'pretty sure' it was Patterson. Although she had vividly testified of a '.45 caliber pistol' held by Patterson, she finally acknowledged under cross-examination that she did not know one gun from another. She recalled that it was Patterson who fired the gun, although she could not remember that at Scottsboro, less than two weeks after the incident. She became hopelessly confused about where she was struck, or how hard, or how seriously."

The prosecution called Orville Gilley. Like both alleged victims and defendants, Gilley spent much of his time going from place to place on freight trains. However, he asserted that he was no run-of-the-mill hobo. "I am an entertainer," he proudly testified. "I recite poetry and take up a collection after I finish, in hotel lobbies, restaurants, out on the streets, any place." Gilley backed up Price's story.

Leibowitz cross-examined Gilley on events prior to the alleged attacks. Gilley said he and Price had been together in Chattanooga but Callahan cut off the line of questioning.

Then Leibowitz pointed up something odd about Gilley's story: that he testified to witnessing these horrors and doing nothing about them. Gilley admitted that at "no time while this raping was going on did I ever make any attempt to notify any engineer, or any officials of that train what was going on in this gondola car."

The defense badly wanted Ruby Bates to testify to her recantation but was forced to make do without her because she was in the hospital.

At this trial, for the first time, the prosecution did not call either doctor who had examined Price and Bates in the aftermath of the alleged rapes.

So when the defense commenced, Leibowitz called Dr. Bridges to the stand on November 28 as a witness. The doctor testified that there was "no blood at all" dripping from Price's vagina. He continued, "I saw no blood on her face or her forehead."

In summation, Prosecutor Bailey conceded that Price and Bates were not the sort of women that most Southerners idealized. He argued that these impoverished women were to be respected for seeking honest, humble work rather than "to rouge their faces and stand on the street corners." Bailey ridiculed the defense suggestion of a frame-up and appealed to the jurors' sense of local pride.

In the defense summation, Leibowitz once again tried to appeal to distaste for women who engage in non-marital sex. He claimed he would not be defending the accused had the accusations been brought by a "decent, respectable, Southern white woman." However, he said that Price was a "lewd woman" and a "girl tramp."

He discussed the conflict between Price's testimony and that of Dr. Bridges and asked, "Who's on the level in this case, this doctor or Victoria Price?"

The jury retired to consider the fate of Haywood Patterson. Within minutes, the court was filled with white, male prospective jurors for the trial of Clarence Norris.

The next day, Patterson's jury returned with its verdict: "We find the defendant guilty as charged in the indictment and fix his punishment at death."

## Leibowitz Kept Trying

The next trial of Clarence Norris began before Judge Callahan and an all-white, all-male jury. The dedicated, unpaid Leibowitz plugged away. Carter writes that when Price "testified that she was struck in the face with the butt end of a pistol, Leibowitz borrowed one of the deputy's pistols, handed it to her, and demanded to know which was the butt end and which was the muzzle. She stared at it for a moment and then mumbled that she did not know; the only thing she knew about pistols was what she had 'been told.'"

Repeatedly Leibowitz sought to bring out Price's sexual history and just as repeatedly Judge Callahan blocked that line of questioning even when it concerned extremely recent history directly relevant to the semen doctors had found in her after the alleged rapes.

On December 6, 1933, the jury returned with its expected verdict and sentence: Norris was convicted and sentenced to death.

Judge Callahan sentenced Patterson and Norris to be executed on February 1, 1934, but the appeals Leibowitz filed soon after automatically gave them stays.

As appeals wound their ways through the higher courts, Leibowitz found himself reeling under an unexpected blow. As Carter put it, "Two ILD attorneys had been caught red-handed trying to bribe Victoria Price."

In June 1934, a man named J.T. Pearson, claiming to represent Victoria Price, wrote to ILD officials that Price might retract her accusations for a payment. Using the alias Daniel Swift, Samuel Schriftman, an attorney associated with the ILD, began negotiating with Pearson.

Pearson had not actually been working with Price's knowledge or on her behalf but he knew how to get in contact with her and did so when the ILD told him she could get $500 for recanting. When Pearson relayed this offer to Price, she refused it. Without telling Pearson about it, she contacted Huntsville police and reported the attempted bribery. They advised her to play along.

In late September, Pearson offered her $1,000. She appeared to accept.

Schriftman and Brodsky associate Sol Kone arranged to meet Price in a Nashville hotel where the pay-off was to take place. Carrying a briefcase filled with $1,500 all in $1 bills, Schriftman and Kone flew to Nashville. They may have taken along $500 more than was agreed upon because they thought Price could attempt some last minute dickering.

Pearson picked up Price in a car and they headed for Nashville. On the way to that city, police forced Pearson to the side of the road and arrested him. At the same time, other police arrested Schriftman and Kone.

Meeting up with Brodsky, Leibowitz raged that the ILD had "assassinated the Scottsboro Boys with that sort of business."

When Leibowitz denounced the ILD, they fired him.

The committed Leibowitz believed only he could rescue the Boys from being executed and was determined to hold onto the reins of the case. He won over several black ministers to his side and they obtained affidavits from Norris and Patterson firing the ILD and re-hiring Leibowitz.

The ILD was also determined to hold onto the case. William Patterson, whom Acker describes as "a black attorney from Harlem and the national secretary of the ILD," appealed to Mrs. Wright and Mrs. Patterson. On October 31, attorney Benjamin Davis and Josephine Norris were at the prison. At their urging, Clarence Norris and Haywood Patterson signed affidavits turning their cases back over to the ILD.

A Leibowitz representative was at the prison the next week. He got affidavits from both Boys returning the case to Leibowitz.

So it went, back and forth, with the young convicted men turning in one direction and then another.

In October, the American Scottsboro Committee (ASC) was formed at Leibowitz's behest. It boasted a prestigious line-up of officers: Its chair was executive secretary of the Federal Council of Churches' department of race relations, Dr. George E. Haynes, and its directors included famed performer Bill "Bojangles" Robinson.

Leibowitz and ILD lawyers hammered out a compromise: Leibowitz and Chamlee (no longer associated with the ILD) would defend Norris and ILD attorneys Fraenkel and Pollak would defend Patterson.

The U.S. Supreme Court review began on February 15, 1935. Leibowitz argued that Norris's conviction should be overturned because "Negroes" had been systematically excluded from the jury. ILD attorneys argued similarly for Patterson.

The defense attorneys won. A new trial was ordered for Norris and Patterson's case was ordered to be again reviewed by the Alabama Supreme Court.

Several opposing organizations that were concerned about the Boys began negotiating over control of the case. The NAACP, the ACLU, the ILD and the League for Industrial Democracy (LID, affiliated with the Socialist Party) met to discuss the Scottsboro Boys. They agreed that Leibowitz, who had done so much for the Scottsboro Boys, nevertheless presented a problem because of prejudice against him as a Jew and a Northerner, coupled with the offense occasioned by his outburst against previous jurors.

These groups met with Leibowitz. They said that they would support him as chief counsel if he would allow a Southern attorney to take the more prominent role in the courtroom proceedings. Leibowitz agreed.

In December 1935, the NAACP, the ILD, the ACLU and the LID formed a "Scottsboro Defense Committee."

Civil rights activist Allan Knight Chalmers became SDC chair. At the 1936 trial of Haywood Patterson, Huntsville, Alabama attorney Clarence Watts sat beside Leibowitz.

Carter reports, "On Tuesday morning, January 21, the trial finally got underway as Victoria Price told her story for the eighth time." Once again, Judge Callahan presided before an all-white, all-male jury.

Watts devoted much of the defense to pointing out contradictions in Price's claims. As Carter reports, Watts pointed "out contradictions in her account of how she had fallen and supposedly fainted. W. W. Hill, the station master at Paint Rock, and Tom Taylor Rousseau, the young part-time Jackson County deputy, both said they had first seen her standing at least 10 cars farther back than the gondola where she claimed she had fainted as she got out."

Leibowitz left all cross-examination to Watts with the exception of one prosecution witness. That witness was Obie Golden, a guard at the Kilby State Penitentiary, who testified that in 1934 Patterson had called out to Golden that he wanted to speak to him and then told the guard, "I am guilty of that crime. Also Clarence Norris and also those other seven up there in Birmingham Jail." Leibowitz brought out that Golden had not notified the warden about this supposed confession, had not written it down, and had waited over a year and a half before reporting it to the prosecution.

The defense called Lester Carter to the stand to suggest a source for the small amount of non-motile semen found in Price.

Morgan County Solicitor Melvin Hutson, who had succeeded Wade Wright in that office, made the initial prosecution summation. He praised Price, asserting, "She fights for the rights of the womanhood of Alabama" who, whether "in overalls or furs," are entitled to freedom from attack."

In the defense summation, Clarence Watts approached the jury in a quiet manner. He told them that he was a "friend and neighbor" of theirs. Watts pointed to the many contradictions in Price's story and the medical evidence refuting it. He appealed to the jury to "do the right thing" and pointed out that when justice is unfair "there is not protection for anyone, man or woman, black or white."

The trial had lasted all of three days, beginning on a Tuesday and going to the jury on a Thursday.

While the jury deliberated Patterson's fate another was impaneled in the new trial of Clarence Norris.

As the last juror for Norris was being selected that afternoon, word came back that the Patterson jury had reached a verdict.

The clerk read its verdict: "We, the jury, find the defendant Haywood Patterson guilty as charged and fix his punishment at 75 years in prison." The conviction did not come as a surprise but the less than maximum sentence did.

The jury had settled on less than execution because foreman John Burleson argued long and hard for the prison term. His reasons were hardly enlightened. Burleson said blacks had "more animal in 'em than white folks. The beast in 'em overrides 'em and they go temporarily insane and do things they swear they never would do."

### The Shock of the Slashing

On January 25, heading back to the Birmingham jail after a day in court, Ozie Powell, Clarence Norris, and Roy Wright were riding in a car driven by Morgan County Sheriff J. Street Sandlin. Deputy Edgar Blalock was in the car to help guard the prisoners.

Sometime before 4 p.m., Ozie Powell slashed Deputy Blalock with a knife, cutting him across the fleshy part of his chin. Although he was behind the wheel, Sandlin reached back to push Powell before stopping the car which was by this time careening from side to side on the highway. After he halted the vehicle, Sandlin fired on Powell.

According to Carter, this scene was witnessed by filling station operator G. F. Anderson, who ran over to the commotion just in time to see Norris and Wright with their hands over their heads, and one of them shouting, "Boss we haven't got anything on us. You can search us. We haven't got anything at all." Anderson saw Powell slumped in the seat, blood streaming from the bullet wound in his head.

Two versions of this altercation emerged. Norris and Wright claimed Powell found a pocket knife in the cell and put it in his pocket. While the three manacled prisoners were in the car, Sandlin and Blalock started bad-mouthing the Boys's attorney. Powell talked back and Blalock slapped him on the mouth. Then Powell slashed Blalock.

The officers claimed the attack had been unprovoked.

Powell sustained permanent brain damage.

On June 14, 1936, the Alabama Supreme Court upheld Patterson's conviction.

On July 12, 1937, a new trial began for Clarence Norris before Judge Callahan and an all-white, all-male jury, despite the fact that the U.S. Supreme Court had granted him a new trial based on the all-white composition of his previous jury. Thomas Lawson headed the prosecution team. Watts and Leibowitz sat at the defense table.

The prosecution case remained what it had been.

Leibowitz read the previous testimony of the late Dr. Bridges into the record. The trial lasted three days.

The jury took two hours and 30 minutes to convict Norris and sentence him to die.

The trial of Andy Wright began with a surprise move from the prosecution: Lawson announced the state would not seek the death penalty.

Local attorney Watts was not there. The defeats of the previous trials had left him too discouraged to continue. Leibowitz slogged on, giving everything he had to rescue innocent men from injustice.

After a trial of a little over one day and deliberations that lasted an hour and 15 minutes, Andy Wright's jury returned a guilty verdict and a sentence of 99 years.

The trial of Charley Weems, with Leibowitz as sole counsel, began. Again, the prosecution did not ask for the death penalty.

Weems's trial went to the jury on the second day. They deliberated for three and a half hours on an afternoon and two and a half hours the next morning before convicting him and sentencing him to 75 years.

## Four Set Free

On July 24, 1937, the prosecution dropped the rape charge against the now brain-damaged Ozie Powell. It is likely the state did not want to bother with a rape trial since the disabled man was willing to plead guilty to assault of a police officer. Judge Callahan sentenced him to 20 years.

Lawson and Leibowitz went to the bench where they spoke in hushed tones to Judge Callahan. Then Leibowitz went to the county jail. He handed a court order to a jailer. Montgomery, Roy Wright, Roberson, and Williams were let out of their cells and allowed to follow their attorney into waiting cars.

The state had agreed to drop charges against these four. They were free.

Many people were flummoxed at this bizarre compromise. The evidence against all nine Scottsboro Boys was essentially the same so how could these four be innocent and the others guilty? It seemed like either the state had agreed to freedom for four guilty rapists or four other men (Powell being incarcerated for an assault) were unjustly imprisoned.

Lawson read an explanation. He said that the state was convinced of the guilt of those convicted but believed Roberson and Montgomery were innocent because their disabilities made it unlikely they could have committed the crimes. Lawson said the state still believed Price but thought she had made an error of "mistaken identity." Lawson continued that charges against Roy Wright and Williams had been dropped because they had been 12 and 13 at the time of the rapes and the six and a half years they had spent behind bars was adequate punishment for attacks committed when they were so young.

The U. S. Supreme Court refused on October 26, 1937 to hear Patterson's appeal.

The SDC went directly to Alabama Governor Bibb Graves, asking him to consider pardoning Patterson, Norris, Andy Wright and Weems. Graves agreed to consider it.

In June 1938, the Alabama Supreme Court upheld the sentences of Norris, Andy Wright, and Weems. Governor Graves commuted the Norris death sentence to life imprisonment.

In the meantime, the four set free went to New York City with Leibowitz who attempted to steer them into a stable life of vocational training and regular jobs.

The Boys believed they could get rich quick on their notoriety. Thomas S. Harten, a black minister, approached them, offering to become their manager. Harten soon had them on stage where they were billed as "the Scottsboro Boys ... the symbol of a struggle for enlightenment and human brotherhood which will go on and on until it is won!"

Much of the money from the engagement went into the pocket of their manager while they had to buy new suits at their own expense. Instead of raking in a fortune, they plunged into debt.

Eugene Williams, Willie Roberson, and Leroy Wright eventually settled into fairly normal lives. The nearly blind and alcoholic Olen Montgomery careened from one low-paying job to another and was often jailed for public intoxication and drunk and disorderly conduct.

In October, Governor Graves met with the imprisoned Scottsboro Boys.

Graves informed Chalmers and Hall that the interview had been a disaster. Graves claimed that Patterson and Norris were enraged at each other and that a file fashioned into a knife had been found on Patterson. Said the Governor, "They are anti-social, they are bestial, and they are unbelievably stupid and I do not believe they can be rehabilitated in freedom."

According to Carter, many observers believed the hostilities between Norris and Patterson were just Graves's excuse for avoiding action. There was no evidence that Andy Wright and Weems (Powell was a special case) had been anything other than perfectly polite. It is likely Graves simply feared the political repercussions of pardoning the remaining Scottsboro Boys.

Weems was paroled in November 1943.

Andy Wright and Norris were paroled in January 1944 on the condition that they work at a lumber company near Montgomery. The two men also had to live in a small room and sleep in the same bed. Finding these conditions little better than imprisonment, they fled North.

After receiving official assurances that neither man would be returned to prison if they came back to Alabama, Chalmers persuaded the fugitives to return. Alabama officials broke their word and clapped Andy Wright and Norris behind bars.

In late 1946, Norris received a second parole. Powell was also paroled.

In 1948, Patterson was in a prison work gang. He ran from it, made his way to Detroit, and took refuge with his sister. Two years later, he was arrested by the FBI. Michigan Governor G. Mennen Williams refused to sign extradition papers. Alabama officials had no interest in pursuing the matter, thus setting him free.

In 1950, Andy Wright was paroled. Surrounded by reporters, the man who had served 19 years for a non-existent crime said, "I have no hard feelings toward anyone." Asked about Price, he commented, "If she's still living, I feel sorry for her because I don't guess she sleeps much at night."

## Tragedies and a Triumph

Not surprisingly, several of the Scottsboro Boys, who had grown to manhood in prison, met with tragic fates.

About a year after Andy Wright's release, a black woman accused him of raping her teenaged daughter. He was tried and acquitted. However, he saw this as further evidence that he could never escape his past. He said, "Everywhere I go, it seems like Scottsboro is throwed up in my face. I don't believe I'll ever live it down."

In 1959, 22 years after gaining his freedom, Roy Wright found his wife with another man. He stabbed her to death and then shot himself.

With the help of journalist Earl Conrad, Patterson wrote a memoir entitled *Scottsboro Boy*. In 1950, Patterson got into a barroom brawl and stabbed a man to death. Convicted of manslaughter, Patterson died in prison from cancer in 1952.

By the early 1970s, Clarence Norris was married and working as a vacuum sweeper in New York City.

One day, he phoned the Alabama Governor's Office. He asked to speak to then-Governor George Wallace. An official came on and Norris related that he was one of the Scottsboro Boys. Norris told how he had "broke my parole" and wanted "to know if Alabama still wants me." He was told to call the Department of Corrections. Norris did and learned that he was indeed still a wanted man.

Norris asked for assistance from the NAACP. Their attorneys pressured the Alabama Board of Pardons and Paroles into reviewing the case. After an extensive re-examination of the evidence, the board voted to grant Norris a pardon. However, the governor had to approve it for it to go into effect.

Governor Wallace had achieved fame as a fiery segregationist. He had once tried to block blacks from attending a previously all-white university by standing in a doorway and had proclaimed "segregation forever." More recently, he had abandoned the segregationist cause and sought, with some success, to make political alliances with blacks.

He signed the pardon.

Several months after being pardoned, Norris met with Wallace who shook Norris's hand and told him he was glad to have signed the pardon. Many observers speculated that Wallace had signed the pardon as a ploy to get black votes. Goodman writes, "After leaving the governor's office, Norris was asked if he cared to comment on Wallace's motives. He said he didn't: 'I'm grateful to the governor, and I told him so. I'll tell him every time I see him."

### "Do I look dead?"

A made-for-TV film entitled *Judge Horton and the Scottsboro Boys* aired on NBC in 1976. The version of events recounted in this movie drew largely from Dan T. Carter's *Scottsboro: A Tragedy of the American South*.

According to Gilbert Geis and Leigh B. Bienen in *Crimes of the Century: From Leopold and Loeb to O. J. Simpson*, "The television drama mercilessly portrayed Price as a whore, a perjurer, and suborner of perjury."

The day after *Judge Horton and the Scottsboro Boys* was broadcast, Victoria Price went to an attorney's office and introduced herself to the lawyer. "Does the name Victoria Price mean anything to you?" she asked.

The attorney replied, "But they said you were dead."

Price pointedly queried, "Do I look dead?"

Carter's massive book was for the most part meticulously researched but ended with two errors. He wrote that both Price and Bates were deceased. When his book was published in 1969—and indeed when the film aired in 1976—both women were still living, although Bates was ailing.

Both women filed lawsuits against NBC. Bates died later that year before a court delivered an opinion on her case.

Price sued NBC for slander, invasion of privacy, and libel. She asked for $6 million in damages. Geis and Bienen report, "The judge declared a mistrial on the ground that there existed no material evidence upon which the jury could find in Price's favor on claims of slander or invasion of privacy. When all the evidence had been heard, the same result was reached in regard to the libel claim." She appealed and an appellate court ruled against her.

The U.S. Supreme Court agreed to hear her next appeal. NBC and Price came to an agreement in which she dropped the case in exchange for an amount of money that was not made public. Geis and Bienen write that Price used the money to leave a residence that would usually be called a "shack" and "buy a small house, a dream she said she had carried with her all her life." Crewe and Uschan note, "She died without ever apologizing for ruining so many lives with her lies."

## Bibliography

http://www.imdb.com/title/tt0074723/#comment, Judge Horton and the Scottsboro Boys.

Acker, James R. *Scottsboro and its Legacy: The Cases That Challenged American Legal and Social Justice.* Prager Publishers. Westport, CT. 2008.

Carter, Dan T. *Scottsboro: A Tragedy of the American South.* Louisiana State University Press, Baton Rouge, Louisiana, 1969.

Crewe, Sabrina and Uschan, Michael V. *The Scottsboro Case.* Gareth Stevens Publishing. Milwaukee, WI. 2005.

Geis, Gilbert and Bienen, Leigh B. *Crimes of the Century: From Leopold and Loeb to O. J. Simpson.* Northeastern University Press, Boston, Massachusetts. 1998.

Goodman, James. *Stories of Scottsboro: The Rape Case that Shocked 1930s America and Revived the Struggle for Equality.*Pantheon Books. New York, NY. 1994.

# CHAPTER FIVE

## The Murder of Marilyn Sheppard
## and Trials of "Dr. Sam"

Many points in the Sam Sheppard case remain in dispute to this day but this is certain: in the wee hours of the Fourth of July in 1954, Marilyn Sheppard was brutally beaten to death in her suburban bedroom.

Four months pregnant, pretty, brown-haired Marilyn Sheppard, 31, was married to her high-school sweetheart, successful neurosurgeon Dr. Sam Sheppard, 29.

The couple resided in the Cleveland, Ohio suburb of Bay Village in a two-story, lakeside house.

Sam Sheppard is backed up by neighbors and close friends Spencer "Spen" and Esther Houk in his claim that he called their home at 5:40 a.m. that morning.

"My God, Spen, get over here quick!" Sam shouted. "I think they've killed Marilyn!"

Spencer woke his wife, Esther, and they drove to the Sheppard home. Spencer was a butcher who also served as Bay Village mayor.

The Houks got to the Sheppards' unlocked kitchen door. Inside the house, they found a shirtless Sam, his pants drenched in water, leaning against a chair in the den. He moaned as his hands pressed the back of his neck.

"What happened?" Spenc asked.

Sam said he had fallen asleep on the living room couch after last evening's party only to be awakened by Marilyn screaming, "Sam!" Sam ran up the stairs where "somebody clobbered me." He said he lost consciousness after being struck.

Esther rushed upstairs and found a scene of horror. As James Neff reports in *The Wrong Man: The Final Verdict on the Dr. Sam Sheppard Murder Case*, "On the bed ... Marilyn's body lay face up. Her legs hung over the foot of the bed ... under a wooden bar that ran from post to post across the foot of the bed. It looked as if someone had pulled her legs under the bar, pinning her like a giant specimen. Her body was outlined by blood ... About two dozen deep, ugly crescent-shaped gashes marked her face, forehead, and scalp."

Marilyn's pajama tops were pushed up to her neck so that her chest area was bared. There was a blanket around her middle. Underneath that blanket, her pajama bottoms had been partially removed so that her pubic area was exposed.

Esther checked Marilyn for a pulse—and found none. Then she ran back downstairs and yelled, "Call the police! Call the ambulance!"

Sam asked her to return upstairs and check on his and Marilyn's son, seven-year-old Sam, Jr., nicknamed "Chip."

Esther did as Sam asked. The boy was sleeping soundly. Amazingly, he appeared to have slept through an extraordinary battle waged in the room across from his. Later it would be revealed that Chip, like his father, was an extraordinarily sound sleeper.

At about 6:00 a.m., Bay Village police officer Fred Drenkhan arrived at the Sheppard house. He noticed a doctor's bag on the hallway floor, turned upside down with its vials and prescription pads in a mess. When Drenkhan entered the den, the police officer found Sam—and another mess.

As Neff writes, "Two trophies lay on the floor, broken: one of Sam's treasured high school track trophies and Marilyn's bowling trophy."

Drenkhan asked Sam what had happened and the doctor told a fuller version of the story he told the Houks. He had heard his wife cry out, ran upstairs, been clobbered and passed out. When he came to, he heard noises downstairs and ran down there and after someone. In this and subsequent conversations, he variously described that someone as "a light form" and "a bushy-haired man." The form ran out of the house and Sam chased it, catching up with it on the sand. The pair fought and Sam was again knocked unconscious. When Sam came to, he was at the edge of the lake, with his upper body in the sand and his lower body in the water.

Dr. Richard N. Sheppard, Sam's oldest brother, arrived on the scene. Spen had called Richard who took Chip home with him.

A Bay Village police officer drove to the small farm of Bay Village Police Chief John Eaton. Eaton headed to the Sheppard residence.

Dr. Steve Sheppard, another Sheppard brother, drove up with his wife, Betty. Steve immediately thought that Sam had sustained a serious neck injury.

Steve drove Sam to the Bay View Hospital.

## Who could do this?

Chief Eaton phoned Cuyahoga County coroner Dr. Samuel Gerber. Gerber phoned a close associate and the pair arrived at the Sheppard home around 8:00 a.m. Drenkhan told Gerber what Sam said had happened. Gerber found Sam's vague account alarmingly suspect. He also thought he saw evidence of a staged scene in the living room. Three drawers of a desk were pulled but not taken out of a desk and their contents were not thrown about. As he went upstairs, Gerber saw drops that appeared to be dried blood. There was also what looked like smeared blood on the doorjamb and knob plate of the door that led to the screened porch. That blood suggested that the person who opened it had a bloody hand and may have had a cut on it.

A technician from the Scientific Investigation Unit, Michael Grabowski, arrived on the scene at 8:10 a.m. Gerber pointed out objects and areas he thought relevant and Grabowski photographed them. Then Grabowski dusted for fingerprints. Later, Grabowski went to the beach where, according to Neff, Grabowski "photographed two sets of footprints, one of them barefoot." Gerber went to Bay View Hospital to interview Sam. Gerber then returned to the Sheppard house to find two Cleveland homicide detectives, Robert Schottke and Pat Gareau, already there. The three conferred and agreed this was probably a domestic homicide staged to simulate a burglary. They thought Sam had gotten rid of his T-shirt because it was covered with blood. They also believed he had plunged his lower body into the water to wash off blood. "It's obvious that the doctor did it," Gerber said.

However, the relative absence of blood on Sam's clothes was puzzling. As Cooper and Sheppard note in *Mockery of Justice: The True Story of the Sheppard Murder Case*, "None of Dr. Sam's clothes were spattered with blood: not his pants, not his leather belt. It's hard to wash blood out of cloth (and even then it can be seen microscopically), but it is virtually impossible to remove blood from leather. The only blood on his clothing was a splotch, which matched perfectly a mark on the sheets where Dr. Sheppard said he had leaned over his wife to check her condition."

Dr. Lester Adelson performed the autopsy on Marilyn Sheppard. He set her time of death as between 3:30 a.m. and 5:30 a.m. with the most probable time being "at about 4:30 a.m." Nevertheless, Gerber told reporters that she had died at about 3:00 a.m. This earlier time made Sam's story especially suspicious. He had called the Houks at about 5:45 a.m. Observers naturally wondered what Sam had done in the two hours and 45 minutes between his wife's death and his attempt to seek help.

As Neff relates, Adelson found that "the killer had fractured her skull plates with 15 blows, but none of the strikes were powerful enough to push bone into the dura, which encased the cerebellum just under the bones." This was significant for it suggested that either the killer was not physically strong or was deliberately dragging things out or had mixed feelings about the battering and so did not put full strength into it. Two teeth were torn out. Marilyn also had several injuries to her hands, including a fingernail torn off, that indicated she had fought hard for her life.

Perhaps because Adelson may have already heard that his superior, Gerber, was convinced this was a domestic homicide, he did not examine Marilyn's vagina for the tearing that might indicate rape. He removed a male fetus from her womb and preserved it in a large jar.

Around the Sheppard residence, Gerber and Eaton gathered a group of neighbors to look around the area for a discarded weapon. Mayor Houk's 16-year-old son Larry found a cloth bag. Among other things, it held a watch that had stopped at 4:15 a.m. Dried blood was on the band. This seemed to clinch Sam's guilt. He claimed he did not check on his wife after being knocked unconscious, so how had the blood got there unless it had spattered while he was beating her?

At Gerber's request, Dr. E. R. Hexter examined Sam and found that he had a few injuries, none of which were serious.

Dr. Charles Elkins examined Sam at the request of the Sheppards. Neff writes, "Elkins said that Sam had a cerebral concussion, a spinal cord injury that robbed him of reflexes on one side." He also found that Sam's neck went into spasms, a response impossible to simulate.

Sam's family retained a respected attorney named Bill Corrigan. Since the prosecutor at Sam's second trial was named John Corrigan, the two men will be called B. Corrigan and J. Corrigan in this article. On the advice of B. Corrigan, Sam refused to take a polygraph test.

## Sam and Marilyn

Newspapers related the Sheppard family's history. Samuel Sheppard was born on December 23, 1923, the youngest of three sons. His parents were Dr. Richard Sheppard and Ethel Sheppard. The senior Richard Sheppard was a doctor of osteopathic medicine or D. O. Osteopaths are similar to allopathic physicians or MDs. As Cooper and Sheppard observe, "osteopaths would take the same or similar medical exams and had specialties, such as surgery or gynecology or pediatrics. Like M.D.'s, osteopaths served internships and residencies, prescribed drugs, and ordered X rays." However, they also note, "Osteopaths also believed in the integration of treatment, approaching the body as a whole and incorporating body manipulation with other treatments."

Along with his brothers, Sam grew up in a Cleveland suburb.

The ambitious elder Dr. Richard Sheppard founded the Cleveland Osteopathic Hospital in 1935. He wanted each of his three sons to follow in his footsteps and grow up to be physicians but it seemed at first that Sam would disappoint his father.

In his elementary school years, Sam earned lackluster grades. In eighth grade, he became an outstanding athlete.

Marilyn Sheppard had been born Florence Marilyn Reese on April 14, 1923, into the affluent home of Thomas and Dorothy Reese.

By the time he was in high school, Sam had developed a determination to become a doctor that led him to study hard. His grades rapidly improved.

After graduation, Sam went to Hanover College in Indiana. Sam accumulated about three years of undergraduate credits before attending to the College of Osteopathic Physicians and Surgeons in Los Angeles.

He and Marilyn wed on February 22, 1945.

After a difficult birth Marilyn delivered Samuel Reese Sheppard on May 18, 1947.

Sam returned with Marilyn and little Chip to Cleveland to join his brothers in their practice.

### The Days Before the Day of Doom

On July 1, 1954, a visitor arrived at the Sheppard residence. His name was Dr. Len Hoverstein. A close friend of Sam's, Len had just been fired from a hospital. He asked to stay for a while and Sam agreed.

Marilyn was displeased by Len's arrival. According to Cooper and Sheppard, Len had stayed at the Sheppard house before and Marilyn had found him "sloppy and inconsiderate." Neff writes that Len had also made advances at Marilyn that she had rebuffed.

On Saturday, July 3, Len decided he wanted to spend the night with friends about 40 miles away. Cooper and Sheppard speculate that since Sam and Marilyn "were throwing a hot dog roast for the hospital interns on the next day," Len "wanted to avoid the uncomfortable comments that might arise about his lack of job prospects."

Thus, Len was gone when neighbors Don and Nancy Ahern arrived at the Sheppard home for a dinner party. Sam went to sleep on the daybed. The visiting couple left after midnight through the kitchen door. Neff writes, "Nancy later told the police that she could not remember locking the kitchen door. And, no, she could not remember if Marilyn had locked it either."

### A Philanderer who Flaunted it, the Other Woman, and the Lie

Gerber, Schottke, Gareau and others were convinced that Sam had killed his wife. They soon believed they had a motive in a classic marital problem. Nancy Ahern revealed that Sam was frequently unfaithful and had been seeing a Bay View Hospital nurse. People speculated that Sam and Marilyn had gotten into an argument about his infidelity that had tragically escalated or that he had killed Marilyn so that he could be free to marry another woman. In 1954, a divorce was difficult to obtain if either husband or wife opposed it and still slightly scandalous.

Marilyn knew about her husband's wanderings. At one point, they discussed divorce but Marilyn did not want to become a single mother.

Marital difficulties were exacerbated by Sam's lack of discretion in pursuing extra-marital relationships. In his affair with nurse Susan Hayes, Sam flaunted their relationship. He and Marilyn attended an office Halloween party. At the party, Susan whimsically grabbed Sam's pipe and put it in her mouth, saying she was in character as the doctor. The two of them openly flirted and Marilyn left the party.

During a working vacation in California in which Sam received advanced surgery training, Marilyn stayed apart from her husband to enjoy the natural beauty of Big Sur. Sam called Susan Hayes who soon joined him. He brought his mistress into the home of a friend with whom he was staying. Susan stayed in the bedroom Sam was using and was with him while his host and hostess socialized. Neff notes, "Most of the women there knew Marilyn and resented being put in such an uncomfortable situation by her husband."

When Sam met up again with Marilyn, he told her that he definitely wanted to stay with her. She became pregnant during these days.

Investigators learned that infidelity might have sparked the killing in another way. They spoke to a neighbor who claimed Marilyn had said she could not get pregnant again because Sam was sterile due to X-ray exposure. The neighbor was unclear as to whether this was said in a serious or joking manner but if the former, it suggested that Marilyn might have been pregnant by another man and Sam had exploded in rage over it.

A laboratory attempted fetal blood typing of the fetus. Such blood typing could not establish paternity but could rule particular men out. However, that blood typing was unsuccessful so nothing about its paternity could be proven.

Spen was sometimes with Marilyn for coffee and Steven Sheppard suggested Spen had a romantic interest in her.

Neff reports that a woman named Jessie Dill told investigators that Marilyn was having an affair. Dill claimed the two of them had struck up a conversation and that Marilyn had confided that she had been seeing another man. Police found Dill's account credible because it included specifics about the Sheppard marriage that had not been in the papers such as the name of one woman with whom Sam had been involved.

On July 14, the case seemed to get a break. A few yards from the Sheppard property, Neff reports, a torn man's T-shirt of about Sam's size was discovered "snagged on a prong of reinforcing wire in a crumbling concrete pier." It was turned over to technician Mary Cowan for examination for blood-stains. Tests returned negative results for blood but Gerber pointed out that there was no proof the T-shirt was Sam's.

An inquest into the death of Marilyn Sheppard was held July 22, 1954.

Gerber summoned Sam.

He asked him if he had an affair with Susan Hayes. Sam stoutly denied it.

## Trial by Press?

Louis Seltzer, editor of the *Cleveland Press*, was convinced of Sam's guilt and Seltzer's newspaper crusaded for Sam's arrest. The paper ran an editorial entitled, "Why Don't Police Quiz No. 1 Suspect?" That editorial asserted that Sam was receiving kid-glove treatment because he was an upper-middle-class doctor: "You can bet your last dollar the Sheppard murder would have been cleaned up long ago if it had involved 'average people.' They'd have hauled all the suspects to Police Headquarters. They'd have grilled them in the accepted, straight out way of doing police business."

Other *Cleveland Press* headlines included "Why Isn't Sam Sheppard in Jail?" and "Quit Stalling and Bring Him in!"

On July 30, 1954 Sam Sheppard was arrested as he walked out the front door of his house. Along with the police was an angry crowd taunting, "Murderer! Murderer!"

Sam Sheppard's trial began October 28, 1954. Judge Edward Blythin presided. The lead prosecutor was John Mahon.

B. Corrigan headed Sam's defense.

When Gerber took the stand, he made a startling assertion about the bloodstains on Marilyn's pillowcase. Cooper and Sheppard report that he testified that the stains "showed two blades, each about three inches long, joined in the middle like a wishbone, and separated at its widest part by two and three-quarters inches, each blade having a toothlike indentation at the end."

Gerber asserted that the stains were made by an instrument. The prosecutor asked him to specify what type of instrument and the coroner answered, "A surgical instrument."

On cross-examination, B. Corrigan asked if Gerber had compared the pillowcase stains to surgical instruments in the Sheppard home and Gerber replied that he had only done a "casual inspection" and could not identify any as the source of the stains. When asked if he had compared surgical instruments at Bay View Hospital to the stains, Gerber said, "No."

Mary Cowan testified. On cross-examination, Neff writes, "Corrigan tried to use Cowan to counter the state's theory that Sam had washed blood from himself by jumping into the lake." Cowan conceded that microscopic traces of blood would remain on fabric even after being drenched in water. Neff elaborates, "Corrigan felt her revelation helped Sam's case immensely. There should have been a few dozen spatters of blood on the front of Sam's pants if he had killed Marilyn, not just one large stain at the knee."

Prosecutors called Sheppard housekeeper Elnora Helms to the stand. She testified that police had asked her to examine the bedroom after the slaying and that she could find nothing missing from it. Neff writes that this indicated premeditation as the killer must have "brought the unknown murder weapon into the room" rather than having grabbed something available as might have been the case with a sudden explosion of temper.

Susan Hayes testified. A prosecutor asked what Sam had said about divorce. Hayes answered, "I remember him saying that he loved his wife very much, but not so much as a wife. He was thinking of getting a divorce, but that he wasn't sure that his father would approve."

## The Defense Begins

Neff writes, "For their defense, Corrigan and Garmone followed the game plan outlined in opening statements: first, that Sam was not the kind of man who would kill, second, the evidence proved that he could not have done it; and, finally, evidence pointed to a third party at the crime scene – in particular two independent witnesses who saw a strange man near the Sheppard home about the time of Marilyn's murder."

Dr. Richard Sheppard testified that it would have been impossible for someone to batter Marilyn as she had been battered without getting the clothing on his lower body splattered with blood.

Two witnesses testified they had seen a man with bushy hair in the vicinity in that early morning.

Dr. Sam testified to running upstairs to see a "form" and chasing "it' to the beach. Then he seemed to have a clearer view and described the "person" as having "a good-sized head—with a bushy appearance at the top of his head—his hair."

On cross-examination, Mahon asked Sam repeated questions about his extra-marital affairs.

The cross-examination ended with the following exchange.

Mahon: "Doctor, what is the best way to remove blood from clothing?"

Sam: "I couldn't tell you, sir."

Mahon: "Is cold water more effective to remove blood from clothing than hot water?"

Sam: "I am certainly no authority on that, and I have never tried to remove blood from clothing, sir."

Mahon: "Now, Doctor, the injuries that you received, didn't you receive those injuries from jumping off of the platform down on the beach?"

Sam: No, sir, I think that would be impossible."

The defense called Dr. Charles Elkins. He testified that Sam had been severely injured. Normal reflexes had been missing from his left side and when his neck was pressed his muscles had gone into involuntary spasms. However, the reality of his injuries did not necessarily exculpate Sam as Marilyn could have injured him in their struggle or he could have injured himself, as the prosecution suggested, in a suicide attempt after killing her.

## Closing Arguments and the Verdict

Tom Parrino made the first closing argument for the prosecution. Parrino stated: "If this was a burglary, then this was the neatest burglar in history." He pointed out that Sam was large and strong and asked incredulously, "This man was rendered senseless with a single blow?"

Pete Petersilge led off the defense closing. He said, "The state still does not know with what weapon she was killed, the state still doesn't know why she was killed. And yet on the basis of that rather flimsy evidence, the State of Ohio is asking you to send Sam Sheppard to the electric chair."

Petersilge argued, "If Sam had then tried to cover up, he could have done a lot better than he did... It certainly would have been a very easy thing to put on another T-shirt." He continued that the lack of blood on Sam's belt, shoes, and socks constituted "mute evidence, but very powerful evidence, that Sam Sheppard did not kill his wife, because the person who killed Marilyn" would have to have been heavily sprayed with blood.

Mahon said Sam had injured his neck when he flung himself into the water in a suicide attempt, "pursued by his own conscience as he ran away from the foul act that he had just committed."

Judge Blythin told the jury that they had five possible verdicts: not guilty, manslaughter, second-degree murder, first-degree murder with a recommendation for mercy, and first degree murder minus the recommendation for mercy. About the final option, Blythin reminded them, "If you do find the defendant guilty of murder in the first degree and do not recommend mercy, it will be the obligation of the court to sentence the defendant to death."

The jury deliberated five days. On December 21, they found Sam Sheppard guilty of murder in the second degree. Judge Blythin sentenced him to life imprisonment.

## Enter Criminalist Dr. Paul Kirk

After the conviction, B. Corrigan sought the help of Dr. Paul Kirk in finding grounds for appeal. Neff writes that Kirk was "known as the founding father of criminalistics, a term he coined."

Kirk agreed to research the Sheppard case but warned B. Corrigan that he would follow the evidence wherever it led and that Kirk would not shape his findings to reach any particular conclusion. In fact, Kirk's initial impression was that Sam was guilty. He found Sam's amorphous description of the intruder suspicious and thought the neatly pulled out drawers indicated staging.

Kirk arrived in Cleveland on January 22, 1955. At the Sheppard house, Kirk vacuumed the floor of the bedroom in which the murder had taken place with a special instrument that, as Neff writes, possessed "a customized filter to trap minute particles." He took multiple photographs and made measurements.

After closely studying the blood patterns on the walls, Kirk found a gap in the blood spatter. He believed this gap was accounted for by blood having spattered on the person of the killer. He thought the weapon had been roughly a foot in length.

There was one blood spot that Kirk believed stood out from all others. Neff notes, "It was the largest by far, one inch in diameter and nearly round. It adhered to the lower third of the wood closet door, about three feet from where Marilyn's head rested, and did not display the beading characteristic of impact spatter."

Still troubled by Sam's vague description of the intruder, Kirk tested the story. At night, Kirk had Dr. Richard dress in a white shirt and dark pants and stand at the foot of the bed. All lights were off save a dim one in the dressing room. Kirk ran upstairs. Cooper and Sheppard write that Kirk saw "a whitish 'form,' exactly as Dr. Sam described it."

Kirk went to the prosecutor's office and examined the spatter on Marilyn's pajama bottoms. He concluded that they were already pulled down at the time of the battering and believed that indicated sexual assault. Large parts of Marilyn's teeth had come off. He believed it unlikely her teeth were broken by her face being battered because she had no swelling around her lips. Rather, Kirk thought she had bitten down on her attacker's hand. Experiments in his laboratory led him to think that the puzzlingly unique spot on the wall was made from a bleeding wound.

Kirk believed many of the blood spots through the house came from a wound and that the murder weapon was likely to have been a flashlight.

Kirk wrote a 19-page report that he gave to B. Corrigan in 1955. B. Corrigan cited the findings in an appeal but was turned down by the Ohio Appeals Court that criticized Kirk's conclusions as "highly speculative and fallacious."

In 1956, Karl Schuele, who lived next door to the Sheppard's empty house, discovered a corroded flashlight in the shallow waters of Lake Erie. He turned it in to Bay Village police chief John Eaton. According to Neff, "Eaton filed a report, noting that the flashlight was dented and battered at one end as if someone had used it for 'striking something repeatedly.'" Neff reports that no one in the coroner's office examined it for trace evidence.

### The Triumph of F. Lee Bailey

For years, B. Corrigan filed appeal after appeal, all of which were turned down. In 1961, B. Corrigan died. However, there was a bright spot that year for Sam: the publication of *The Sheppard Murder Case* by Paul Holmes, a book that argued for Sam's innocence. An ambitious young attorney named Francis Lee Bailey, who would become famous with his first name abbreviated to its first letter, read the book and wanted to defend Sam. Bailey soon started work on the case that would catapult him to glory.

Bailey believed he worked in a more favorable environment than B. Corrigan had because the U.S. Supreme Court was then headed by Chief Justice Earl Warren and was starting to dramatically expand the rights of the accused.

Bailey went before federal Judge Carl Weinman with a long list of wrongs. Neff reports that the following were among them: "Dr. Sheppard was arraigned without his lawyer, despite asking for a short delay so he could arrive. The trial judge refused to move the trial to another city despite venomous pretrial publicity … Detectives testified repeatedly about Sheppard's refusal to take a lie detector test. In violation of Ohio law and without the judge's permission, jurors, while deliberating, were allowed to make unmonitored telephone calls."

In March 1964, Bailey was a guest at a discussion with columnist Dorothy Kilgallen. Kilgallen stated that, prior to the trial, Judge Blythin had told her Sam was "guilty as hell." She said she had not originally reported this because it had been said to her "in confidence." Bailey had something to add to the list of Sam's legal grievances.

On July 15, 1964, Weinman overturned Sam's conviction. Judge Weinman blasted the 1954 trial as a "mockery of justice." Neff writes that Weinman cited five reasons for overturning the verdict, each one sufficient by itself to require a new trial: Judge Blythin's failure to disqualify himself after making biased remarks about the case; Blythin's failure to move the trial to another city; allowing detectives to testify that Sheppard refused to take a lie detector test, letting jurors make unsupervised phone calls in the middle of their deliberations; and Blythin's failure to shield jurors from slanted news coverage." Sam was released from prison. He wed Ariana Tebbenjohanns, a woman with whom he had pursued a romance through the mails.

On March 4, 1965, the U.S. Court of Appeals for the Sixth Circuit in Cincinnati overturned Judge Weinman's reversal. Sam remained free on bail while Bailey appealed to the U.S. Supreme Court.

In front of the Supreme Court, Bailey argued that Sam "was so thoroughly tried and convicted by the news media that a fair trial in the courtroom could not and in fact did not occur." Bailey also pointed to Kilgallen's deposition in which

Judge Blythin told her prior to the trial that Sam "was guilty as hell."

On June 6, 1966, the U.S. Supreme Court overturned Sam's conviction. In the majority opinion, Associate Justice Tom Clark wrote that "virulent publicity" had violated Sam's right to a fair trial and that Judge Blythin had not properly warned the jury against getting information about the case from sources outside the trial.

## The Second Trial

The lead prosecutor at the second trial was Cuyahoga County prosecutor John T. Corrigan. His co-counsel was prosecutor Leo Spellacy.

The presiding judge was Francis J. Talty. He ordered the jurors sequestered and calls to their families monitored.

Russ Sherman was Bailey's co-counsel.

In a bold move, Bailey told the jury that they would not only hear evidence suggesting Sam was innocent but learn of a plausible alternative killer. Bailey intended to put forth a theory first proposed in Holmes' book.

Holmes theory was as follows: Marilyn had been having an affair with a man who lived close by and was also married. Her lover saw the house dark except for a light in the dressing room and took this as a signal that Sam was gone. He snuck into the house and did not see Sam sound asleep on the day-bed. The man's wife was alarmed by his absence but figured out where he was. The jealous wife came into the house and attacked Marilyn. Sam woke to Marilyn's screams and was later knocked unconscious twice by the man who had decided to aid the wife he had betrayed. The man staged a burglary.

Holmes named neither villain nor villainess in his book but anyone familiar with the case knew he meant Spencer and Esther Houk.

In Bailey's opening, he stated that the killer's "physical strength was compatible with that of a woman."

Dr. Lester Adelson took the stand and detailed Marilyn's wounds. Under Bailey's cross-examination, Adelson said it was possible that Marilyn's teeth were broken by being pulled from inside. Bailey wanted to suggest that the bitten killer had a flowing wound that Sam did not.

The prosecution called Spen Houk. He testified to Sam's morning phone call.

When Bailey cross-examined Spen, Bailey brought out that the Houks had not called the police after Sam called nor had they brought a weapon to the residence. Bailey asked if they had any reason to believe the killer was gone and Spencer answered, "I just didn't give it any thought."

Bailey asked Spen if he remembered a Spang Bakery driver at the Sheppard residence. Spencer replied, "Quite possibly." He also elicited from Spen the statement that he had once brought a meal to Marilyn when she was sick in bed.

Esther Houk testified to seeing Marilyn's bloody corpse. Questioned by Bailey, she testified that she had started a fire in her living room fireplace that morning. Neff writes that Bailey "hoped to suggest that the fire may have been used to burn evidence such as bloody clothing."

Gerber testified to finding Sam's watch in the green bag in the bushes and to the bloodstains on Marilyn's pillow. When the prosecution questioned him, he refrained from speculating as to what the weapon was.

Bailey eagerly cross-examined Gerber on this point and that cross is recounted in *The Defense Never Rests* by F. Lee Bailey with Harvey Aronson.

Gerber: "It looked like a surgical instrument to me."

Bailey: "Just what kind of surgical instrument do you see here?"

Gerber: "I'm not sure."

Bailey: "Would it be an instrument you yourself have handled?"

Gerber: "I don't know if I've handled one or not."

Bailey: "Do you have such an instrument back at your office?"

Gerber: Shakes head.

Bailey: "Have you ever seen such an instrument in any

hospital, or medical supply catalogue, or anywhere else, Dr. Gerber?"

Gerber: "No, not that I can remember."

Bailey: "Tell the jury, doctor, where you have searched for the instrument during the last twelve years."

Gerber: "I have looked all over the United States."

Bailey: "By all means, tell us what you found."

Gerber: "I didn't find one."


The prosecution called Mary Cowan. She testified that Sam's watch had blood spatter on it. The implication was that it was spattered while Sam wore it while he beat Marilyn.

Bailey asked her if she had examined a rivet hole on a broken link of the watch's band for blood. He was suggesting that blood inside it would mean it got there after it was broken.

Cowan conceded she had not.

Bailey called Jack Krakan to the stand. He had delivered bread to the Sheppards for Spang Bakery. He testified to seeing Marilyn kiss a man and to walking in as Marilyn handed the man a key and said, "Don't tell Sam."

Kirk testified that the blood spatter pattern indicated a left-handed swing. Sam was right-handed. He also testified that although the unique bloodstain was type O, as was Marilyn's, it probably came from a different person because there was a difference in the rate of agglutination, or clumping, between it and the other spots.

He also testified that the spots on Sam's watch could have been from contact rather than spatter.

Bailey called Richard Eberling to the stand. Eberling once owned Dick's Window Cleaning Service and had regularly washed windows for the Sheppards.

Eberling said he had told police a few years after the murder, when he was arrested for stealing, that he had cut his hand and bled in the Sheppard home.

Bailey did not call Sam to testify. In *The Defense Never Rests*, he writes that this was because Sam had turned to "booze and pills" to cope and was often "unaware of what was going on around him."

The case went to the jury on the morning of November 16, 1966. They had a verdict that same day: not guilty.

After Sam's release, a book he had written in prison, *Endure and Conquer*, shot to the best sellers list. However, much of the profits went to pay Bailey's fees. Sam was re-instated as a surgeon but his skills had deteriorated due to lack of use and alcoholism. Twice he was sued for malpractice due to patient deaths. He and Ariane divorced.

Sam eventually had a new career as a wrestler with the moniker "Killer Sheppard." He married the daughter of his manager. On April 6, 1970, Sam died at 46 of an illness that often strikes alcoholics.

The Sam Sheppard case may have been immortalized in the TV series *The Fugitive* that started running in 1963. Although series makers always denied the connection, the parallels between its plot and Sam were glaring. In the show, David Janssen plays Richard Kimble, a Midwestern physician unjustly convicted of the murder of his wife. Kimble had left the house after an argument with his wife. When returning, he saw a one-armed man running away—then found his wife beaten to death.

Convicted of the crime, Kimble was sentenced to death. The train taking him to the execution is derailed and Kimble escapes. He chases the mysterious one-armed man and police officers, most prominent among them Lieutenant Phillip Gerard (Barry Morse), chase Kimble. There is often conflict as Dr. Kimble must risk getting caught in order to treat someone injured or sick.

The program possessed a great deal of dramatic tension for, as Neff notes, it was "a cop show, a doctor show, and a chase show all in one." It was probably more than coincidence that the show aired its last episode—one in which Kimble and Gerard join forces to chase the one-armed man and Kimble is vindicated and set free—about a year after Sam's acquittal.

### Sam Reese Sheppard's Crusade

When "Chip" grew up, he shed his nickname and determined

to vindicate his father. Sam Reese's interest was piqued in late 1989, when Richard Eberling was convicted of murder.

Sam Reese and others wondered if Eberling had been involved in Marilyn's death. In 1960 Eberling was convicted for a series of thefts. The window washer had taken cash, jewelry and figurines from homes in which he worked. He often took gems from their setting and sold them. However, he had kept two rings intact: those of Marilyn Sheppard. He had not stolen them from the home she shared with Sam but from a box labeled "Personal Property of Marilyn Sheppard" in the home of Dr. Richard Sheppard. When questioned, he said he did not know why he kept Marilyn's rings. He also told police he had cut his hand at the Sheppard residence a few days before the murders and dripped blood through the house.

The murder for which Eberling was imprisoned had originally been identified as an accident. He had worked as a caregiver for the elderly Ethel Durkin. Her 1983 death was initially recorded as the result of an accidental fall. In 1987, a woman who had partnered with Eberling in a fraud scheme reported to police that Eberling had murdered Durkin after forging a will giving him most of her estate. Her body was exhumed and autopsied, showing that she had been struck on the head and neck.

An amateur detective who used the moniker "Monsignor" phoned Sam Reese to inform him that Eberling had a story to tell Sam Reese. Sam Reese wrote to Eberling who wrote back indicating he knew the true story of Marilyn's murder. Eberling claimed, "Her death was not intentional" and "The pressure build-up caused temporary insanity." Sam Reese assumed Eberling was referring to himself.

Sam Reese visited Eberling at the Lebanon Correctional Institute. Neff writes that Eberling recalled being in the Sheppard house two days before Marilyn's murder and hearing Esther Houk scream at Marilyn, "I will kill you if you don't leave my husband alone."

In 1995, Reese filed a lawsuit against the state of Ohio, on behalf of Sam Sheppard's estate, for Sam's "wrongful imprisonment." Sam Reese asked for $2 million, one third of which would have gone to his attorneys.

While Sam Reese waited for the case to be heard, Eberling died in prison of a heart attack.

Cuyahoga County Common Pleas Court Judge Ronald Suster presided at this civil suit. Terry Gilbert was lead attorney for plaintiff Sam Reese. George Carr was Gilbert's co-counsel.

William D. Mason was lead attorney for the defendant, the state of Ohio. His co-counsel was Steve Dever. Assisting them were Dean Boland and Kathleen Martin.

Gilbert declared in his opening statement, "Dr. Sheppard was a victim of this crime, too. He was attacked, beaten, unconscious." Gilbert then pointed out that Sam's wounds did not bleed so he could not have contributed to the blood trail in the house. Gilbert argued that even after Sam's acquittal, "He literally died a broken man. This is the product of wrongful imprisonment." Gilbert asserted that Gerber's identification of the likely murder weapon as a "surgical instrument" was a "false claim [that] was enough to convict [Sam] alone."

Then Gilbert suggested an alternative suspect: Richard Eberling who "had motive, opportunity and he confessed."

Gilbert called F. Lee Bailey to the stand. Bailey stated, "This man was so badly injured, somebody else had to be there."

Dever used Bailey to undercut the plaintiff's theory of the case. Bailey testified, "I did not form an impression that Richard Eberling killed Marilyn."

Expert on blunt trauma Dr. William F. Fallon Jr. took the stand. He testified a study of the X-rays indicated that Sam had suffered "possibly life-threatening injuries." Dever pointed out that a chip fracture appeared in an early X-ray but not a later one.

Dever asked, "Can you rule out that the X rays had been substituted or switched?"

"No," Fallon answered.

The Ohio defense suggested that Dr. Steve Sheppard had switched Sam's X rays with those of a patient who really was severely injured.

The plaintiff called Kathy Wagner, now remarried with the last name of Dyal, former nurse's aid for Ethel Durkin. She testified that one evening, when she and Richard Eberling were exchanging confidences, he mentioned Marilyn Sheppard. Dyal testified, "He told me that he had killed her and that he hit her husband in the head with a pail and that 'the bitch bit the hell out of me.'"

Forensic psychiatrist Dr. Emanuel Tanay testified that Eberling's statements meant, "He is sending signals that he did it." Tanay saw Marilyn's murder as the act of a "sexually sadistic killer" and not a homicidal husband.

Dever asked, "Did you find any evidence of any type of burns, bite marks, any type of trauma caused to the breast or genital area of Mrs. Sheppard?"

Tanay said he had not.

Then Gilbert had professor of dentistry Dr. Michael Sobel testify. Gilbert displayed a close-up of Eberling's wrist. It showed a scar that Sobel said could be from the cut of a fingernail and that Marilyn might have scraped Eberling's wrist with the fingernail that was torn off.

On cross-examination, Dever queried, "There should be a piece of Richard Eberling under the fingernail, right?"
Sobel said no because her hands were not bagged.

Blood-pattern analyst Bart Epstein testified for the plaintiff. He cited the relative absence of blood on Sam as supporting his innocence. Gilbert asked about the blood pattern on Sam's watch. Epstein testified that the spots were made by contact rather than by blood flying. On cross, he conceded that Sam might have lost some blood on the lake but that it still would have been on his shoes and belt if he wore them during the homicide.

Dr. Mohammad Tahir took the stand. He testified that, according to his DNA tests, the blood on Sam's pants was neither his nor Marilyn's and that a vaginal swab contained sperm that was not Sam's.

On cross-examination, Dever drew forth the admission that the slides might have been reused and dirty. Tahir also conceded that the sperm could have been from consensual sex up to two days before the murder and that the sperm was scantier than one would expect if the man had fully ejaculated. Dr. Ranajit Chakraborty testified that markers in the closet stain were found in about 2.4% of the population and that Eberling was in that group.

Then the defense of the state of Ohio began calling its witnesses.

Blood-pattern expert Toby Wolson testified that the blood trail might not have been from a bleeding person because the spots were very small. He also testified that, after examining copies of the photos Tahir had used in his analysis, he believed the photos were not clear enough to interpret.

Paul Gerhardt, brother of Esther Houk, testified for the first time that he remembered repairing a lamp for the Sheppards and leaving it in an upstairs bedroom. He believed he had left it in the bedroom in which the murder took place.

Ohio's defense called retired FBI criminal profiler and crime analyst Gregg O. McCrary. He testified that he had studied the crime photos and other records and firmly concluded that the killing "was a staged domestic homicide." Neff writes that McCrary based this opinion on four things: "that the Sheppards' marriage was under stress; Dr. Sheppard was not injured; the crime scene was staged; and that Marilyn's murder was an 'overkill.'"

On rebuttal, Gilbert called criminalist Terrence Laber. On cross-examination, Dever showed the court a slide of the pillow stain, then pulled a lamp from under the chairs where the bailiff and law clerk sat. He asked if the stain could have come from a lamp like this one and Laber replied that it could not. However, the stem of the lamp resembled a long flashlight that Kirk had postulated was the weapon.

The suit went to the jury. They reached their verdict within hours: the plaintiff, Sam Reese Sheppard, had not proven that his father had suffered wrongful imprisonment.

Sam Reese appealed and the Eighth District Court of Appeals ruled in February 2002 that the case should never have even been heard in the first place as a claim for wrongful imprisonment could only be brought by the individual who had been imprisoned. In August 2002 the Supreme Court of Ohio upheld that decision.

While the Sam Sheppard case appears to have reached its end as a legal matter, it continues to haunt the culture.

One of the things that has kept the Marilyn Sheppard murder alive in the annals of true crime is that the case has an extraordinary line-up of plausible suspects without any of them being proven to have committed the crime.

## What about Esther and Spencer Houk?

The Houks had not called the police after Sam phoned them with the message that Marilyn had been killed. They headed over to the Sheppard residence without bringing a weapon even though they had no way of knowing that a murderer was not still there. When they got there, Esther ran up to the bedroom in which Marilyn had been killed without being told where Marilyn was. The Houks did not attend Marilyn's funeral.

Spen was hospitalized with a nervous breakdown a few weeks after Marilyn's death.

F. Lee Bailey and Paul Holmes both subscribed to the belief that Esther killed Marilyn because Spen had a tryst with Marilyn and that Spen got into a fight with Sam in order to cover up for Esther.

In 1989, Sam Reese received a letter from the imprisoned Richard Eberling in which Eberling claimed to know "the entire story." The two began corresponding and Sam Reese started visiting Eberling in prison. The journalist working with Sam Reese, Cynthia Cooper, also visited Eberling. Eberling also fingered Esther but his scenario was different.

Eberling said he had been washing windows at the Sheppard home two days before the murder. Spen came over while Sam was still there with Marilyn. Spen stayed after Marilyn left. After Spen left Esther came over. Eberling was not in the room with the women but heard Esther scream, "If you don't leave him alone, I'll kill you!"

Later Eberling said he knew another secret: Spen had been having a homosexual affair with Sam. Eberling claimed to have learned this through an employee who had been washing windows at a hotel in which the two men enjoyed a rendezvous. Eberling believed Esther had been mad at Marilyn thinking Spen was having sex with the wife when he was actually having sex with the husband.

Eberling claimed to have run into Sam shortly after Sam's acquittal and that Sam had confided the following story. On the murder night, Spen went to Sam's for a tryst. Esther, thinking Spen was going to see Marilyn, followed. Esther went upstairs and attacked Marilyn. After her rage was spent, she claimed to have gone crazy. Sam felt sorry for her and agreed to help Spen stage a cover-up. Sam assumed his story of the "bushy-haired man" would be believed and felt stuck with the lies he had agreed to even after being wrongly convicted.

However, it seems odd that Sam would not have come clean during the decade he was imprisoned.

### The Mysteriously Murderous Major Call

In a book published in 2002, *Tailspin: The Strange Case of Major Call,* author Bernard F. Conners suggested a new suspect, the mysterious James Arlon Call

Call's story is indisputably bizarre. He made his career in the United States Air Force and attained the rank of major in February 1951.

In 1952 Call's beloved wife, Muriel, died suddenly.

Crushed by grief, Call asked for and was granted an extended leave from the military.

By the fall of 1952, Call was back on active duty. He volunteered for combat assignments in Korea.

On May 13, 1954, Major Call went absent without leave (AWOL) from the air force base in Shreveport, Louisiana.

Call traveled to the Adirondack mountain range in northeastern New York state. There he camped out around the village of Lake Placid where he committed stick-ups and burglaries. Conners notes that Call always, "shaved and cut his hair regularly, using a mirror and scissors, to avoid the scraggly woodsman-like appearance" that people might expect of someone hiding in the woods.

Call invaded an empty house on the edge of a camp called the Perkins camp on August 5, 1954. Police spotted him, leading to a shoot-out that left one officer dead.

Call pled guilty to second-degree murder. He served over 13 years before being paroled on July 30, 1968.

He died in a one-car accident on May 5, 1974.

Conners goes beyond known facts to argue that Call murdered Marilyn Sheppard. Call used a crowbar in some of his burglaries. Conners believes this made an imprint in Marilyn's blood. He had an injury on a finger after the Sheppard murder that Conners argues was Marilyn's bite. Among the items confiscated when Call was last taken into custody was a meerschaum pipe. Sam Sheppard smoked pipes. Conners thinks the blood stain on the Sheppard pillow suggests the shape of the Luger Call carried.

The composite drawing of the "bushy-haired man" bears a resemblance to Call—although photos show Call's hair as solidly down with an occasional wisp of hair sticking out. Conners argues Call failed to tame his hair into submission on July 4, 1954.

Conners case is strong but flawed. Call's known violence was gunplay and against men. There was never a suggestion of a sexual motive in any of Call's crimes as there is in Marilyn's murder.

### Did Sam really do it?

There is also the possibility that Dr. Sam really was guilty as charged. DeSario and Mason argue for this position in *Dr. Sam Sheppard on Trial*. The dust jacket of their book has the words "case closed" on it although they are probably optimistic to believe that everyone will accept their version of events. However, they spiritedly defend the original investigators and prosecutors.

They do not pretend to know the precise motive. The idea that Dr. Sam planned to kill his wife so he would be free to marry another woman without the stigma attached to divorce in the 1950s seems far-fetched. After all, he disregarded the stigma attached to open philandering. It would seem more likely that he erupted in rage during a heated argument. That could have occurred because Marilyn took him to task for his infidelity.

It is also possible that Sam was infuriated because Marilyn confided that her pregnancy may have been sired by another man. That scenario also seems weak because of the timing of the pregnancy.

It also leaves us with the puzzle of the broken sports trophies. Sam would be unlikely to destroy the sports trophy he cherished. Of course, it is possible that he might do so as part of a staged scene but that opens the question of why other items were not randomly destroyed. Another possibility is that he and Marilyn initially got into an argument downstairs and that each smashed the other's trophy.

Sam Reese lost his suit because Sam cannot be definitely ruled out as Marilyn's murderer. However, neither can the slaying be definitely attributed to him.

### Richard Eberling:
### Window Washer turned Millionaire turned Murderer

James Neff, Sam Reese, and Cynthia Cooper all point fingers at Richard Eberling as Marilyn's probable murderer. Both *The Wrong Man* and *Mockery of Justice* devote a great deal of space to the singular odyssey of the orphan turned window washer turned millionaire turned convicted murderer.

Richard Eberling was born Richard Lenardic to Louise Lenardic, an unmarried 19-year-old Yugoslavian immigrant. His paternity was never established. Louise could not care for them but would not sign him over for adoption. Soon after his birth, Richard began shuffling between foster homes. Cooper and Sheppard write that the boy was in five different homes before he reached seven. A fussy baby, he had temper tantrums and blackouts.

When of school age, he stole, lied, wet his bed, and engaged in sex play with other boys. He got in trouble at a new school for forcing kisses on girls.

As an adult, Richard claimed that when he was seven a foster father raped him.

However, he was industrious in an unexpected manner: he loved cleaning houses and arranging furniture.

At eight, Richard was placed as a foster child with the farm family of George and Christine Eberling. Richard got along well there although he often stole small items from the Eberlings and their acquaintances.

George Eberling died in 1946. By then, Richard was a teenager. He wanted to participate in sports. Christine forbade him to because she insisted he need to work at home and feared his getting injured.

Christine told Richard he should become a doctor. He liked this idea but his low grades made it impractical.

Although never adopted by the Eberlings, Richard persuaded a court to change his name to Richard George Eberling. As a young adult, he began a window washing business. Eberling's life often appeared plagued by accidents. In 1955, a fire destroyed Christine Eberling's barn shortly after he arrived home. Some Eberlings griped that a disproportionate amount of the insurance pay-off went to Richard because of furniture he had stored in the barn.

In 1956, Richard crashed his car into a parked truck and his date was killed. An autopsy determined that the death was an accident.

In 1960, Eberling met Oscar B. "Obie" Henderson. The two men were instant friends. They were soon housemates, a relationship that would last 30 years. They stoutly denied being gay but friends spoke of them as a couple.

Around the same time, began working for Ethel May Durkin. He and the elderly, childless, affluent widow hit it off immediately. He was soon doing odd jobs around her home and keeping her company. His presence did not sit well with

Ethel's sister, Myrtle Fray. Once when Eberling was in another room of Ethel's home, Myrtle berated her sister, saying, "You've got to get rid of him. He's a crook." Ethel retorted, "He's over all that." They continued arguing and Ethel pointed out that Richard could hear Myrtle who answered, "I don't care if he hears me or not!"

Myrtle was murdered in 1962. She was found with her face beaten and her body exposed because her nightgown had been ripped open. Apparently no effort made to test for semen.

Years later, Richard would say he had a theory about the murder. "It had to be a woman," he said. He believed this because he thought it would be difficult for a man to leave her apartment without being spotted by the neighbors. However, he speculated that if a man killed Myrtle, he had dressed in women's clothes.

Myrtle's Fray's murder was never solved.

In 1970, another Durkin sister, Belle, who lived with Ethel, fell down a flight of stairs and died a few months later.

The 1970s appeared to be good years for. Dick's Window Cleaning branching out into putting up screens and storms and into interior decorating to be re-born as R. G. Eberling & Associates. In 1972 Cleveland mayor Ralph Perk hired Richard to remodel the mayor's office. The job finished in 1976. According to Cooper and Sheppard, it "was declared an aesthetic success." However, the next mayor did not retain Richard's services.

Eberling and Henderson were often seen about town, hobnobbing with the elite and in the company of single women. One of Eberling's friends said, "He was always looking for old ladies to take care of. He'd be really nice to them. If you'd be nice to them, they'd be nice to you."

After Eberling's dismissal from city hall work, he spent increasing time with Ethel. Henderson as well as Eberling frequently kissed her and flirted with her. Henderson sometimes fixed her hair.

Cooper and Sheppard report, "From 1979 to 1982, Ethel suffered a series of falls." She signed a power of attorney making Obie executor of her will. In November 1983, Ethel became disturbed when a caregiver resigned. Ethel persuaded the woman to return. Then Ethel called her before she was supposed to show up and said, "Richard says no."

On November 15, 1983, Eberling phoned police to say medical personnel were needed. They found Ethel lying on the floor, breathing but unconscious. Eberling told them she had fallen. She was hospitalized, unable to speak, until she died on January 3, 1984.

Ethel's will named Henderson as executor and left him four percent of her estate. 70% of that estate was left to Eberling. The friends lived lavishly for several years.

In 1987, a woman contacted police claiming to know Ethel's will was fraudulent and suspected foul play in Ethel's death. She had been in cahoots with Eberling and had been one of the witnesses to the will.

Investigation revealed that the will had been typed after it had been signed. Eberling persuaded Ethel to sign a blank sheet of paper by telling her he wanted to have her handwriting analyzed. Ethel's body was exhumed and the coroner found that she had died from blows to the back of her head and face.

Henderson went to prison for several years for fraud and theft. Eberling was convicted of similar crimes and also of Ethel's murder. Claiming innocence, he died in prison.

There are many reasons Cooper, Sheppard, and Neff pin Marilyn's murder on Richard. Having worked at the home regularly, he was intimately familiar with it. A large man, he might have been able to defeat a confused Sam in a physical fight. If the jury in the Ethel Durkin murder decided correctly, Eberling was capable of murder. Moreover, the beating death of Ethel resembled the beating death of Marilyn. Although he was only charged with one murder, the string of mysterious deaths in his wake lead some people to suspect he was a multiple murderer.

Cooper and Sheppard note, "Eberling, who was ever conscious of money, did not present the information that he later claimed to have when a ten-thousand-dollar reward was offered by the Sheppard family."

If he were the murderer, puzzling aspects of the case would make sense. He might have smashed sports trophies because of his long simmering frustration at his having been denied a chance to go out for sports in high school. Turning over Sam's medical bag may have grown out of his regret at not being able to fulfill his foster mother's dream for him of becoming a doctor. Even the neat pulling out of drawers makes sense in light of Richard's penchant for tidiness.

Then there is the strange story he told of his having dripped blood in the house just days before the murders. It had not been suggested that Eberling's blood was in the house so why would he try to account for its presence? In 1990, Vern Lund, a dying man who had once worked for Dick's Window Cleaning, contacted Sam Reese, to say that he, not his boss, had worked in the Sheppard home days before the murder.

Over the years, Eberling made several comments about Marilyn. Asked if he might have dated her if he had met her before Sam, he answered, "Probably not. I was an orphan, she was a golden girl… I wasn't good enough." He said, "She was a lovely lady … I think she was lonesome because she let a lot of family dirt out to me." Neff quotes him saying that she wore, "Tight little brief shorts and a very little blouse. She was immaculate, all in white." Neff also reports that Richard said Marilyn hospitably invited him to enjoy milk and brownies with her and Chip. Neff comments, "He was describing an ideal mom—feeding him comfort food." Eberling describes Marilyn as both an idealized mother and a sexual tease: a particularly alarming combination considering his history of abandonment by mother-figures and possible sexual confusion.

DeSario and Mason show a photograph of Richard Eberling, already balding in 1954, and pointedly ask, "Is this the bushy-haired man?" However, Cooper and Sheppard report, "He wore toupees and ones that, by the account of a friend, gave him a 'bushy-haired' appearance in 1954."

However, there is no evidence conclusively proving Richard was in the Sheppard house on the night in question.

The Marilyn Sheppard murder remains officially un-solved. With its line-up of suspects both colorful and plausible, it is a tantalizing mystery.

## Bibliography

Bailey, F. Lee with Aronson, Harvey. *The Defense Never Rests.* Stein and Day. New York. 1971.

Bailey, F. Lee with Rabe, Jean. *When the Husband is the Suspect: From Sam Sheppard to Scott Peterson — The Public's Passion for Spousal Homicides.* A Tom Doherty Associates Book, New York. 2008.

Conners, Bernard F. *Tailspin: The Strange Case of Major Call.* British American Publishing, Ltd. Latham, New York. 2002.

Cooper, Cynthia L. and Sheppard, Sam Reese. *Mockery of Justice: The True Story of the Sheppard Murder Case.* Northeastern University Press. Boston. 1995.

DeSario, Jack P. and Mason, William D. *Dr. Sam Sheppard on Trial: The Prosecutors and the Marilyn Sheppard Murder.* The Kent State University Press. Kent and London, 2003.

Neff, James. *The Wrong Man: The Final Verdict on the Dr. Sam Sheppard Murder Case.* Random House. New York. 2001.

# CHAPTER SIX

## The Alice Crimmins Case

The Alice Crimmins case broke in 1965 and grabbed headlines for the next twelve years. Like Joey Buttafacao in the 1990s, the name of Alice Crimmins became, in the latter half of the 1960s and most of the 1970s, synonymous with tabloid sensation. For example, lesbian activist Jill Johnston wrote that she had hit the big time when she got as much media attention as "a new episode in an Alice Crimmins murder trial or the sinking of the Queen Mary."

This odd real-life mystery was the subject of two true-crime books, two best-selling novels, and a made-for-TV movie. Indeed, as recently as 1994, the case inspired a film, Beth B.'s *Two Small Bodies.* The Neal Bell play of the same name was first presented in 1977.

The incident that would transfix the public for over a decade involved a previously obscure family with a sad but in many respects, all-too-familiar family history. That family lived in the Queens borough of New York City and consisted of airline mechanic Edmund Crimmins, homemaker Alice Crimmins and their children, Eddie, Jr., aged five, and Alice Marie, always called Missy, four. Edmund Crimmins was a six-foot-tall, sandy-haired and ruggedly handsome man who was starting to get a paunch and double chin. He towered over his wife Alice, a blue-eyed redhead with delicate features who was both slim and buxom.

As couples usually are, the two had been very happy during the early years of their marriage. However, that marriage had crumbled, in large part, because Eddie spent very little time at home with his family; he preferred working overtime or drinking with the boys. Lonely and frustrated, Alice had found solace in a series of extra-marital affairs.

Their children have been described as well-behaved and cheerful youngsters. The two sometimes sat on the windowsill of their room, waving and saying "hi" to passersby. Unlike many children who are born so close together, they did not seem much afflicted by sibling rivalry. Missy was a "girly girl" and her chubby older brother had adopted a protective attitude toward her, calling her "my Missy."

One time another little boy pulled some hair from one of Missy's dolls. In a typically childlike way, Eddie interpreted an offense against one of his sister's toys as an attack on her and he charged at the larger boy, shouting, "Don't you ever touch my Missy! Don't you ever touch my Missy!

During the separation from Eddie, Alice, who had previously been a full-time homemaker, had gotten a job as a cocktail waitress. Also during their separation, she had attended a bon voyage party — one that led to her husband's custody suit. The party was held on a boat and Alice had attended it with Anthony Grace, one of her major boyfriends. He was a 52-year old wealthy building contractor who sported a pencil thin mustache and was given to silk suits and a diamond pinky ring. Short and thickset, he had many friends amongst prominent New York City politicians and was rumored to have a few amongst its hoodlums.

Grace and the other men had playfully locked the women in a washroom. Then the boat set sail. Unable to get off it, Alice Crimmins found herself on the way to the Bahamas at the very time when she should have been going home to relieve her children's babysitter.

That babysitter called Edmund Crimmins who immediately came to pick his kids up. He took them to the residence of his mother-in-law, Alice Burke, and decided that he would file suit for their custody. "You're not fit to bring up those kids!" he angrily told their mother.

The trial for that suit was only a week away. Her attorney had told her to expect a court agency inspection in connection with so Alice had spent the much of previous evening doing a lot of housecleaning and fixing up.

However, on that hot, sunshiny morning of July 14, 1965 she found little Eddie and Missy were not in their rooms. She made a frantic phone call to Edmund who strongly denied taking them, then went over to her place to help her look. Unable to find them, he called police to report that his children were missing.

## The Catholic Cop and the Made-Up Mom

At the station house, one detective immediately wanted the case of the missing children. He was Detective Gerard H. Piering, a 30-something father of six who sported an out-of-style crew-cut and yearned to make second-grade detective. He and his more easygoing partner, George Martin, met both parents at the mother's residence.

That residence was a ground-floor apartment in a working-class development of red brick called the Regal Garden Apartments. The Crimmins home was modestly furnished but neatly kept.

The window of the children's room was wide open, and a carriage was underneath the window. It appeared that Missy and Eddie had either been enticed out of the window or, as they had done before, crawled outside on their own.

When Piering saw Alice Crimmins, the strait-laced Roman Catholic was instantly taken aback: her children were missing yet this mother was neither sobbing nor hysterical. Rather, she was heavily made-up and sharply dressed, looking chic and sensuous in tight toreador pants and a flower-print shirt and high-heeled white shoes. Her short red hair was elaborately teased. By his own recollection, Piering disliked her on sight, thinking, "She looks like a cold bitch to me." He told Martin, "You interview the guy. I'll take the bitch."

Missy Crimmins was discovered a few hours later in a vacant lot. She had been strangled to death. Detective Piering was informed that the body of a little girl matching Missy's description had been found but did not immediately inform the parents of the daughter's death. Rather, he decided to give the mother whom he suspected a sort of "test."

## The Puzzle of Personality

Taken to the vacant lot without knowing in advance what she was going to see, Alice was escorted directly to the corpse of her four-year-old daughter. Tiny Missy, a delicate-featured blonde, lay on her side. The girl was dressed in a white T-shirt and yellow panties. A blue flower-patterned pajama top was ominously wound and knotted about the child's neck.

Crimmins swooned and Piering caught her. "It's Missy," she mumbled.

She had to be assisted back to the unmarked police cruiser. However, she did not cry, a fact that struck the detectives as damning. Indeed, all during the drive back home, this mother —who had just suffered what would be, to a normal person, the most grievous loss imaginable—shed no tears. Rather, she sat in the car, staring into the distance and answering questions in a flat, expressionless tone.

When she arrived home, she stepped into a swarm of photographers' lights popping off in her face—and suddenly started sobbing.

That settled it in the minds of the investigating officers. Alice Crimmins did not care about her children. Her swooning at her dead daughter's side was theatrical; she only cried on camera in a calculated attempt to simulate grief.

Their very negative opinion of her would soon be reinforced and hardened for the next morning she was to keep the officers who wanted to question her waiting while she finished putting on her makeup. As Ken Gross wrote in *The Alice Crimmins Case*, both police and public were outraged at the idea that "a woman who was supposed to be in the ultimate stages of grief and anxiety (her son was still missing) was more concerned about her appearance!"

Her son's badly decomposed body was found several

days after his sister's was. Then, within a week of the funeral, Alice Crimmins, mother of two small dead children, appeared to simply resume her normal life. "Normal life," in this case included not just doing housekeeping chores and cooking for herself and her husband—she and Edmund had reconciled—but evenings at bars and nightclubs where she drank and danced the nights away.

Perhaps this behavior did indeed point, as so many believed, to an abnormally callous mentality and one that was capable of murder. Then again, all of it is subject to less sinister interpretations.

It is commonly accepted that shock can dam emotional expression. Perhaps the visual flash of camera bulbs suddenly jolted it out of Crimmins. Subsequent events would show Piering hasty in judging the swoon as faked since Alice would show a tendency to faint under most extreme pressure.

There is a poignant explanation for her apparently obsessive concern with her appearance. "It was an important part of her, the makeup," Gross wrote, "Later it would be misunderstood, dismissed as cold vanity. But the adolescent acne of her well-scrubbed Catholic girlhood had burrowed into her a permanent feeling of inferiority. It would take her the better part of an hour but that great affliction of her acne-scarred complexion would be disguised with expert care." Finally, her resumption of an active nightlife and, soon after that, an active extra-marital sex life might also be viewed as a coping mechanism. Just as she had previously fought off loneliness through sensuality, so now she tried to escape an overwhelming grief with the pleasures of the flesh.

Husband Edmund Crimmins had his own share of peculiar personality traits. Since their separation, he had installed a wiretap on her phone and another wiretap from her bedroom to the basement so he could listen to her making love to other men when he surreptitiously entered the home. In one instance, he had been in the basement while Alice was in bed with another guy. Edmund Crimmins had burst into the bedroom and chased the lover naked into the street. He would sometimes sneak into the home when he knew she was not there simply to be around the items she owned.

Even more disturbingly, he had told Alice that, during their separation, he had once exposed his genitals to some little girls in a park. Later, he claimed that he made up the story to ease Alice's guilt feelings about the demise of their marriage and make her think he was as "bad" as she was. However, whether the story was true or false, telling it certainly marks Edmund Crimmins as an odd man.

But the cops saw Alice as the more sinister of the two.

## Dust, Disputed Dinners, and an Ill-Preserved Crime Scene

Part of the reason the police soon focused their attention on Alice was that Detective Piering recalled seeing things that threw her story into question and she remembered items conflicting with other people's reports.

When Piering first went into the children's room to investigate, he moved a lamp from the bureau over which the youngsters would have had to scamper on their way out the window. In doing so, he says, he noticed a thin film of undisturbed dust over the top of it because the lamp itself left a clear round ring. However, Piering did not order the photographer to record this vital evidence nor did he even make a written note of it.

A photograph of the bureau showing a layer of undisturbed dust would be especially welcome since that area had seen some action recently whether or not the Crimmins kids scrambled over it. During her housecleaning, Alice had unbolted the screen because she had found a hole in it, intending to replace it with the screen from her own bedroom. However, she found a bit of dog excrement on that screen. So she returned to the children's room and put the screen with the hole in it back in the window but did not refasten it to its bolts. She simply propped it against the glass. Later, in his frantic search for the children, Eddie Sr. had leaned out the window to yell for them.

As Piering would later recall, Alice told him that she had fed the kids some manicotti and he saw a slice of the same in the refrigerator and a box of frozen manicotti in the trash. He did not save either bit of evidence, have it photographed, or make a note.

However, when Alice talked to other detectives, she said that the kids had eaten veal that night. The autopsy showed that Missy's stomach contained pasta but no meat. Child molesters frequently pretend to be children's "friends" and caregivers. Could a pedophile have fed the Crimmins kids before murdering them? Stranger things have been known to happen. Then again, perhaps Alice Crimmins was innocently mistaken.

There were other conflicts between her recollection of that fateful evening's events and those of others. She recalled getting gas for her car at a Gulf station at 9:00 p.m. on the fateful evening; the two attendants remembered her being there around 5:00 p.m. However, this was a matter that was, in and of itself, irrelevant to the case.

Then there was the issue of the precise time Missy died. It was initially determined by Dr. Richard Grimes, by the temperature of the deep tissues of Missy's body, that she had died at least six to twelve hours before her body had been discovered and perhaps earlier than that. The Medical Examiner's office was headed Dr. Milton Helpern, a respected coroner, and he had been present at the little girl's autopsy. He found that the child's stomach was quite full and concluded that she had died no more than two hours after this meal.

Alice claimed that, on the fatal night, the family had eaten at 7:30 p.m. and she had checked on the children at midnight.

Was she lying? Was she mistaken? Or had the kids been kidnapped and fed a last meal of macaroni before killed? The public wondered and increasingly became critical of the authorities for not bringing the killer of the Crimmins kids to trail as the investigations continued for two more years.

## Turning the Heat up on a Hot Lady

During those years, the cops followed Alice Crimmins constantly, watched her every move and—as her own husband had—tapped her phone. They had good reason to expect such activity to bear fruit. If Alice was the killer, she had to have accomplices because the locations and times at which the bodies were found meant that someone else had transported at least one dead child (she had been under constant surveillance when little Eddie's body was unceremoniously dumped in a vacant lot). Even if she was such a "cold bitch" that she never needed to unburden herself to anyone, her co-conspirator(s) would surely want to talk about payment or silence or both.

But there were no such conversations.

However, there was much to keep the police listeners entertained since Alice Crimmins and her many sweethearts engaged in sexually oriented conversations. The cops could count themselves doubly lucky, even by today's "dial-a-porn" standards, since they were being paid to listen to titillating sex talk.

The cops also waged a campaign of embarrassment and harassment against Alice Crimmins in the hope that the tension might "break" her. During the months that she and Eddie were reconciled, they phoned him to let him know she was entertaining another man in the marital bedroom. They went to her various employers and informed them that the efficient secretary working for them under the name "Alice Burke" was actually the notorious Alice Crimmins, a promiscuous woman suspected in the deaths of her two young children, leading to her sudden firing.

So Alice Crimmins went from one employer to another, working for a few weeks as a secretary here, a receptionist there, an airline travel agent on one occasion and then, inevitably, unemployed and looking for work again. She drank more heavily and became increasingly hostile to the investigators she knew were trying to pin a double murder rap on her. She learned that her phone was tapped and began opening conversations with a message to the third parties listening: "Hi, boys, drop dead!"

## The Window Woman

Finally, more than a year and a half after the Crimmins children were killed, the police believed they had an important break in the case. Sifting through the multitude of letters purporting to offer clues, they came across one dated November 30, 1966, and addressed to then-District Attorney Nat Hentel that said as follows.

*Dear Mr. Hentel:*

*Have been reading about your bringing the Crimmins case to the grand jury and am glad to hear of it.*

*May I please tell you of an incident that I witnessed. It may be connected and may not. But I will feel better telling it to you. This was on the night before the children were missing.*

*But as the press reported that a handyman saw them at the window that morning, it may not be related at all.*

*The night was very hot and I could not sleep. I went into the living room and was looking out the window getting some air. This was at 2 a.m. A short while later, a man and woman were walking down the street toward 72 Road. The woman was about five feet in back of the man. She was holding what appeared to be a bundle of blankets that were white under her left arm and was holding a little child walking with her right hand. He now hollered at her to "hurry up." She told him "to be quiet or someone will see us." At that moment I closed my window, which squeeks [sic] and they looked up but did not see me.*

*The man took the white bundle and he heaved it into the back seat of the car. She picked up the little baby and sat with him in the back seat of the car. This woman was then with dark hair, the man was tall, not heavy, with dark hair and a large nose. This took place under a street light so I was able to see it quite planly [sic]. The car turned from the corner of 153 St. onto 72 Road and out to Kissena boulevard.*

*Please forgive me for not signing my name, but I am afraid to. Wishing you the best of luck.*
*A reader*

*P.S. — About one hour later I thought I saw just the man getting into a late model white car.*

The police were both elated (they knew that the report of a handyman seeing the kids at the window in the morning was unsubstantiated) at receiving the letter and initially despairing at the probability of finding its author.

However, they found a clue in the phrase "down the street towards Seventy-Second Road" that enabled them to narrow the search down to a reasonable block of residences. They then reduced that to those not having air conditioners beside their windows. The sleuths came up with a possible 39 apartments. Handwriting in the anonymous letter was compared with samples of complaint letters from those apartments leading them to Sophie Earomirski, a middle-aged, heavyset blonde who often suffered from insomnia.

When the investigators interviewed her, they found her story somewhat revised from that in the fateful epistle. Sophie told the police that she now recalled the woman saying, "My God, don't throw her like that." While the letter described an incident that "may be connected and may not," Sophie now identified the woman she had seen as Alice Crimmins. Earomirski knew Alice from around the neighborhood and Alice's photo was regularly in the newspapers so it seems rather odd that, in the letter, Earomirski saw her only as a woman "with dark hair" and was uncertain as to whether the group she had seen was even connected to the Crimmins case.

However, the police were elated by Earomirski's evidence and viewed it as just what they needed to secure an indictment.

Drawing on Earomirski's story, the investigators put together a scenario of a murderous mother aided by a man with mob ties. For some reason Alice strangled Missy to death, they theorized. Perhaps Missy had intruded on Alice when she and a boyfriend were going at it hot and heavy. Alice had been murderously enraged and her horrified lover had made a quick exit, never to be seen or heard from again.

Alice had told Piering that she had made a phone call to a bar called the Capri's that night and spoken to Anthony Grace. They decided that call must have been about Missy's killing and that Grace, eager to shield a ladylove from the results of her impulsive actions, had placed a fatal call from that busy bar. He had called a hoodlum and told the thug to go over to Crimmins' place to silence little Eddie. Earomirski had seen a dead Missy being carried in a blanket and her older brother obediently trudging to his doom.

## A Romeo Named Rorech

At the same time that investigators were tracking down the writer of an anonymous letter, they were applying pressure to Joseph Rorech, one of Crimmins' major boyfriends.

The tall, muscular Rorech had chiseled features and wore his dark, wavy hair combed straight back from his forehead. He was a high-rolling, hard-drinking home repair contractor with a loud and blustery manner who had lived a very compartmentalized life. There was the devoutly Roman Catholic family man with seven children and the compulsive womanizer. Far more secretly, he was a bisexual who sought and enjoyed the company of men who cross-dressed.

At the time of the Crimmins case, Joe Rorech was a man in serious trouble. His business dealings were going sour and he was drowning in debt. His long-suffering wife had a job selling encyclopedias door-to-door. He had written a raft of bad checks to attempt to hold off his creditors and was in serious legal trouble. Trying to stay one step ahead of cops and creditors, he had taken to using a variety of aliases.

The Crimmins case investigators put a wire on him to listen in to his conversations with Alice but she said nothing indicating culpability in the deaths of the children. The sleuths also repeatedly interviewed him. He recalled Alice talking about the custody suit and saying, "I'd rather see them dead than with Eddie." Had she actually murdered her kids so that her ex-husband would not get custody of them? There were people willing to believe so. However, the investigators realized that a jury could regard this statement as hyperbole. Throughout several months of intense drilling, Rorech denied that she had ever said anything directly incriminating

Then he received "immunity from prosecution for all crimes except adultery and murder" and changed his mind, recalling that she had told him something quite damning.

### "Sexpot" Tried in "The Hippodrome"

On September 11, 1967, two years and two months after the deaths of little Missy and Eddie, Alice Crimmins was arrested for the first-degree murder of her daughter. She was not charged in her son's death because it could not be medically proven that he had been murdered.

An all-male jury was impaneled, partly because prospective female jurors tended to say they were biased against Alice Crimmins. Some people thought it would work in the defendant's favor to be judged by members of the sex that had been so very important in her life. However, the sad fact is that the same men who are all-too-eager to bed a woman may also judge her harshly for her "easy" ways.

The press, especially the tabloid press, had a field day with the case. Alice Crimmins was invariably called the "ex-cocktail waitress" even though it was a position she had held for only a few months. As Ann Jones has noted, the word was used "as a pejorative to sneer at Alice Crimmins and a whole category of women workers at once" despite a future attorney's sound judgment that "it was actually a very hard job." But people see the tight-fitting, frilly outfit, not the constant walking and serving.

Crimmins' sexual escapades were raked over for both their titillation value and as a source of moral outrage. Front Page Detective labeled her "Sexpot on Trial" and described her as "an erring wife, a Circe, an amoral woman whose many affairs appear symptomatic of America's Sex Revolution."

The courtroom trial began in May, 1968 with Judge Peter Farrell, a long-nosed man with thinning silver hair, presiding. It was sensational in the extreme, partly because of the sex-related testimony and partly due to Crimmins' emotional outbursts.

The physician who had first inspected Missy's body when it was found in the lot was named Richard Grimes. He testified: "I saw the body of a girl who appeared to be about five years of age … She was clad in a cotton undershirt, a pair of yellow panties—"

"No!" The doctor's recitation was broken by a shout from Alice Crimmins who began to weep.

Judge Farrell demanded order and told Dr. Grimes to continue. "Around the little girl's face there was a cloth tie," Dr. Grimes said. "The loose ends of the tie appeared to be the arm of some type of garment. The tie was over the mouth of the child, the knot encircling the neck, and the tie was rather loose. … "

Alice Crimmins, supposedly a cold and unfeeling woman, wailed and sobbed uncontrollably during this testimony. A few spectators started crying with her and the judge put the court in recess.

A different kind of explosion from Alice took place during Joe Rorech's testimony. Rorech had to be repeatedly reminded to speak up as he testified in what was, for him, an oddly subdued voice. He told the packed courtroom that prior to the murders, Alice had discussed Eddie's custody suit and had speculated that she might simply take off with them if she thought she might legally lose them. He also repeated her statement that she "would rather see them dead than with Eddie." Later, he said that the two lovers had been talking about the children and a teary-eyed Alice had sadly said, "Joseph, please forgive me, I killed her."

At this testimony, Alice Crimmins leapt to her feet and screamed, "Joseph! How could you do this? This is not true! Joseph … you, of all people! Oh, my God!"

Sophie Earomirski may have been the trial's most dramatic witness. On direct examination by prosecutor James Mosley, she told how she had seen a woman carrying a bundle, a man, and a little boy on that sleepless night at the window. "He took the bundle and he swung the bundle under his arm ... and he walked very quickly to the car," Earomirski testified as the courtroom listened in hushed anticipation. "... he took this bundle and threw it in the back seat of the car. She ran over to him and she said, 'My God, don't do that to her.' And then he looked at her and said, 'Now you're sorry?' and ... she said, 'Please don't say that.'"

When asked if she recognized the woman in the courtroom, Earomirski didn't hesitate. She pointed an accusing finger at Alice Crimmins and said, "That's the woman."

Again Alice jumped to her feet screaming. "You liar! You liar!" the defendant yelled. "You liar! You liar! You liar! You liar!"

Judge Farrell pounded his gavel and demanded Alice Crimmins get a grip on herself.

One of Crimmins' attorneys, Martin Baron, tried to point out inconsistencies between the story she related to this jury and that she had told to the grand jury. However, Sophie was very popular with the courtroom audience, most of who were strongly convinced of Crimmins' guilt. The spectators often laughed or even applauded at her answers until the judge admonished them that, "This is not the Hippodrome." She held up well under cross-examination and, during a court recess, triumphantly held up her hands in a boxer's salute.

### Alice Takes the Stand

At her first trial, Alice Crimmins took the witness stand in her own defense. She spoke in a thin voice that did not carry well so the judge the judge recessed the court until the next day so a microphone could be installed in front of her.

Baron took her through her background and marital troubles. When the questions turned to her children, Crimmins began to shake uncontrollably and tears began streaming down her heavily made-up face. Judge Farrell declared a recess but the trial had to be postponed until the next day because Crimmins had fallen into a semi-faint.

She repeated the story she had told the police of her activities on the terrible night her children disappeared. She strongly denied that she had ever confessed killing Missy to Joe Rorech.

Crimmins was aggressively and belligerently cross-examined by prosecutor Tony Lombardino. Due to the rules of evidence in New York courtrooms, he had complete leeway to delve into anything that might reflect adversely on her character even if it had no direct connection to the issues at trial. He used that leeway to bring out every possible detail of Alice Crimmins' active sex life. This was 1968 when the Sexual Revolution was in its infancy and the working-class people of Queens were outraged by active non-marital sex, especially by a woman. Some of their exchanges were quite lurid. Lombardino established that Crimmins knew a fellow named Carl Andrade and that he had visited her at 1:00 a.m. during her separation from Eddie when the children were in their room sleeping.

LOMBARDINO: Where specifically in your apartment was Andrade?

CRIMMINS: In my bedroom.

LOMBARDINO: Where were you, Mrs. Crimmins?

CRIMMINS: In the bedroom with him, sir.

LOMBARDINO: I see. Did your husband come into the apartment that morning? [As previously noted, Eddie Crimmins was often, unknown to Alice, in the basement of the home listening to her activities through the wiretaps he had installed.]

CRIMMINS: Yes, he did.

LOMBARDINO: What were you two doing when he got there?

CRIMMINS: We weren't doing anything at the moment.

LOMBARDINO: You weren't doing anything? How was Carl Andrade dressed?

CRIMMINS: He was in a state of undress.

LOMBARDINO: Will you tell the men of this jury panel what you mean by a state of undress?

CRIMMINS: Just what I said, sir. A state of undress.

LOMBARDINO: What was your condition of attire?

CRIMMINS: I was also in a state of undress.

LOMBARDINO: Did your husband see Carl Andrade?

CRIMMINS: Yes, he did.

LOMBARDINO: What did he do when he saw Carl Andrade.

CRIMMINS: They had a scuffle and Eddie chased him.

LOMBARDINO: Was Andrade in a state of undress when Eddie chased him?

CRIMMINS: Yes, he was.

LOMBARDINO: How did he get his clothing, Mrs. Crimmins?

CRIMMINS: I got dressed and brought them out to him.

LOMBARDINO: Where was he when you brought him his clothes?

CRIMMINS: In his car.

In another particularly damaging exchange, Lombardino was able to juxtapose the pitiful deaths of her children with the apparently callous hijinks of their promiscuous mother.

LOMBARDINO: Does Joe Rorech have a swimming pool?

CRIMMINS: He does.

LOMBARDINO: Did you swim in it?

CRIMMINS: Yes, I did.

LOMBARDINO: What were you wearing when you swam in Joe Rorech's pool?

CRIMMINS: One time, a bathing suit; one time, no bathing suit.

LOMBARDINO: And where were your children while you were swimming in Joe Rorech's pool without a bathing suit?

CRIMMINS: They were dead.

Alice Crimmins left the stand on shaky legs. She knew that she had damaged herself in the eyes of the conservative, old-fashioned men who made up the jury and indeed, one of the jurors, Sam Ehrlich, commented to another that, "A tramp like that is capable of anything."

## A Conviction, a Collapse, and a Fresh Start

In its summation to the jury, the prosecution hypothesized that Alice had killed her daughter in momentary anger. The jury came back with a verdict of guilty of first-degree manslaughter. The shock of the verdict caused Crimmins to lapse into a coma. She was in the jail hospital for two weeks after her conviction. Transferred to prison, she became briefly hysterical, then appeared to settle down into prison routine. She was assigned to secretarial chores and, as she had in the free world, performed them in an excellent manner.

Her attorneys were soon back in court asking for a mistrial. Three of the jurors, one of them the Sam Ehrlich quoted above, had made trips to the crime scene despite the judge's warning that they were not to visit it. The court denied the motion for a mistrial and sentenced Crimmins to a prison term of from five to 20 years.

Crimmins got a new lawyer, Herbert Lyon, an attorney well-known and well-respected in New York City. Many people were perplexed that he took the case, however, because he was an expensive lawyer and she was a pauper. Her family's savings had been spent paying for her first set of defense attorneys.

It turned out the Lyon and his partner, William M. Erlbaum had taken on the case for idealistic reasons: they were completely convinced of her innocence and were working for her free of charge. Lyon asked a Queens County Supreme Court judge for bail on the grounds that there was a good chance the conviction would not stand. It was granted and, after 24 days in prison, Alice Crimmins was free. The appellate court did not get around to considering the appeal until a year and four months later. They threw the conviction out.

The second trial began in March 1971, six years after the deaths of the Crimmins children. This time, the stakes were even higher than they had been in the first trial for Alice had been indicted in both deaths. She was charged with the first-degree murder of her son Eddie and first-degree manslaughter in the death of Missy (the earlier verdict in Missy's case had in effect acquitted her of the girl's murder).

Public sentiment had shifted somewhat. Female promiscuity was no longer as shocking as it had been only three years previously. The women's liberation movement was a hot item in 1971, and some early feminists as well as other observers believed that Crimmins was being tried for her sex life and not for homicide. Not surprisingly, Alice Crimmins, whose self-esteem was so intimately tied to her appearance and who was so very dependent on men, was far closer to Marabel Morgan than Gloria Steinem in her beliefs about sex roles. Asked what she thought of feminism, she replied, "Oh, I'm for equal pay for equal work but not for all the far-out stuff. I don't hate men. I believe that women are put on this earth to serve men. A man should be dominant. I believe in women's liberation, but not at the price of my femininity."

## An Out-of-Control Defendant and a "Snarl of Charge and Counter-charge"

This trial would become, as writer Ann Jones noted, a "snarl of charge and counter-charge." Moreover, the years of her ordeal had taken a toll on Alice Crimmins. She remained a shapely and attractive woman but she had a hunted, hounded look. She also lost control of herself even more often during her second trial than her first.

While prosecutor Thomas Demakos was questioning prospective jurors, he commented, "She is presumed to be innocent … but she is not innocent!"

Alice cried out, "I am too innocent! You know I'm innocent!"

The bespectacled and balding Judge George J. Balbach told the prosecutor to avoid making such assertions when he was interviewing potential jurors.

Later, the other prosecutor Vincent Nicolosi said in his

opening statement that, on the last evening of their lives, their mother "fed them manicotti." Alice said, "I did not!"

Edmund Crimmins, now divorced from Alice, testified in this trial as he had in the last. While he said nothing that implicated his ex-wife, he stated that he had "no feeling for her really."

Once again, Detective Piering testified, recalling the unrecorded dust on the bureau and the vanished manicotti box in the trash as clearly as before. This time, he added something previously unmentioned. He claimed that Alice had told him that during the trip to the gas station, "The children were acting up in the back of the car and she swung and hit the girl."

Lyon was instantly on his feet, asking for a mistrial. He pointed out correctly that it is not unusual for parents to use corporal punishment but said that bringing it out in the trial was prejudicial. His motion was denied.

Anthony Grace took the stand and the prosecutor often seemed to be placing Alice's beau on trial, repeatedly asking Grace if she had requested any "help" and if Grace had sent "anybody over to that apartment that particular night." Grace denied firmly that he had anything to do with the children's deaths.

Detective John Kelly testified that he had a conversation with Alice Crimmins about possible immunity in her son's death and a good "deal" on the charges relating to her daughter if she would "tell the whole truth." He said that she had told him she would "have to talk it over" with her lawyer. He also testified that she had complained about many of the prosecution's witnesses lying in her first trial. He recalled retorting, "If all those people lied, why didn't I lie?" She supposedly had told him, "Well maybe the DA couldn't make you lie."

This provoked another Alice outburst: "But he did now!"

Once again, Sophie Earomirski gave dramatic testimony about the group that she had supposedly seen from her window. Again she was asked to identify the woman. "Alice Crimmins," she replied.

Alice Crimmins stood and shouted, "It is not! You liar! In

God's name, tell the truth!"

The judge gaveled for order and Crimmins continued screaming, "You liar! You swore to tell the truth up there! Do you know what the truth is? You're so sick you don't know how to tell the truth!"

Again the judge called for Crimmins to get a grip on herself.

DA Demakos asked Earomirski, "Was it Mrs. Crimmins you saw out there that night?"

"I swear to God," Earomirski replied.

"You swear!" Crimmins cried. "It wasn't me! I didn't do it! You don't know what God is!"

The judge declared a recess.

## Comedy in the Courtroom

Lyon attempted to cast doubt on the witness' veracity by raising doubts about her mental health. He questioned her about the accident at the World's Fair, something which had occurred only nine months prior to her fateful night at the window.

"There's nothing to it," Earomirski said. "I reached down to take my pocketbook from the little bin and a mouse ran up my arm and I fainted."

"A mouse?" Lyon asked.

"Yes, a mouse," Earomirski replied nonplussed. "You know, a little itty–bitty thing with a tail on it: a mouse."

Both spectators and jurors rocked with laughter while the judge brusquely called for order.

Asked if she had reported the mouse was yellow, Earomirski replied, "Because upstairs in the gourmet shop they had a giant cheese which all the mice used to eat and the cheese was yellow and the mouse was yellow. Yes, sir." Earomirski smiled in delight at the titters her story elicited.

She denied that the time she had overdosed on tranquilizers was a suicide attempt.

Lyon pointed out that her stomach had been pumped.

"That's right," a smiling Earomirski readily agreed. "And

then I went with my husband across the street to a diner and had a hamburger."

Lyon questioned Earomirski about the extensive and dramatic dialogue she testified that she had heard. He asked her to point to where those people were and she indicated a spot 150 feet from her window. Lyon then showed a diagram from the first trial in which Earomirski had placed the people some 60 feet farther from her vantage point at her window.

"Were they speaking loud, were they yelling," Lyon rather understandably wondered.

"No, in normal tones," Earomirski replied.

"And from 200 feet away you heard them talking in normal tones?" Lyon asked in amazement.

"That's not unusual," Earomirski informed him. "My girlfriend, I hear from the window when she asks me what I want from the store."

Lyon asked where the girlfriend lived and Earomirski went to the diagram and pointed to an apartment some 200 feet away from hers.

"The acoustics carry differently in that area because we are downhill," Earomirski told him.

"And if your girlfriend calls you in a normal tone from her window and you are in your kitchen, you can hear her?"

"Of course," the unflappable Earomirski replied, as if it were the most obvious thing in the world. After testifying, she again strutted in the courtroom hallway with her hands clenched in a boxer's salute.

### The Surprise Witness and Alice's Desperate Gambit

Once again Joe Rorech took the stand to claim that Alice "said, 'Forgive me, Joseph, I killed her.'"

A weeping Crimmins shouted, "You miserable, lying worm!"

Then Rorech said what he could not say at the first trial, when Crimmins was being tried for the death of the girl only. Rorech stated: "She then said, 'I didn't want him killed. I agreed to it.'"

A surprise witness soon appeared. As the courtroom listened in stunned silence, a short and skinny housewife named Tina DeVita testified that she had seen a group consisting of "a man carrying a bundle, a woman, a dog, and a boy" walking on 150th Street in the area of the Regal Gardens apartments. Alice Crimmins listened with widened eyes and gasped as she heard this testimony.

During a recess, Crimmins approached reporters to make an obviously desperate plea. "I've come here to make an appeal," she began in a shaky voice. Tears blurred her blue eyes. Alice Crimmins was clearly terrified. "I'd like anybody that lived in my neighborhood to come forward," she said. "Anybody that lived in my neighborhood who might know something about what happened on the night of July 13th or the morning of July 14th. I am asking for anyone that was out that morning between 1:30 and 2:30. Anybody that saw something—or didn't see something. It doesn't make a difference either way because it's just as important to me if they didn't see something or if they did see something. They are coming with people for six years. Now, I don't know where these people are coming from. But I'm asking for help from my side."

Crimmins voice cracked and it seemed like she might collapse into sobs but she managed to choke out, "I need that help because I did not kill my children. Anybody that just didn't see anything is just as important to me as someone who might have seen something … I didn't kill my children. I swear I didn't kill them."

## A Repercussion and a Startling Result

The prosecutors were furious. Crimmins had been ordered by the court to refrain from press interviews. The judge warned her lawyers that if she broke that order again, Crimmins bail would be revoked and she'd be slammed behind bars.

The next day another surprise witness appeared. This time, it was the prosecution side that was stunned by the testimony.

That witness was Marvin Weinstein, a travel agency manager who claimed that he had been walking on 153rd Street in the wee hours of July 14th of 1965. He had been visiting a friend named Anthony King.

"Who was with you?" Lyon inquired.

"My wife, my son, my daughter, and my dog," Weinstein answered. He went on to say that his son was three-and-a-half at the time and his daughter was two years-old. Weinstein had carried his little girl in his arms wrapped in a blanket.

Weinstein's wife appeared in the courtroom and she bore more than a passing resemblance to Alice Crimmins.

Had Alice Crimmins' desperate gambit paid off? Many observers believed so. After all, if the group seen by Earomirski and DeVita was not Alice Crimmins and a shadowy hit man with a doomed little Eddie and a dead Missy but the Weinstein family, the primary basis upon which the prosecutors first drew up their indictment so many years ago would collapse.

Did it?

## Who was Lying?

Anthony King came into the court and said that the Weinsteins had not visited him that night. Lyon cast doubt upon King's testimony by bringing out that he and Weinstein had once been friends and business partners, but were now personal enemies. He then brought in a witness who told the court that King was a notorious liar.

Vincent Collabella, the gangster said to have been the hit man, was brought into court by the Crimmins attorneys. Tall, handsome, and swarthy, Collabella had a lengthy and serious criminal record. The arrogant career criminal denied knowing Alice Crimmins, Anthony Grace, or even having ever been to Queens. The prosecutors tore into him but were unable to get any sort of admission out of him.

The trial was winding down and the Crimmins attorneys were in a quandary. Should Alice take the stand in her own defense? They knew that, although they are admonished not to, juries hold it against defendants when they remain silent. However, they also knew that the last time she had been on the stand, she had been hammered at because of her sex life and that had, and probably would again, prejudice a largely working class, middle-aged, and old-fashioned jury.

Herb Lyon asked for a meeting in the Judge's chambers. He requested that the justice rule that Alice could not be questioned about her sexual history during cross-examination. The judge refused to do so. Fearing that another rundown of her amorous dalliances would prejudice the jury, Alice didn't take the stand.

Lyon's summation was eloquent and impassioned. He decried the prosecution's case as "a bunch of garbage." He described Rorech as a man scorned. "[Anthony] Grace replaced Rorech in Mrs. Crimmins affections," Lyon told the jury. "He can't match Anthony Grace in business and now he has lost out to him with Mrs. Crimmins."

Earomirski "started this whole thing," Lyon said. "And I'm going to finish it. I don't care if Mrs. Earomirski's compensation case runs into a big award. But I do care when it runs into a murder case." He pointed out the way her recollections dramatically changed from the letter about "something that may not be connected at all," and noted that a doctor's report said that Earomirski had "neurotic tendencies to subconscious exaggeration." He asked the jury to ponder Earomirski's bizarre assertion that she could hear people talking in normal tones from 200 feet away. "I don't know if you need a doctor to explain that kind of hearing," he said. "This is worse than the yellow mouse."

Finally, Herb Lyon wound up with a moving plea on behalf of a client he strongly believed had been grievously wronged. "Mrs. Earomirski said she heard the children crying from their grave. If they are crying from their grave, they are saying, 'Let our mother go! You have had her long enough. Six years of torture. In addition to loving us, she is accused of killing us. Six years based on a letter that comes anonymously, based on a snake who stings like a viper, and based on a misconception of the analysis of the food."

Thomas Demakos was no less passionate in his People's summation. He told the jury, "She doesn't have the courage to stand up here and tell the world she killed her daughter – "

"Because I didn't kill my daughter!" Crimmins wailed.

"And the shame and the pity of it is that this little boy had to die too," Demakos said. He ridiculed the idea that she was being persecuted. "If the people think that all the district attorney's office has to do is go out and frame a woman for publicity, then God help this country of ours!"

## Shock and Aftermath

The jury came back with the harshest possible verdict: guilty of first degree murder in Eddie, Jr.'s death and first degree manslaughter in that of Missy. Many in the courtroom burst into tears. Alice sobbed, "Dear God, no! Please, dear God!"

Her mother, Alice Burke, wailed, "Sweet Jesus, no! Not again!"

John Burke, her brother, said, "She didn't kill her children. She didn't kill them."

Her ex-husband Edmund Crimmins cried, "This isn't justice," as tears streamed down his cheeks.

A male spectator, who had sent Alice a greeting card with the message, "We're with you, Alice" only the day before, shouted, "They ought to kill the jury!" as he fell into tears.

Herb Lyon appeared stunned in defeat, saying, "I guess I convinced everyone but the jury."

The second trial of Alice Crimmins ended and Crimmins went to prison for what was assumed would be the rest of her life.

She had served more than two years behind bars when she was released in 1973. The Appellate Division of the Supreme Court in Brooklyn reversed her conviction in Eddie Jr.'s case, ruling that there was no evidence of murder. It also reversed the manslaughter conviction in Missy's case because Demakos' assertion that "she doesn't have the courage to stand up here and tell the world she killed her daughter" suggested that a defendant who exercised the right to refrain from testifying was admitting guilt.

The DA appealed both rulings; in the meantime, Alice was free on $25,000 bail. Then in February 1975, the Court of Appeals upheld the reversal of the murder conviction but reinstated the manslaughter conviction and sent her back to prison.

Even that was not the end of the Crimmins saga. In 1977, a New York tabloid broke the story that she was participating in a work-release program and, like other inmates in the program, she was allowed every other weekend free. She had also been permitted to marry Anthony Grace.

The newspaper showed Mrs. Alice Grace with her husband on board a yacht. The next day its cover featured another picture of the furloughed Mrs. Grace about to step into her husband's white Cadillac. New York politicians cried out that she should not be paroled but in Nov. 1977, after more than three years of imprisonment, she was released. Although free, she still wanted vindication, but her appeal for a new trial was denied and the courts ruled that she could appeal no further.

## Mystery Most Frustrating

A close, objective look at the matter shows that, despite two convictions, the "guilt" of Alice Crimmins remains problematic. For one thing, the case was "solved" with major loose ends dangling. According to the prosecution's own theory of the crime, the mother could only have murdered with the help of at least two accomplices, yet no one else was ever even charged, much less tried, in connection with the deaths.

At a time when the issue of memory and its reliability is so prominent, when "False Memory Syndrome" v. "Recovered Memory" is debated by psychologists and the courts, the Crimmins case takes on a special relevancy because the trustworthiness of the human memory played an extraordinary role in it.

First, there was the strange certainty of Alice Crimmins' own memory. She said that she had fed her kids veal at 7:30

p.m. on the evening of July 13, 1965. Then she had taken them for a ride, gassed up her car at nine o'clock, returned home, and put them to bed. She looked in on them at midnight and took little Eddie to the bathroom. Missy had stayed in bed because she didn't have to go.

After returning the boy to bed, she attached the hook-and-eye latch that she had put on the door. (This lock, Crimmins said, was to stop the chubby boy from raiding the refrigerator at night. The cops thought it was to prevent either child from walking in on their mother when she was with a boyfriend.) Then she fell asleep in her clothes, awakened, walked her dog, took a bath, and finally retired for the night—at four o'clock AM.

Questioned repeatedly about these mundane events, Crimmins remained stubbornly positive. No, she could not possibly be off by, say, an hour as to the time they ate. She checked on them at midnight, no earlier, no later. When two gas station attendants said that she had come to the station at 5:30 p.m., she called them "liars," refusing to acknowledge that she might be in error about a matter that was, in and of itself, irrelevant.

The veal or macaroni question is one of the most troubling aspects of the case. Many observers, including, most importantly, two juries, have found Crimmins' insistence that she fed her children veal and the Medical Examiner's failure to find meat in Missy's stomach utterly damning. However, one must ask why Crimmins would make up such a story. As writer Albert Borowitz has noted, it is highly unlikely that Crimmins knew enough about forensics to deliberately create such an enigma. Furthermore, she specified buying it that very day at a deli at which she was well known and where her story could be checked out. As it happened, the deli owner couldn't remember what she had bought but there was no way she could bank on that. Nor could she know that Piering would not better preserve or record the crime scene.

Detective Gerard Piering was so confident of his memory that he "forgot" more substantial methods of evidence gathering like taking photographs, making notes, or just preserving it.

Joe Rorech and Sophie Earomirski also had fascinating memories.

In the first trial, Rorech testified that his ex-girlfriend had confessed, "I killed her." Since Crimmins was accused of killing her daughter only, tying her to the death of her son would have been grounds for a mistrial. Thus, if she had told him that "I killed my kids," it would have been inadmissible.

If she had confessed to the killing of Missy only, Rorech would have been of no extra value in the second trial. But he testified at that event that Alice Crimmins had told him, "Forgive me, Joe, I killed her," and, "I didn't want him killed. I agreed [to it]." This precise wording that Crimmins used, at least as he remembered the conversation, gave Rorech's testimony maximum prosecutorial impact at both events.

The memory of Sophie Earomirski seemed to grow with time. In her initial epistle, she said she had seen something "which may be connected or then again it may not." By the time she testified before a grand jury, Sophie Earomirski not only knew with certainty that the woman was Alice Crimmins but recalled dramatic dialogue—even though she had heard it from some 200 feet away.

Moreover, there is something inherently fishy about that family grouping. Albert Borowitz asks if, having just witnessed his sister's death, little Eddie would so very passively have gone to his own. Perhaps it is even more unbelievable that he would not have shown more concern for the "bundle" that his mother carried. At five years old, he would not have developed the defense mechanism against emotional displays that most adult males—and some females like Alice Crimmins herself—acquire. Wouldn't he have been crying in his grief? Wouldn't he have been demanding to hold the little sister he loved so dearly and so protectively?

Was Alice Crimmins "railroaded?" Not quite. As Ann Jones wrote: "She was granted no presumption of innocence." The common prejudice against sexually adventurous women tipped the scales of justice toward conviction and blackened her name. While she lives out the rest of her life in freedom and anonymity as well as -- perhaps -- the material comfort and security of her second husband's affluence, in the annals of murder cases, she remains "Alice Crimmins, Child-killer."

There is a crying need for closure and solution when an outrage has been committed and that is especially true when the victims are children. However, to those who take the time and trouble to familiarize themselves with the details of the Crimmins case, the deaths of little Eddie and Missy remain that most frustrating of puzzles, an intractable mystery.

## Bibliography

Carpozi, George. *Ordeal by Trial: The Alice Crimmins Case.* Walker & Co. April 1972.

Gross, Ken. *The Alice Crimmins Case.*

Jones, Ann. *Women Who Kill.*

# CHAPTER SEVEN

## Jean Harris: The Case for her Innocence

On March 10, 1980, the bestselling Complete Scarsdale Medical Diet by Dr. Herman Tarnower received a publicity boost. Tarnower could not enjoy the fruits of it since it was his killing. Called "The Headmistress and the Diet Doc," the case grabbed international headlines because of the social prominence of Tarnower's slayer, Jean Harris, the 56-year-old headmistress of the exclusive Madeira School, as well as that of the victim.

In addition, as Diana Trilling observes in Mrs. Harris, "To many women ... it had only to be known that Tarnower had replaced his mistress of 14 years with a woman 20 years her junior and more than 30 years younger than himself for Jean Harris to be regarded as embattled female spirit."

Trilling continues, "Whoever had known sexual jealousy, that most destructive of emotions—and this would be so for men no less than for women—had known madness" and could sympathize with Jean Harris. Prominent feminist Betty Friedan saw no feminist implications in the case and derided Harris as a "pathetic masochist" for sticking with Dr. Tarnower after their relationship soured.

As more facts emerged about the case, it was learned that Jean Harris had for years suffered a gnawing sense of being "inadequate" and that she believed she could no longer be "useful" as a human being. Long divorced and with her sons grown, she was terrified of a jobless old age. Her romance with

Tarnower had led to her suffering for years under a campaign of extraordinary harassment. By the night of March 10, 1980, she felt that there was nothing solid in her life as both personally and professionally she was being shoved aside. There was overwhelming evidence that she wanted to end her own life.

### The Boy from Brooklyn and the Lady from Cleveland

The man who would author a best-selling diet book but become even more famous in death was born Herman Tarnower in Brooklyn in 1910, into a Jewish immigrant family. He finished his premedical training in two years instead of the usual four. In 1936, he opened a Scarsdale, New York office.

A lifelong bachelor, he hired husband and wife Henri and Suzanne Van der Vreken in 1964 to run his house. In the spring of 1966, Tarnower was at a dinner party when he found himself smitten with divorcée Jean Harris, mother of two teenagers. Days later, Harris was bedridden because back trouble flared. Tarnower surprised her with a get-well present, the book *Masada*, about finds at the ancient Israelite fortress where, in A.D. 73, Jewish men, women, and children committed suicide rather than accept defeat by Rome. "It's time you knew more about the Jews," the card said. Tarnower showered Harris with cards, presents, and calls.

The woman who inspired his attention was born Jean Struven in Cleveland, Ohio in 1923, the second of the three daughters of Albert and Mildred Struven. Albert Struven was a civil engineer and vice-president of the Arthur G. McKee, Inc., construction firm. He had a terrible temper, exploding into rage over such problems as a broken light bulb or stalled car.

Jean admired her father for his brilliance but feared his tirades. Mildred sometimes called Jean "Miss Infallible" for her self-righteousness. In high school, Jean won a prize for her essay, "The Man I Took For Granted." It refers to *Life With Father* by Clarence Day when she writes, "Oh, Mr. Day, had I your talent with which to tell the story of an equally deserving father! I have not the eloquence to bring it forth. Or perhaps this realization is not entirely an appreciation of father, but a step toward appreciating men in general. It is possible that some-day my subject will be, not 'The Man I Took For Granted,' but 'The Man Who Took Me For Granted.'" When they married, Jean was 23 and Jim Harris, 27. Jean later recalled thinking quiet Jim a nice contrast to blustering Dad.

David Harris was born in 1950, and Jimmie in 1952. In 1964, Jean, feeling stifled in her passionless marriage, divorced Jim. Jean moved from school teaching to school administration, getting a job as director of the Middle School at Springside, a private school in a Philadelphia suburb. She was working at Springside when she met Tarnower at a dinner party given by Jean's close friend Marge Jacobson. Jackson described the at-traction of Harris and Tarnower as "Instant take!"

Within months of meeting Harris, Tarnower gave her a diamond ring and proposed marriage. She enthusiastically ac-cepted. However, the wedding was delayed – by Harris. She explained to a friend, "I cannot marry Hy for a year. I cannot take those children out of school again."

As that year passed so did Tarnower's interest in mar-riage, something Harris would discover when she pressed him for a new wedding date. In a phone call Harris told Tarnower, "School is going to start, and I have to know where I am to start, and I have to know where I am going to be living, and where the children are going to be in school." Tarnower re-plied, "Jean, I can't go through with it. I'm afraid of it. I can't go through with it and I'm sorry." She mailed the ring back.

Harris and Tarnower continued dating despite Harris's feeling of discomfort in a relationship that could not lead to marriage. Her strongly held old-fashioned morality inevita-bly gnawed at her even as she gave in to her passion for Tar-nower. Springside's headmistress retired in 1970 and Harris hoped she would be the replacement. She was not. Harris then learned the Thomas School in Rowayton, Connecticut was searching for a headmistress. She applied and was hired. Ro-wayton is about a half hour's drive from Tarnower's Purchase, New York home.

On April 26, 1973, Harris celebrated her 50th birthday with sons David and Jimmie. Tarnower was not there. He had long ceased telling Harris he loved her. Instead, as Shana Alexander writes in her book, *Very Much A Lady*, he repeatedly told Harris, "I don't love anyone and I don't need anyone."

He seemed oddly oblivious to the pain this caused her since she was adamant in acknowledging that she loved him deeply. Then again, perhaps he was aware of it and just did not care.

Or perhaps it gave him a certain sadistic pleasure.

### Nasty Phone Calls

At about this time, Lynne Tryforos, a separated mother of two small daughters, became Tarnower's secretary/receptionist. Although he was 30 years older than Tryforos, Tarnower soon began an affair with her.

In 1974, Harris and others worked out a plan in which the Thomas School merged with another school, a move Harris believed necessary to solve Thomas's financial troubles. In 1975, Harris began receiving anonymous phone calls at her home. The caller would graphically describe Tarnower having sex with another woman, jeer at Harris that she should take sex lessons, called her "old and pathetic" and suggested she "roll over and die."

During this same time period, Harris often received a message at work that she should call a number. She called the number and found she had called Tryforos. Tryforos would demand Harris quit harassing her, changing her unlisted phone number several times. Each time it changed, it was sent to Harris.

Harris consulted with a private detective and with two phone company employees in an unsuccessful effort to stop both the anonymous calls to her house and the calls to her work leaving messages to call a certain number that was inevitably the unlisted phone number of Lynne Tryforos. Unable to track down the source of these calls, Harris felt besieged by them. Her sleep was frequently disturbed, leaving her fatigued the next day, and she was made terribly anxious and self-conscious.

Shortly after making the deal that merged Thomas with another school, Harris was hired by the Allied Maintenance Corporation in New York City to write bids for industrial cleaning contracts. Although she now lived over an hour's drive away from Tarnower, she continued to visit him on some weekends. She was at his home sunbathing in July 1976 when Tryforos and daughters, Electra and Laura, showed up. The children jumped into the pool while their mother started painting garden furniture.

"Does it not seem bizarre to you, Lynne, that you are here painting his furniture while I am here?" Harris asked.    Tryforos stared and said nothing.

Harris said, "Lynne, why in hell are you here?"

"I'm here because I'm allowed to be," she answered.

"Not while I'm here, Lynne," Harris said.

Tryforos and daughters left.

Tarnower was negligent in keeping evidence of a visit from one woman away from the other. When Harris visited Tarnower, items belonging to Tryforos often confronted Harris. Despite Tarnower's indifference to her pain, as well as his repeated insistence that he loved no one, Harris could not bring herself to end the relationship.

That same July, Harris learned that the Madeira School in McLean, Virginia sought a headmistress. On December 15, 1976, Harris, then 53, was appointed Madeira School headmistress. She moved into an on-campus house in Virginia in 1977. She continued to see Tarnower even though it meant a drive of about six hours.

At Madeira, the new headmistress quickly became known as "Integrity Jean" because in her lectures on morals and ethics she often mentioned the word "integrity."

### The Making of a Best-Seller

Since overweight can cause heart problems, Tarnower had

for years been giving patients diet advice mimeographed on a single page. That page advised eating a high-protein, low-carbohydrate, low-fat, low-sugar diet, and teetotalling.

In the late 1970s, Bantam Books President Oscar Dystel suggested Tarnower write a book based on his sheet. He suggested Samm Sinclair Baker, a practiced self-help book writer, as co-author.

Tarnower and Baker, together with the Van der Vrekens, Harris, and Tryforos, expanded the one page into a book. Alexander writes, "Tarnower talked, Samm took notes, wrote them up, and returned them to the doctor for revisions. Suzanne Van der Vreken created and tested new recipes.

Jean Harris read sections of the manuscript, often re-writing parts in her own hand. Lynne Tryforos sometimes took manuscripts in Jean's handwriting and corrected and clarified portions for the typist. Recipes appeared with names like Mustard Sauce Henri, Borscht Suzanne, and Spinach Delight à la Lynne.

When published in 1978, *The Complete Scarsdale Medical Diet* by Dr. Herman Tarnower and Samm Sinclair Baker shot to the top of the bestseller lists. At the beginning of the book, Dr. Tarnower explains what he sees as the reason for the popularity of his diet in two words that he italicizes: "It works."

Dieters were advised to go on the Scarsdale Medical Diet (SMD) for a period of 14 days. They should be on it no less than that for best weight-loss results and no more than that to maintain maximum health. After the two weeks of SMD, they were advised to switch to the less restrictive Keep-Trim Diet (KTD).

The book states, "The average person's food intake contains approximately 10-15 percent protein, variations of between 40-45 percent fat and 40-50 percent carbohydrates." By contrast, the SMD "averages 1,000 calories or less per day and averages 43 percent protein, 22.5 percent fat, and 34.5 percent carbohydrates."

When the book appeared, Baker was upset over the first sentence on the acknowledgments page: "We are grateful to Jean Harris for her splendid assistance in the research and writing of this book." Baker thought her contributions did not merit such prominence and called Tarnower to object. Tarnower stood firm, "Samm, please leave it just as it is," he said. Then he gently added, "I like to make people feel good and I want to make her feel good."

In October 1978, Harris bought a handgun, telling the store clerk it was for "self-protection." Later, she explained, "I felt if I couldn't function anymore, I could handle it." Alexander reports that Harris believed she had picked the one weapon likely to end in her suicide rather than rendering her disabled as she also said, "A gun was the one way I knew I wouldn't mess it up."

## Destroyed Dresses

Harris suffered a major trauma in March 1979. Returning from a trip with Tarnower, Harris found the clothes that she had left in a closet in his home destroyed.

Duncan Spencer writes in Love Gone Wrong: The Jean Harris Scarsdale Murder Case, "Suzanne [Van der Vreken] said, '[Harris] found her clothes ripped and slashed ... One sleeve was ripped from the body of a dress, there was a slash in every dress and all of the dresses there were slashed and ripped.' Suzanne went on to say that Mrs. Tryforos had visited the Tarnower house before the doctor and the headmistress returned from Jamaica."

Reluctant to complain right after their vacation, Harris said nothing to Tarnower – even though one-third of her wardrobe had been viciously destroyed.

This was not the only time Harris found her property destroyed. On one occasion, she found a nightgown covered with orange stains. Even more upsettingly, she found a new dress still in its box, no longer folded, but rolled up and smeared with human feces.

Harris believed Tarnower was responsible for the cost of these two damaged items of apparel. She also knew he kept two wallets filled with cash. She took money that would cover the cost of the two destroyed items from one of those wallets.

In Christmas 1979, Harris and Tarnower vacationed in Palm Beach, Florida. Harris writes in *Stranger in Two Worlds,* "We were there for two very happy weeks. Mrs. Tryforos outdid herself this time. In addition to phone calls and telegrams, she placed an ad on the front page of *The New York Times* to tell the doctor, long distance, that she loved him forever. It was something that might be considered 'cute' if you could spare the $250 that it cost, if you were in your teens, and if the person you addressed it to wasn't a 69-year-old man spending a two week vacation with another woman.

Under the circumstances it would be hard to imagine anything more tasteless and deliberately mean." Harris continues that Tarnower reacted with "horror" and exclaimed, "Jesus! I hope none of my friends see it."

Harris writes that she thought, "I'm your friend, Hy, and I see it." However, she tried to make light of her pain by saying, "Why don't you have her try the Goodyear blimp next time, Herm?"

## Troubling Times at Madeira

In 1979, just over two years into Harris's tenure as headmistress, the Madeira Board hired professional school consultants Russell R. Browning Associates to examine how the school rated with potential donors. In May 1979, the Browning Report was complete. Shana Alexander reports, "One director said Jean Harris was the most controversial head of school in the nation."

The report quoted one parent saying, "Mrs. Harris doesn't care what she says, and isn't careful to whom she says it." It also criticized her lack of ability to handle disciplinary situations effectively, a shortcoming that one "friend" of the school said caused several sets of Madeira parents to try to dissuade prospective new families from applying.

While the report quoted people who made positive comments about Harris, its recommendation was to "get rid of Jean Harris immediately" and install an interim headmistress while searching for her replacement.

The board voted to ignore the Browning suggestion.

Nonetheless, the report devastated the emotionally fragile Harris. She now believed it was likely only a matter of time before she lost her job. It seemed like everything in her life was slipping away from her. Her boys were grown and out of the house. The man she deeply and desperately loved only tolerated her. She was being repeatedly and cruelly harassed. Now she feared losing her job. There seemed to be nothing solid in her life, nothing on which she could depend.

On September 18, 1979, a Madeira clique that called itself the "Brazen Hussies" played a prank that misfired. A member accidentally poured caustic toilet bowl cleaner instead of shampoo over the heads of new members. One girl's face was badly burned. Harris drove the girl to the hospital. When the injured girl returned to Madeira, she became Harris's special protégée and friend.

In March 1980, a Madeira official informed Harris about marijuana use in a dorm. "I'll have a talk with the house mother," Harris said. The official stated that the house mother was said to be involved. Room searches were made. Marijuana seeds and stems were found along with paraphernalia.

The girls in those rooms were taken to a meeting of both adult officials and Student Council members. Some students said, "If you're not expelled for this, what do you have to do to get thrown out of this place?" Others said this activity was so common it made no sense to make a big deal out of it.

Harris sided with kids who believed the malefactors should be expelled. A vote was taken and four seniors were expelled only two months before graduation. A student protest developed, leading to a rally in support of them.

In the immediate wake of this blow-up, Harris wrote Tarnower a long, rambling letter in which she pled for his affection and complained about the wrongs she claimed Tryforos had perpetrated. She told him about having one-third of her wardrobe slashed and ripped, about finding a nightgown covered with orange stains, and a dress smeared with excrement. She told him about years of being repeatedly awakened in the middle of the night by a jeering caller.

## The Fateful Day

On the morning of March 10, 1980, Harris read a letter from the girl who was injured in the Brazen Hussies incident. The teenager wrote, "This isn't a 'hate' letter at all. I just feel that you are not handling the situation correctly." The girl said people knew pot smoking was common so punishing four with expulsion was "hypocritical."

This gentle criticism from a girl Harris had singled out for protection and special friendship devastated the headmistress. Spencer reports that Harris showed the letter to Madeira's second-in-command, Kathleen Johnson, and to English teacher Ruth Katz. Johnson, who later took over as Madeira's acting headmistress, recalled, "It's too bad that letter upset her." Johnson said the letter appeared to have an extraordinarily traumatic effect on Harris. "It was as though she had something pulled down in front of her eyes," Johnson commented. "She hadn't understood what we had said to her."

According to Spencer, Katz recalled, "I simply came down the hall to wish her a pleasant holiday, and I observed her over the letter. It was clear to me that Mrs. Harris was weary and discouraged; numb and very quiet—maybe glazed." Sympathetic to the "drain" Katz saw in Harris, she gathered a bunch of daisies and placed them on the seat of Harris's car.

The critical letter from a girl Harris had aided and taken under her wing led Harris to a terrible decision. Later, she said in a courtroom, "It sort of put a box on my life." Spencer reports Harris recalling, "If she thinks I've failed her, too [like the board, like Tarnower, like the students], I've really blown the whole thing. I've failed everyone. I was doing the best I could do; it just wasn't enough. I didn't have the strength to do more."

She decided that she had failed completely and had no reason to live.

## Shots in the Night

At 5:16 p.m., she called Tarnower. "Hy, it's been a bad few

weeks," she said. "I'd like to come and talk to you for a few minutes." He replied that a niece was coming for dinner.

"That's all right," Harris said. "She always leaves early. I couldn't get there before 10:30."

"It would be more convenient if you came tomorrow," Hy said.

"I won't be able to see you tomorrow," she said. "Please, just this once, let me say when."

"Suit yourself," he replied.

After that phone call, Harris picked up the gun. She loaded it, trying to ensure all chambers were filled. Harris felt she no longer had anything to offer and could no longer function. Thus, she would die. Her death would be peaceful. She would enjoy a last few minutes with Tarnower, talking with him and feeling "safe" one last time. Then should would go to the pond on his property, the one around which the lovely daffodils grew, and shoot herself. Her drive was oddly peaceful for she knew what she would do and how her life would end.

At one point she thought, "What if Hy says something to spoil my resolve to die?" Then she thought, "I won't let him know what I'm going to do, I won't stay too long, and I won't let him spoil my resolve."

She knew the dedicated doctor was used to getting up in the middle of the night to help people. She arrived at 10:45 p.m. She expected the front door would be unlocked but it was not. Holding her pocketbook and the daisies she had found in her car, she went through the garage as she often had before and up the circular stairway.

"Hy," she called. "Hy, Hy." Harris heard him stirring. She sat on the bed that was "hers" when she stayed at his house. She turned on the light and saw Tarnower in his blue pajamas. "I thought you'd put a lamp in the window," she said since she had called to let him know she would be coming over. "It's black as pitch out there."

Tarnower angrily barked, "Jesus, it's the middle of the night and you wake me up!"

"I only want to talk, Hy, and I won't be long."

"I don't feel like talking in the middle of the night," he

answered.

"I brought you some flowers," she said. "Have you written any more on the book?" Tarnower had decided to write another book, this one on the subject of longevity.

"Shut up and go to bed," he said. "I don't want to talk."

"Won't you really talk to me for a little while?" she begged. Silence. Then Harris broke that silence by saying, "There's a shawl here. I want to be sure Kathleen [a daughter-in-law] has it. I'll just get it."

Harris headed for the nearest bathroom. She turned on the light and saw a greenish blue satin negligee. Believing the owner of that item had destroyed Harris's clothes, she picked up the negligee and took it to Hy's bedroom where Harris tossed it on the floor. Denied the final "safe" feeling she craved, Harris returned to the bathroom where she was confronted by a box of hair curlers she knew to be those of Tryforos. Harris threw the box and it crashed into a side window.

Tarnower jumped up from bed. When Harris walked back into the bedroom, he struck her across the mouth. She ran back to the bathroom, picked up another box, and tossed it so it smashed a mirror. She went back to the bedroom and he struck her again on the mouth.

After the second blow, Harris felt all agitation drain out. The last few minutes of pleasant talk with the man she loved were not to be. Why bother even going to the pond? She sat on "her" bed and pulled her hair behind her ears. Calmly, she raised her face to Tarnower, shut her eyes, and urged, "Hit me again, Hy. Make it hard enough to kill me."

"Get out of here," he growled. "You're crazy!"

"Never mind," she said. "I'll do it myself." She zipped open her pocketbook and took out the gun. She raised it to her head. Tarnower lunged at her, knocking the gun down, and making it go off in the process. The bullet went through the palm of a Tarnower hand. Harris dropped the gun.

Tarnower shouted, "Jesus Christ! Look what you did!" Then he went to the bathroom to treat the (relatively minor) wound.

Spencer notes, "There is one lapse in Tarnower's reaction that merits examination. He knocked the gun out of Harris's hand even at the expense of the shot to his own hand. But then, having painfully gotten control of the situation, he didn't take advantage of it by getting the gun and throwing it out the window, unloading it, tossing it down the spiral staircase, or merely hanging onto it with his good hand while he took a close look at the wounds in the bathroom. The logical, consistent explanation is that he knew the first shot had been fired by mistake."

While Tarnower was in the bathroom, Harris was on her knees looking for the gun under "her" bed. She pulled it out and pointed it at her head. Tarnower was back. He grabbed her upper arm tightly, causing her to drop it. With the gun in Tarnower's wounded right hand, he moved to the head of "his" bed and buzzed for his servants. That he buzzed with his left hand and held the gun in his right is provable, as Spencer observes, "by the fact that blood was found on the gun and the bed and none on the buzzer." A desperate Harris begged, "Hy, please give me the gun, or shoot me yourself, but for Christ's sake let me die."

"Jesus, Jean, you're crazy, get out of here!" Tarnower shouted.

She pulled herself up and grabbed for the gun. Tarnower left the buzzer to grab her wrist. He lunged forward. She believed she had the gun in her control. She felt what she believed was the muzzle in her belly and pulled the trigger. Despite the loud noise, Harris thought, "My God! That didn't hurt at all! I should have done it long ago."

Tarnower fell back. Harris jumped up. She ran out of his reach. She put the gun to her head. She took a very deep breath, a breath she expected to be her last breath, and pulled the trigger.

The gun clicked.

Astounded, believing she had filled all chambers, she lowered the gun and gazed at it. She pulled the trigger. Boom! A shot rang out. She raised the gun to her head again. She repeatedly pulled the trigger and empty chambers repeatedly clicked.

One thing that must be noted is that Harris could only recall pulling the trigger twice at times when Tarnower was shot. She remembered the time when he brought her hand down from her head, making it go off and into his hand. She remembered consciously firing at herself when she believed the muzzle was poking in her belly, a shot that probably went through Tarnower's arm.

However, all doctors who examined his corpse believed he was shot at least three times. Most believe he was shot four times. Harris simply could not recall or account for those shots. She may have had a temporary blackout when they were struggling.

She ran to her coat. She knew there were bullets in a pocket. The coat was beside the bedroom TV. She retrieved the coat but realized the gun was full of spent cartridges. She could not put fresh bullets in until the cartridges were out. Harris went to the bathroom to try unloading the cartridges by banging the gun against the bathtub. The bathtub was chipped by her efforts but no cartridges dislodged and the gun flew out of her hand and into the tub.

Harris went back to the bedroom where she saw Tarnower. Harris shouted, "Somebody turn on the goddamn lights! I'm going for help!"

She ran into the rain, got in her car, and raced out of Dr. Tarnower's driveway. As she began to turn into a parking lot with a phone booth, a police car flashing its lights bore down on her. Making a U-turn, she headed back toward the Tarnower residence. The police car followed. Both cars pulled up in front of that house. Harris jumped out and ran over to the police officer. She shouted, "Hurry up! He's been shot!" As they ran up steps, Henri Van der Vrekan shouted, "She's the one! She did it!"

Suzanne Van der Vrekan joined Harris and the police officer in the doctor's bedroom. Shana Alexander writes in *Very Much A Lady,* "Herman Tarnower was now on his knees between the two beds, slumped against the white telephone, its bloody receiver dangling down. With Suzanne's help, the police officer gently laid the wounded man down on his back between the beds." The cop ran downstairs for emergency oxygen as Suzanne took the doctor's hand and softly spoke to him. Harris caressed his face and wailed, "Oh, Hi, why didn't you kill me?"

Additional police officers rushed to the scene. Harris admitted she shot Tarnower but said she meant to kill herself. Harris refused medical attention for the bruise near her eye and for the swelling on her upper lip.

Detective Arthur Siciliano asked, "Who had control of the gun?"

"I don't know," Harris replied.

"Who owned the gun?" he asked.

"It's mine," she said.

"Who did the shooting? Do you recall holding the gun?"

"I recall holding the gun and shooting him in the hand," she answered.

A stretcher with an unconscious and bloodied Herman Tarnower on it was carried past.

Long-time Harris friends Leslie and Marge Jacobson were asleep in their Manhattan home when awakened by Harris's call. "Leslie, I think I've killed Hi," Harris said.

### Charged with Murder

"Do not utter another word!" he ordered. Leslie dressed to meet Harris and told Marge to phone an attorney who worked with Leslie, William Riegelman, and tell him to rush to the police station to see Harris. Riegelman did and found Harris being booked for aggravated assault. Her white blouse was streaked with blood and she was badly bruised on her mouth and right eye. A call came in from St. Agnes Hospital. Tarnower had been pronounced dead and, at the police station, the charge against Harris increased to second-degree murder, the most serious possible in New York unless the victim is a police officer or prison officer on duty.

Friends recommended respected attorney Joel Aurnou.

Aurnou met her. A sobbing Harris said she did not care what happened to her, and wanted no defense. She said she had no reason to live.

Aurnou came up with a reason. He said if she did not defend herself, David and Jimmie would be known as a murderer's sons. Did she want her sons stigmatized? Love for her grown sons motivated her to want to prove her innocence. She told Aurnou all that she could remember of the bedroom struggle, admitting she could only account for two shots.

Prosecutor George Bolen ridiculed this scenario. He insisted Harris had murdered Tarnower. Before trial, he crowed, "All I need to prove intent is Herman Tarnower's body and four bullet holes!"

### A Defense Puzzle

One puzzling aspect of the trial of Jean Harris is that her plea was simply "not guilty." Many observers believed she should have pled guilty to first-degree manslaughter, offering the legal defense of "Extreme Emotional Disturbance" or EED. A legal rather than psychiatric term, New York's penal law in 1967 defined it to state that jurors "may consider all emotions which in fact influence ... conduct, such as, for example, passion, grief, resentment, anger, terror, fright, hatred or excessive excitement or agitation, and these emotions need not necessarily be of sudden or spontaneous occurrence. They may have simmered in the defendant's mind for a long time."

In a major EED case, People v. Patterson, the New York Court of Appeals wrote, "It may be that a significant mental trauma has affected a defendant's mind for a substantial period of time, simmering in the unknowing subconscious, and then explicitly coming to the fore."

Judge Betty D. Friedlander, who represented the defendant in the Patterson case, asserts, "Jean Harris is the person that defense was written for."

Alexander believes it was not used because "it implies a homicidal rather than a suicidal state of mind." In Stranger in Two Worlds, Harris recalls that her lawyers always explained

EED as requiring her to say that she "murdered Hy" but "under extreme emotional disturbance." She writes that she replied, "You're telling me that the way to be acquitted of murder is to say that I murdered a man. I didn't murder Hy, and nothing and no one will ever induce me to say that I did."

However, Alexander believes that the degree of turmoil Harris was suffering makes intent virtually impossible to determine. She also notes, "There is no inconsistency between an EED defense and a 'tragic accident' defense. Indeed, one could have caused the other."

## The People v. Jean Harris

Judge Russell Legget presided at trial. A jury of eight women and four men was impaneled. Four of the jurors were black, three of them women. The foreperson was a male bus mechanic. The other three men were a black social studies teacher, a systems analyst, and a retired school administrator. The black women were a keypunch operator, an anti-poverty worker, and a part-time chambermaid. The white women included a special education teacher, a housewife, and a part-time cardiac therapy nurse.

The trial began on November 21, 1980.

Bolen read the three charges against Harris: count one, murder in the second degree; count two, criminal possession of a weapon in the state of New York, second degree; and count three, criminal possession of a weapon in a place not the defendant's home or place of business, third degree. In his opening statement, Bolen said, "No one's going to appear in the court with a movie camera and a screen, or a videotape and play for you what happened at the residence of Dr. Herman Tarnower March 10 and particularly what happened in his bedroom."

Bolen discussed the way Tarnower juggled sexual partners, primarily dividing his romantic and sexual attentions between defendant Jean Harris and office assistant turned bedmate Lynne Tryforos. Bolen stated that after dinner, Tarnower "went up to the bedroom and retired for the night. Several hundred miles away, Jean Harris placed keys into the ignition of one of the school's cars and with her in the car was a revolver and a number of cartridges." He promised to prove that the defendant "consciously, volitionally, and intentionally fired five shots."

Opening for the defense, Aurnou asserted, "There came a time on that night when both Jean and Dr. Tarnower struggled over the gun, when both Jean and Dr. Tarnower fought over her life—and both of them lost. He lost his life in what we will show you was a tragic accident, and she was left with a life she no longer wanted to live." Aurnou also said, "We contend what happened in the case did not happen in the way the prosecutor described it … Facts will show you a very different version; when we say facts, we mean physical facts found and available at the scene."

After Bolen finished direct examination of one of the first officers at the scene, Daniel O'Sullivan, Aurnou asked in cross-examination, "Did you hear [Harris] indicate that it was her intention that she never return to Virginia alive?" O'Sullivan answered, "Yes." Aurnou asked, "Did you hear her answer that she did not know [who had control of the gun]?" Again, the officer said, "Yes." He answered, "That's correct" when Aurnou asked if she had said she did not know who pulled the trigger. Aurnou asked, "Did you also hear my client say, sir, that she asked the doctor to kill her because she wanted to die?" Yet again, O'Sullivan answered, "Yes."

Bolen called surgeon Dr. Harold Roth who arrived at the Tarnower residence as the wounded man was being put in the ambulance and accompanied him to the hospital. He administered cardiac massage but Tarnower was dead by the time he got to the hospital. His right arm was "totally disarticulated."

On cross-examination, Aurnou asks, "If you had had seven or 10 minutes more … would that have made a difference in his ability to survive?"

"It might very well, yes," Roth testified. "Any minutes would have made a difference."

Thus, Aurnou laid support for the defense contention that

the failure of the police to rush Tarnower to the hospital was part of the "tragic accident" resulting in his death. Alexander writes, "The two fatal bullet holes, one in front, one in back, lined up so perfectly that it appeared to everyone, doctors and medics as well as the cops, that Tarnower had sustained a single, superficial flesh wound clean through the shoulder, an illusion strengthened by the fact that there was surprisingly little external bleeding."

On redirect examination, Bolen got Roth to say that police consider a hand wound that goes from front-to-back a "classic defense wound." The prosecutor argued that Tarnower sustained this wound when he held his hand up to ward off a direct and murderous shot.

Bolen called Westchester County Deputy Medical Examiner Louis Roh, M.D. to the stand. When Roh autopsied Tarnower, he found five wounds, four wound tracks, and three bullets. "The one bullet that caused the wound to the hand is the one that caused the wound in the right anterior chest wall," Roh testified. He supported the prosecution contention that the hand wound was sustained when Tarnower vainly tried to ward off a shot because the hand and chest wounds could be lined up and because when the bullet dropped into the chest cavity after hitting the collarbone and cutting a big vein, it did not have much force. He further testified, "It is my opinion that it is consistent with a defense wound."

Trilling reports, "To counter Aurnou's claim that the police delay could have caused Tarnower's death, Bolen questioned the pathologist as to how much blood the doctor would have had to lose to go into intractable shock. Roh believed that the doctor went into intractable shock within five to 10 minutes after he sustained the injuries."

Harris moaned during this testimony.

Bolen asked if the wounds were "consistent" with a struggle over a gun between a man of Tarnower's size and a woman of Harris's. "It is not consistent with a struggle for the gun. ... Number 1, the multiplicity, the person receiving three gunshot wounds and four wounds on the body ... Secondly, the location of these wounds. If two persons are struggling over the gun and discharging during the struggle, I would expect to see the wounds mainly in the front part of the body," Roh responded.

Aurnou got Roh to admit on cross that in his original autopsy report, he said that four bullets had struck Tarnower instead of the three to which he testified at trial. The suggestion was made that Roh changed his opinion to bring it more in line with the idea that the hand wound was a classic defensive wound.

The prosecution soon rested.

One of the first defense witnesses was Madeira Board Chair Alice Faulkner. Harris trembled and wept as Faulkner testified to finding a letter from Harris as well as a companion document stating, "I want to be immediately CREMATED AND THROWN AWAY." Both were found on a chair by the living room door of the home Madeira furnished for the headmistress. The letter reads:

*Alice –*

*I'm sorry. Please for Christ's sake don't open the place again until you have adults and policemen and keepers on every floor. God knows what they're doing. And next time choose a head the board wants and supports. Don't let some poor fool work like hell for two years before she knows she wasn't ever wanted in the first place. There are so many enemies and so few friends. I was a person and nobody ever knew.*

The letter was unsigned. The document asking for cremation is signed twice.

Forensic scientist Herbert MacDonell testified to measuring the angle of a bullet hole through a glass door and tracing a ricochet mark to establish the zone within which the gun was fired. Alexander writes, "If the bullet went through Tarnower's hand in the manner Jean had described, the blood would spray in certain specific patterns and parabolas, which would tend to confirm her story. In examining the new close-up photos of the door frame, he spotted dark specks that could be human blood."

He later confirmed they were blood. Alexander continues that MacDonell "discovered on the door frame a 'directional bloodstain,' an oval droplet 1/25th of an inch in diameter, which again confirms Harris's story of where she and Tarnower were standing when the first shot was fired."

MacDonell attacked Roh's testimony. MacDonell testified that if the doctor had held his hand up to ward off the gun in "a classic defense posture," his face and entire pajama sleeve would have been covered with a thin spray of blood – they were not. This testimony powerfully rebutted the contention that Tarnower was trying to ward off a shot from a Harris who came barreling down on him with the gun.

He also testified that his reconstruction indicated that the shot Harris fired when she thought the gun barrel was pointing at her stomach had broken Tarnower's arm. MacDonell found small bloodstains in the bathtub – exactly the right size to have been put there by someone banging a gun filled with fresh blood against enamel. MacDonell asserted that the gun was filled with blood when Tarnower held it in his injured hand.

Alexander writes, "By examining the primer in the base of the spent cartridges under low-power magnification, the professor [MacDonell] can tell whether the firing pin has struck the primer once, or more than once ... Since he found four shells double-struck, and one single-struck, he has been able to calculate the precise sequence of the five shots fired from the six-cylinder weapon: bang, bang, bang, bang, click, bang, click, click, click, click." That sequence precisely supports Harris's recollections.

Bolen asked MacDonell if he had examined the blood-stained bed sheets. MacDonell admitted he had not and said he would like to. The expert spent a lunch hour looking at the sheets. Back in court, he pointed out how the patterns supported Harris's story. For example, he said a stain looked like someone might have laid a gun across it. MacDonell laid his own gun across it and the fit was perfect.

Over a weekend recess, Bolen talked to a defense pathologist who said that if a bullet passed through a hand before entering the chest, one might find tiny palm tissue in the chest. Bolen related this to Roh and asked Roh to look for such tiny palm fragments.

Bolen recalled Roh who testified he found three tiny fragments that could be palm tissue. On cross, he admitted they could be cartilage, cotton fibers, or collarbone fragments. Aurnou put on several pathologists who said the fragments cannot be identified as palm material.

One of those pathologists was the respected A. Bernard Ackerman, M.D. Ackerman testified, "My diagnosis is unequivocal. All three fragments came from tissue other than the [palm] skin of Dr. Tarnower."

Bolen recalled Roh yet again and asked if it would be anatomically possible for Tarnower to have sustained the arm wound in various positions. On cross-examination, Aurnou asked, "Is it also anatomically possible he could have sustained it while sitting on the toilet?"

Harris gasped, "Joel, how could you?"

Harris in Her Own Defense

Harris took the stand. Aurnou asked about her mental state after the marijuana brouhaha at the Madeira school. Her reply was agonizingly slow, "I … couldn't … function." He quotes from her resignation letter that stated, "I was a person and no one ever knew."

Aurnou urged, "Tell the jury what you meant."

She wept as she said, "I think it had something to do with being a woman who had worked for a long time and had done the things a man does to support a family but is still a woman. I always felt that when I was in Westchester I was a woman in a pretty dress and went to a dinner party with Dr. Tarnower and in Washington I was a woman in a pretty dress and the headmistress. But I wasn't sure who I was … and it didn't seem to matter."

Aurnou asked, "It mattered to you, didn't it?

She said, "I was a person sitting in an empty chair."

Later, Aurnou asked, "Did you ever that night intend to shoot or kill Dr. Tarnower?"

"No, I didn't," she replied. "The most violent thing I did

was throw a box of curlers, and I didn't throw them at him. I never for a moment wanted to hurt Hi, never in 14 years. And certainly not that night."

Bolen asked if she was upset Herman dated Lynne Tryforos.

"Yes," she answered. "As I said before, I thought it denigrated Hy ... I think this whole conversation denigrates Hy and I hate it!"

"You were very concerned about the doctor's reputation?" Bolen asked.

"I was indeed, and this thing is tearing me apart," she said.

Later Bolen asked how she referred to Tryforos in the letter she sent Tarnower on March 10.

"I referred to her as what I had experienced her to be ... Dishonest ... adulterous ... a whore," she said.

He asked, "Those were very strong terms to use, aren't they?"

"They are," she answered. "They are very out of character for me to use. But it's not like me to rub up against people like Lynne Tryforos."

Bolen entered the letter that she had written just before Tarnower's death and that would become known as the "Scarsdale Letter" into evidence. Then he read it to the jury. It began, "I will send this by registered mail only because so many of my letters seem not to reach you."

She wrote about years of anonymous taunting phone calls, having her dresses torn, having a nightgown destroyed with orange stains, and the horror of finding a dress smeared with feces.

She writes of her pain when she discovered that he sold the ring he had presented to her as an engagement ring: "I desperately needed money all those years. I couldn't have sold that ring. It was tangible proof of your love and it meant more to me than life itself. That you sold it the summer your adulterous slut finally got her divorce and needed money is a kind of sick, cynical act that left me old and bitter and sick."

The jury convicted Jean Harris of second-degree murder

and of both weapons charges.

Given the powerful scientific testimony of experts like MacDonell and Ackerman stating that the physical facts supported Harris's story, why did the jury convict? Part of it may be that the testimony was too complex for lay persons to adequately follow and understand. Spencer writes, "The jury ignored almost all the evidence and all but a few of the 92 witnesses who appeared at the three-and-a-half month trial." The jurors based their verdict on an inability to act out in the jury room a way for Tarnower to have sustained the hand wound in a struggle.

After the trial, Ackerman wrote an essay entitled, "The Physician As Expert Witness: Is Peer Review Needed?" He argued that prosecution doctors appeared to lose scientific objectivity in finding what would be best for the prosecution.

## Twelve Years in Prison

Sent to the Bedford Hills Correctional Facility, Harris washed dishes and stairs and at one point headed the Inmate Liaison Committee, a post she relinquished due to poor health. She worked in the prison nursery. She also wrote three books: *Stranger in Two Worlds, They Always Call Us Ladies* and *Marking Time: Letters from Jean Harris to Shana Alexander.*

New York Governor Mario Cuomo denied clemency to her three times but granted it in December 1992. Shortly after her sentence was commuted, she moved into a cabin in New Hampshire. *Los Angeles Times* reporter Pamela Warrick described Harris as "slight and delicate" as well as "very sad looking, especially around the eyes." Harris said she entertains few guests other than sons Jimmy and David. After 12 years in unavoidably close quarters with fellow inmates, Harris cherishes privacy. "I can't tell you how wonderful it is to be alone," she said.

Harris told *New York Times* reporter James Feron she wanted to live "where there aren't a lot of people, where I don't have to look into someone else's window." She told Feron that she spent much time "gardening, painting my garage, and writing."

Harris continued working for the Bedford Hills Correctional Facility Children's Center. All profits from books she wrote were donated to the Children of Bedford Foundation that aids the center. However, Harris expressed discomfort with the credit sometimes given to her. "I think I've helped a little bit with that effort, but it is its founder, Sister Elaine Roulet, who is the moral essence of the Children's Center and that prison," she told Warrick.

According to Warrick, Harris rejected comparisons of her case to those of battered women who killed abusers. When Barbara Walters said, "You did become a symbol of the woman wronged," Harris replied, "No. I think I'm the woman who let herself be wronged."

She believes that if her case has any larger implications, it is in the need for individual responsibility. She tells anyone struggling with problem relationships, "It's up to you to make yourself happy."

At the end of Warrick's interview, the reporter asked if she would consider dating.

She answered, "Good heavens, no! Whatever for?"

In December 2012, Jean Harris died at the age of 89 in a New Haven, Connecticut assisted-living facility of complications relating to old age.

## Bibliography

Alexander, Shana. *Very Much A Lady: The Untold Story of Jean Harris and Dr. Herman Tarnower*. Pocket Books. 1986.

Feron, James. *Jean Harris Savors a New Life After Prison*. The New York Times. June 27, 2993.

Harris, Jean. *Marking Time: Letters from Jean Harris to Shana Alexander*. Kensington Publishing Corp.1991.

Harris, Jean. *Stranger in Two Worlds.* Kensington Publishing Corp. 1986.

Luther, Claudia. "Jean Harris dies at 89; killer of 'Scarsdale Diet' doctor.' Los Angeles Times. December 28, 2012

Sack, Kevin. "Clemency Given to Jean Harris in Murder Case." The New York Times. December 30, 1992.

Spencer, Duncan. *Love Gone Wrong: The Jean Harris Scarsdale Murder Case.* A Signet Book. 1981.

Tarnower, M.D., Herman and Baker, Samm Sinclair. *The Complete Scarsdale Medical Diet.* Bantam Books. 1980.

Trilling, Diana. Mrs. Harris: The Death of the Scarsdale Diet Doctor. Harcourt Brace Jovanovich Publishers.

Warrick, Pamela. "'The Myth of Me': Aftermath: Jean Harris rejects the labels thrust upon her after the Scarsdale Diet Doctor murder in 1980, saying she's just a 'tired old lady.' But she still has the energy to speak out for other women still in prison." Los Angeles Times. July 19, 1993.

# CHAPTER EIGHT

## The Jonathan Jay Pollard Spy Case

The driver floored the accelerator in the five-year-old green Mustang. The overweight man at the wheel had black hair with a receding hairline and sported aviator-style eyeglasses. He was in a gut wrenching, dry-mouthed, sweaty-palmed, and heart pounding panic. In the passenger seat beside him sat his portly, attractive, redheaded wife.

Having just undergone an operation, she was in physical discomfort and mentally groggy. Her mind was clear enough, however, to be afraid. She was stroking Dusty, the family cat that was on her lap. The woman also had in her possession a variety of important papers, including birth and marriage certificates and the vaccination records for the feline, that they would need in starting the new life that they hoped against hope that they were speeding toward.

They were driving to the Israeli embassy in Washington, D. C., believing that they would be given refuge there. When they got within sight of the light beige brick building, they saw its flag, made up of a crisp blue Star of David on a background of purest white, flying proud and high. That flag seemed to beckon them to safety and freedom.

The man was named Jonathan Jay Pollard. Family and friends always called him "Jay." The woman was his wife, Anne Henderson-Pollard. Both were terrified that they would soon be arrested on charges of espionage—unless they could get to the Israeli embassy in time.

The gate of the embassy opened up for the car in front of the Mustang and Pollard zoomed in right behind it. He and Anne breathed a sigh of relief. They had made it!

"The FBI is on to me, I need help," 31-year-old Jay Pollard told an Israeli security guard.

Guards left to confer with their superiors. They came back to the Pollards with surprising and distressing news. The security officers informed the American couple that they could not stay at the embassy. They must leave immediately.

Terrified and flustered, Jay Pollard tried to explain. There had to be some kind of mistake. After all, those at the embassy enjoyed diplomatic immunity and could not be arrested for helping him. Surely they would aid one of their best agents!

"Do you know what I have done for Israel?" he asked and pled at the same time. "I'm an Israeli agent."

"Get out," he was told again.

"I want to invoke my right under the Law of Return to Israeli citizenship!" he cried. "We're Jews. We're on Israeli territory. You can't throw us out."

"Get out!" the guard shouted.

Jay Pollard was frantic. His voice broke and he burst into tears as he begged, "Please, you can't do this."

Repeatedly, Jay and Anne were told the same message and it was as implacable as it was unwelcome: "GET OUT!"

Dejected, the anguished Pollard turned his automobile around and drove it out of the embassy. The moment they left, their car was halted. Cars and vans carrying FBI agents surrounded the embassy. As soon as Jay got out of his car, he was arrested on charges of spying, handcuffed, and told his Miranda rights. The contents of the green Mustang were impounded as evidence.

Anne was allowed to go home with Dusty. The next day, Anne too, was arrested.

## Allies Spy

Israel is so closely allied to the United States that some people have called the Jewish nation America's fifty-first state. The US has strongly supported Israel in the wars it has fought throughout its brief and violent history. Moreover, America shares a great deal of the vital intelligence it gathers with Israel and vice versa. Indeed, the vast majority of American intelligence information that Israel would be interested in is voluntarily given over to it.

However, in the arcane world of statecraft, friendly countries do not share every piece of intelligence with each other. Thus, allies spy, a practice called "friendly espionage."

Why would the United States withhold intelligence from Israel? The interests of one country never perfectly coincide with another, no matter how close the two nations might be. As Wolf Blitzer wrote in Territory of Lies, America does not share with Israel (nor Israel with the US) "information that it [feels] could compromise what the intelligence professionals call 'sources and methods'—namely, how that information was collected."

For example, CIA sources within the PLO are kept secret from Israel because the American intelligence-gathering organization believes that those sources would dry up if the Israelis were told about them. American information concerning those Arab states with which we are friendly, such as Egypt, Saudi Arabia, and Jordan, are also not revealed to our Israeli friends. Furthermore, intelligence is shared, even with allies, on a basis of exchange. Thus, if one country has a "mole" implanted in the other, the latter's ability to receive intelligence from the former is greatly weakened.

Moreover, the United States has been known to snoop on Israel. America took satellite reconnaissance photographs of Israeli military installations—which Pollard illegally shared with Israel, helping them to develop better "masking" techniques. The Israelis have been convinced that there were American moles in their country and there has been some evidence to support their suspicion. Republican Senator David Durenberger of Minnesota charged that the CIA had an Israeli spy who started working for the US before Israel accepted the services of Jay Pollard. Immediately after the Pollard scandal broke, the late Yitzhak Rabin, who was then Israel's Defense Minister, said that Israel had found no less than five American spies working inside it during the late 1970s and early 1980s. The spies were expelled from Israel, rather than prosecuted and imprisoned, to prevent too much conflict between the country and its American ally. Such is not possible, of course, in the United States where the rule of law is much stricter.

Americans frequently wondered why the Israelis would risk an international incident in order to obtain what the US withheld from them. After all, the vast majority of data is shared. The answer lies in the extreme degree of concern that the little, tempest-tossed nation has for its security. As noted in an article on the case, "Why Israel spied on U. S." that appeared in U. S. News & World Report, "Officially, the Israeli government regrets the spy case. Unofficially, Israeli officials and private citizens alike repeatedly cite vital security concerns in defense of the action." The article also says, "To most [Israelis], Israel is a nation surrounded by enemies and must risk dispute with its one indispensable ally if it feels that ally is withholding information that Israel needs."

### A Bullied Boy

Jonathan Jay Pollard was born on August 7, 1954, in Galveston, Texas. His father, Dr. Morris Pollard, was a microbiologist. His mother, Molly Pollard, was a homemaker. He was the youngest of three children. Harvey was the oldest and Carol was the middle sister. The family soon began calling their youngest son by his middle name.

When Jay was very young, the family moved to South Bend, Indiana so his father could take a position at Notre Dame University. Dr. Morris Pollard would later recall that he experienced not a whiff of anti-Semitism at the Roman Catholic institution. Rather, he and his family were always made to feel welcome.

Neither Galveston, Texas nor South Bend, Indiana boast-

ed large Jewish communities but the Pollards were deeply involved with the Jewish groups in their areas. The family made
a special effort to instill a powerful sense of Jewish identity
in their children. The parents were devoted to the cause of Israel and impressed their love for the Jewish homeland upon
their youngsters. The Pollard children learned about the Holo-
caust at a young age and grew up knowing that the Nazis had
slaughtered some 70 of the family's European relatives.

That Pollards were affluent and lived comfortably in a
ranch-style home in a little cul de sac. Jay was close to both
parents, especially his mother. He was also, to some degree,
"parented" by his older brother and sister. He was a preco-
cious youngster upon whom his whole family beamed. Musi-
cally talented, he learned to play the cello and became quite
accomplished at it.

School was a different story. He made excellent grades but
outside his family, young Jay was disliked by other children.
He was frequently picked on. On a daily basis, Jay was teased
and taunted and often physically assaulted by his fellow students. Why? There are several possible reasons. The boy was
short for his age. He also wore glasses. Children can be notoriously cruel to "shrimps" and "four-eyes." Additionally, Jay
was obviously bright and envy of a smart kid or "teacher's
pet" often sparks school-age persecution.

Finally, the boy was Jewish in an area that had few Jews.
Jay blamed this factor exclusively for his being the target of so
many taunts. This solidified his interest in, and love for, Israel,
the country where Jews could be "normal."

In 1967, when Jay was 13 years-old, several Arab countries attacked Israel. The teenager was devastated. It seemed
impossible that the little country could hold out against so
many enemies. "They're going to kill Israel!" he sobbed to his
mother. "I'll never get to see Israel." Molly assured him that
Israel would survive.

When Jay woke up the next morning, he found out that
what would become famous as the Six-Day War was over—
and Israel had won! The lad was overjoyed. "Then I'll get to
see Israel!" he shouted.

Thirteen was also the age for Jay's Bar Mitzvah, the ceremony that traditionally marks a Jewish boy's ascent to manhood. A boy gives a speech at his Bar Mitzvah and Jay took the subject of his speech from Isaiah and the message that Israel will be a leader among nations. The rabbi at their synagogue was not a Zionist and discouraged young Jay from speaking on that theme.

The family changed to an Orthodox synagogue. There, Jay gave the Bar Mitzvah speech he wanted to on the subject dearest to his heart.

The next year, 1968, saw the Pollard family visiting Europe. This was also a pivotal experience for Jay. Here he went to Dachau. He saw the palpable evidence of anti-Semitism at its most extreme: the barbed wire, wooden barracks, and crematoria. He was emotionally overpowered. Like so many Jews, he came away with an extra determination that "Never again!" would such a horror befall his people. Israel, he deeply believed, was the key to making sure of that.

In 1970, Jonathan Jay Pollard traveled to Israel as a member of a science camp for gifted students. Jay loved what he found and saw there. He would recall the trip as "one of the most liberating experiences I have ever had in my life." When his parents visited him, his mother found him "in heaven." Even there, however, others saw Jay having difficulty getting along with his fellow teenagers.

Jay had long fantasized about immigrating to Israel. When he returned home, he was more determined than ever to make that dream a reality. His family did not counsel against it but urged him to wait until he had completed his education and could take some marketable skills to the Jewish state.

The young Pollard was accepted to California's prestigious Stanford University. He originally signed up for a pre-medical program, planning to follow in the footsteps of his older brother, Harvey, who had become a doctor. However, Jay found pre-med daunting and soon switched to a political science major. He became known for his great interest in, and increasing knowledge about, military history. He adored spy novels and has read hundreds of them.

As a college student, he spun romantic fantasies about himself, probably patterned after some of the plots in his beloved spy stories, that he earnestly tried to convince his listeners were factual. The stories always involved Israel. He told his friends that he held dual citizenship in the US and Israel which he did not. Pollard variously claimed to be either a captain or a colonel in the Israeli army.

He confided to a buddy that he was a secret agent for the Israeli intelligence agency, Mossad. At that time, Mossad had never heard of him. Seeming genuinely terrified, he told fellows in his dorm that some Israelis were out to kill him. He had a gun to protect himself, he claimed. For whatever reason, he did indeed possess a revolver and showed it to other students. At one point, he told other Stanford students that, while guarding a kibbutz, he had killed an Arab.

One thing he did not do at Stanford was join Hillel, the primary Jewish students' organization, or any other organized campus Hebraic group. He remained a loner. Even when anti-Semitism was not an issue, Jay Pollard had a great deal of trouble making and keeping friends.

In 1976, Pollard graduated from Stanford University with a degree in Political Science. He returned home to South Bend to attend Notre Dame's law school. After a few months, he quit. The other law students, Jay believed, "are just interested in making money. They are not interested in changing anything. I don't want to be a corporation lawyer."

Pollard won admission to the Fletcher School of Law and Diplomacy at Tufts University in Boston. He went there for two years but did not get a degree. The young man suffered a continuing emotional crisis because of his feeling that he belonged in Israel and not America. However, he never felt that one loyalty precluded the other. The US was necessary for Israel. "Israel grows—basks in the sunlight—cast by the American sun," he commented. While at Fletcher, he encountered people who sympathized with the Palestinian cause and they, naturally enough, made Jay's blood boil.

## Polygraphs and Tall Tales

In 1977, Jonathan Pollard applied for a job in the CIA. He did not get it. A polygraph test indicated that he could be a security risk and might not be free of illegal drugs.

A 25-year-old Pollard was hired by Naval Intelligence in 1979 as an Intelligence Research Specialist. He worked at the Field Operational Intelligence Office in Suitland, Maryland. The Navy did not know of the CIA's findings regarding their new employee. He would work in Naval Intelligence for a total of seven years.

The job consisted largely of analyzing data and making reports on it. Jay was not altogether happy at work due, he claimed, to the tendency of some of his fellow employees to make anti-Semitic jokes or remarks. He also heard criticisms of Israel that he regarded as expressions of anti-Semitism. He would later state that workers who made such comments were not reprimanded for them and that, along with the statements themselves, made him extremely uncomfortable as well as angry.

Many people regard the Navy as the least pro-Israel branch of the American service. Access to ports is obviously a major concern and that makes relations with the Arab world in general, and the Persian Gulf states in particular, especially important to the Navy.

What's more, a tragedy occurred in 1967, during the Six-Day War, that had a strongly negative effect on the feelings of many Navy personnel toward Israel. The Israelis bombed an American intelligence-gathering ship, the USS Liberty, killing 34. Israel apologized and claimed, quite plausibly, that it was an accident caused by Israeli pilots mistaking the Liberty for an Egyptian ship. Friction was exacerbated because the Israelis insisted that the US vessel had been in a war zone while the Americans maintained it had been in international waters.

A version of the sinking had been gossiped around the Navy that was far more sinister. It also reflected unfavorably on both the US and Israel as allies. According to this story,

President Lyndon Johnson wanted an Israeli victory but not one that was nearly so quick and decisive as the Six-Day War turned out to be.

The White House wanted to cultivate friendly relations with the Arab nations because of America's extreme reliance on oil and, to that end, the Liberty was there to gather intelligence that would be shared with the Arabs and used against Israel. Thus, the Jewish State deliberately attacked a ship of its most important ally. This account of the tragedy is highly fanciful but the fact that it was believed at all is both symptomatic of and a contributing factor to the alienation of some Navy personnel from Israel.

Jay Pollard got access to classified data after two years on the job. The American government recognizes five different basic degrees of sensitivity concerning secret information. They are, in order of the importance of the secrecy: Confidential, Secret, Top Secret, and Special Compartmented Information (SCI).

Quoting again from Wolf Blitzer: "According to US government regulations, information is classified Confidential if its unauthorized disclosure could reasonably be expected to cause 'damage' to the national security; Secret if its unauthorized disclosure could reasonably be expected to cause 'serious damage' to the national security; and Top Secret if its unauthorized disclosure could reasonably be expected to cause 'exceptionally grave damage' to the national security. SCI is a designation reserved for especially sensitive classified information, 'the dissemination of which is strictly controlled and limited to selected individuals within the military and intelligence community who have special security clearances."

Pollard found himself upset because he did not believe the US was sharing all the data with Israel that it ought to have been. Later Jay would remark bitterly that Soviet military equipment was "quietly entering [the Middle East] unnoticed by the Israelis, who were depending upon the US intelligence community for warning of such activity."

1981 saw a much more welcomed development in Jay's life. He met 21-year-old Anne Henderson, the pretty, shapely, blue-eyed, and flame-haired secretary who would become the first major love of his life. She was also Jewish but somewhat less of a devout Zionist than he was. However, as Wolf Blitzer writes in Territory of Lies, Anne "slowly came to share his feelings and commitment." Henderson had frequent health problems because she suffered from a rare stomach disorder called biliary dyskinsesia that made it hard for her to digest food. However, she pursued a career and generally active life despite occasional flare-ups of this illness.

The couple was soon living together, then planning to marry.

Jay suffered a crisis at work that led to his security clearance getting suspended.

Relations between the intelligence communities of the US and that of South Africa were strained and America needed information about what was going on in the South Atlantic. Pollard approached a superior, saying that he was a friend of Lt. Gen. P. W. van der Westhuizen, South Africa's chief of military intelligence. The two men had become buddies when they were attending Fletcher. Permission was granted to Pollard to establish a "back channel" to Westhuizen.

However, Navy officials began to smell something fishy when Pollard told them elaborate tales of his having lived in South Africa and his father's served as a CIA station chief in the country. They realized that Jay was spinning a tall tale and insisted he see a psychiatrist.

He did. The shrink found Pollard free from mental illness and the young man's security clearance was restored.

In 1984, Jay won an assignment that he heartily welcomed. He was transferred to the Anti-Terrorist Alert Center (ATAC) of the Naval Investigative Service's Threat Analysis Division. He would be working under Jerry Agee, a tall and balding career Navy man who had spent two decades working in intelligence.

As Blitzer noted, "Pollard was assigned duties that included research and analysis of intelligence data pertaining to potential terrorist threats." Agee found his new employee competent. "He was able to do some fairly quick analysis and be, I thought, above average in his analysis of things, what it meant as a threat," Agee would recall. "He was able to write short articles very well and very quickly."

He remembered other things about Pollard. "[He] made comments that he had worked for Israeli intelligence," Agee commented. "[Jay was] a bullshitter. He was always telling tall tales. It was more or less a joke in the office, 'Did you hear the story about Pollard?' There were a lot of Pollard stories."

It does not seem to have occurred to those in this "intelligence" community that a compulsive braggart given to fabricating self-aggrandizing stories, a person for whom the line between fantasy and reality often blurred, was not an individual to be trusted with America's most vital secrets.

In truth, Pollard had already violated his contract against disclosing secrets—although not yet as a spy. In 1982, he removed sensitive documents to show them to social acquaintances. There is an old saying, "Scratch the adult, find the child." The lonely, bullied boy had become a man so insecure that he compromised US security in order to impress his friends.

Pollard was increasingly frustrated and disgusted by things he saw at the NIS. In 1983, President Ronald Reagan had signed a "bilateral intelligence-sharing agreement" with Israel. Pollard was convinced that NIS officials were simply ignoring its directives authorizing release of important data to Israel. He later said that he should have "gone through channels" to report these alleged failures to higher ups. He did not do so.

He claimed that he saw a photograph of a poison gas factory being constructed in Iraq and requested permission to transmit it to Israel. Jay said his superior laughed and said Jews were too sensitive about gas because of their experiences in WWII.

In 1983, Shi'ite terrorist bombed a Marine Corps headquarter in Beirut. The US retaliated with an air raid but Pollard believed it was too little, too late. America was not doing enough to protect its own in the Middle East, Pollard concluded. Thus, it could not possibly be expected to do what it should to protect Israel.

Jay Pollard would have to do it instead, he decided.

## Pollard meets the Pilot

Pollard's plan to spy for Israel solidified when his friend, Steven Stern, described a fascinating lecture he (Stern) had recently attended. The speaker had been the distinguished Israeli Air Force Colonel Aviem Sella, mastermind of the air assault against Syrian warplanes during the 1982 war in Lebanon. Sella's success had been spectacular for his planes had lost none of their own number while shooting down 90 Syrian MIGs!

A lean and handsome man with a high forehead and strong cheekbones, the Colonel had taken a leave of absence from the Air Force so he could study computer science at New York University.

Jay listened to Stern's description of Sella's lecture with undisguised awe. Would it be possible for Stern to arrange a meeting between Pollard and Sella? Jay was more than willing to make a special trip to New York for such a meeting. Stern promised to try to set something up. The next time he saw Sella, he told him of his buddy, Jay Pollard, who badly wished to meet the Israeli Colonel about whom he had heard so much. Sella told Stern he had to think it over.

What he really had to do was clear it with his superiors, for Sella had an inkling of what Stern's friend might be up to. The Colonel contacted Yosef Yagur, a short, well-liked engineer who worked as science counselor at the Israeli Consulate in New York. Yagur also worked for a scientific intelligence-gathering unit of the Israeli Defense Ministry known as LAKAM. Yagur told Sella to wait while LAKAM researched Pollard. After the unit assembled information on the American, Yagur informed the career air force man to go ahead with the meeting but be very careful. After all, Pollard could easily be a plant of some kind, involved in a sting operation.

So Sella told Stern that, yes, he would meet with this Jay

Pollard. No trip to the Big Apple would be necessary on Pollard's part. Rather, he, Sella, would travel to Washington, D. C. Jay Pollard received a phone call. The voice on the other end was that of a stranger but it was friendly. "This is Avi Sella," the man said.

"Shalom!" an awestruck Pollard shouted as he leapt to his feet to stand at attention for the man who could not possibly see him.

At least, this is the version of the initial phone contact that is given in Blitzer's *Territory of Lies*. Knowing that it makes him sound comically childish, Pollard disputes that he jumped to attention at the call.

The pair soon met for lunch at the coffee shop of the Washington Hilton Hotel. Sitting in a corner booth, the two men made some chit chat.

Then Jay came right to the point. "I know I can help you," he told the Israeli pilot. "You have no idea how much vital information the United States is denying Israel."

The military officer was a bit put off. This was much too blunt. Was Pollard setting him up? Sella wondered uncomfortably. While saying little himself, the Israeli allowed the American to wind on. As Sella listened, he became more and more convinced of Pollard's sincerity. The pilot remained cautious.

He asked Jay to produce an example of the kind of material he had in mind. Pollard eagerly assured him that he could and would.

Sella reported back to Yagur who gave him a cautious go-ahead for more meetings with the prospective spy.

### Cloak and Dagger Desk Man

Pollard was soon spying on a regular basis for Israel. He leaked thousands of pages of highly sensitive documents to the Israelis. He was a most valuable and efficient spy for, as Carl Tashian has written, "no one has stolen so much classified information so quickly." Many in Israeli intelligence, who knew of Pollard's work but not his real name, dubbed him "The Hunting Horse." In Elliot Goldenberg's book of the same title, he says that "'Hunting Horse' is a transliteration from the Hebrew, and loosely means he would 'hunt' up information on request and that he was a 'horse' for his handlers; an exceptional agent on whose back his handlers [could] ride up the promotional ladder."

At one of their meetings, Sella raised the issue of payment. Jay replied that he had no interest it. He was motivated solely by his love for Israel. However, Avi insisted that Israel wanted to compensate the agent who was so productive for them.

This was a standard move in the world of espionage, as Dan Raviv and Yossi Melman noted in Every Spy a Prince, their history of Israel's intelligence operations. As they wrote, "The spy who tells his controllers he is acting voluntarily, out of ideological affection for the country he is helping—or disgruntled hatred of the nation he is betraying—can easily be overcome by fear or change his mind. Being a volunteer, he feels he can withdraw at any time." By contrast, "A paid agent cannot. He feels obliged to deliver, and in the background lies the threat of blackmail. The recruiters could always get the agent in trouble with documentary proof of money handed over. By establishing this implied contract, the employer can feel certain of having hired a loyal agent."

On one occasion, Pollard delivered some documents to a suburban home in a Washington suburb. As they were chatting, Sella informed Jay that he would have to travel abroad to meet someone called "the old man." The Israelis would pay for Jay to fly to Paris where details of his payment would be worked out. Sella also suggested a way for Pollard to explain his new riches. The trip to the City of Light would be an engagement gift to Jay and Anne from Jay's fictitious "Uncle Joe Fisher."

Anne and Jay were in Paris in November 1984. Contrary to Sella's repeated instructions, Pollard had always informed Anne Henderson of everything he was doing. They were an extremely close couple and Jay could not keep secrets from her.

In Paris, Jay was introduced to "the old man," who turned out to be Rafael "Rafi" Eitan, head of LAKAM. Eitan was a well-known and seasoned spy who had been involved in the Israeli abduction of the infamous Nazi Adolf Eichmann. Eitan was one of the three men who physically tackled Eichmann and hustled him into a waiting car. Eitan was respected for his extensive knowledge in the ways of espionage but was regarded as something of a social klutz. He was nicknamed "Rafi the Stinker," a name that attached to him in the army, supposedly because he gave off a bad odor from failing to change his socks often enough.

Eitan, together with Sella and Yagur, gave detailed instructions to Pollard about the classified data that they wanted him to obtain. They also discussed payments to Jay. The spy would receive a salary of $1,500 per month. Other gifts would follow, including reimbursements for Pollard trips and an expensive diamond and sapphire ring that ended up on Anne's finger as their engagement ring.

## A Cloud of Suspicion Gathers

In the spring of 1985, James Agee caught Pollard in two outright lies. Neither was about anything of great importance to the agency. Rather, they were fibs designed to make Pollard seem like a bigshot. Agee saw nothing extremely sinister in the man's lying but it raised a red flag as to his trustworthiness.

At approximately the same time, Jay's work for the NIS began to slide in quantity if not in quality. It can be a daunting task to fire someone who works for the government but that was the general direction in which Agee's aims regarding this employee were heading.

Then, by pure happenstance, an incident occurred that made a loud warning bell go off in Agee's head. He was strolling past a clerk's desk and idly picked up a few envelopes. He saw papers that were labeled Top Secret and dealt with intelligence regarding Soviet military equipment going to Arab states. It was also, according to Agee, about "subjects which we, as an organization, had absolutely no interest in – or should have had no interest in."

Agee irritably asked the clerk, "What the hell does this

have to do with anything we're dealing with? Why did we get this?"

"Jay Pollard ordered them," the clerk responded.

"What does he need these documents for?"

"I don't know."

Then James strode to the office of civilian analyst Tom Filkens who was Pollard's immediate supervisor. Agee ordered Filkens to find out the reason Pollard that had ordered these papers "and then get rid of them. Let me know why he got them. Destroy them or send them back. We are not going to keep them here."

So Filkens asked Pollard about the troubling papers.

"They're background for a project I'm doing on terrorist threats in the Caribbean," an unruffled Pollard immediately replied.

The explanation was accepted.

However, the dissatisfaction with Pollard grew worse. He was an unproductive, unreliable employee. James Agee and others believed the division would be better off sans this boastful slacker.

In September 1985, Agee told Filkens to formally warn Pollard that if he did not soon produce a report that was quite a bit overdue, he would get an official notice that he was not performing his duties. That is the initial step toward firing someone.

On a day shortly after that, Pollard was absent from the office from early morning until late afternoon. Agee thought the man was neglecting his work to traipse about at will. He asked Jay where he had been.

"I was doing research at another intelligence library," was Pollard's easy and immediate reply.

Agee had not had the man followed but suspected that he was lying so he decided to call him on it. "That's not true," he replied, bluffing in a firm voice.

"Okay," Pollard said. "You caught me." Pollard claimed he had gone on a job interview but lied because, for obvious reasons, it is not a good practice to tell your present employer that you are putting out feelers elsewhere.

Agee accepted this false story as welcome news. If Pollard would quit, it would save Agee the time and trouble involved in firing him. Privately, he wished the man luck in getting a position elsewhere.

Something happened on October 1, 1985 that filled Jay Pollard with joy and pride. Israel bombed the PLO headquarters in Tunisia. Approximately 60 people, some of them civilians, perished in the attack. Many people expected Yassar Arafat to be killed in the raid because his residence was located at the Tunisian headquarters. However, he escaped uninjured because he was absent at the time.

Jay was proud because he had collected and passed to the Israelis information about Arafat's headquarters and Tunisia's air defense system, together with Libya's air defense system (the Israelis had had to fly over Libya on the way to Tunisia), that had been utilized by Israel in planning the raid.

The raid was in retaliation for triple killing of unarmed Israeli civilians by a PLO group called Force 17. That incident had occurred on September 25, Yom Kippur weekend.

As the month wore on, James Agee became worried that Pollard was not going to quit. Thus, he needed more information to justify dismissing him. He thought he was getting it when one of Pollard's co-workers phoned to say he had spotted Jay leaving the office with what appeared to be Top Secret documents. If he was taking such materials home, he was breaking his contract and could be kicked out. Following up on the lead, Agee discovered that Pollard was regularly picking up such documents on Fridays – documents that were in no way necessary to his work. He began monitoring Pollard closely and examining items around his cubicle.

Early on November 9, 1985, a Saturday morning, Agee was examining everything he could find in Pollard's desk and work area. He had been doing it for several hours when the realization hit him like a bolt of lightning: "I've got a fuckin' spy here!"

Agee immediately phoned Lanny McCullah, the head of counterintelligence at the Naval Security and Investigative Command in Suitland, Maryland. He informed McCullah that a most serious problem was afoot and one that could not be discussed over a telephone. Agee drove to McCullah's home and shared with him all that he had discovered about Jay Pollard.

McCullah came to the same conclusion Agee had: "The guy's a goddamned spy."

When discussing what country it was that could be interested in the data Pollard was gathering, both concluded it was Israel.

Then Agee and McCullah met with other agents to plan how to make a case against Pollard. They all agreed it was vital to catch him off-guard.

## A Peculiarly Prickly Cactus

On Friday, November 15, Pollard, as was his custom, went to the computer center to pick up the package of documents he had ordered.

"It's not here," the clerk informed him.

"What do you mean, it's not here?" Jay exploded. "I ordered it Wednesday."

The clerk checked again but it was nowhere to be found. "Try again on Monday," he suggested.

Pollard was very upset but had no idea that his spying had been discovered. He was looking forward to that weekend: Avi Sella would be visiting.

Sella did indeed visit Washington that weekend and he, Jay Pollard, and Anne Henderson-Pollard enjoyed a night on the town. Pollard happily picked up the tab. He was doing very well financially as a result of his secret work for Israel.

That Monday, a clerk from the computer center phoned Pollard to let him know that the package he had ordered the previous Wednesday had finally arrived. Enormously relieved, he immediately fetched it. Later that afternoon, he left the office and went to his car. Just as he got settled behind the wheel, a NIS agent walked up to the window.

The man was polite but firm as he asked, "Jay, would you

please step out of the car and come back with us into the build-ing?"

Pollard had a sinking sensation. They were onto him. Still, he tried to appear calm but perplexed.

In a NIS office, a group that included both FBI and NIS agents questioned Jay. Pollard insisted that he was only taking the package to another Naval office within the complex. Yes, he knew he was not really supposed to be taking it from the office so late in the day but did not believe it was any big deal. For hours, the agents questioned Pollard who seemed to have no idea what the fuss was all about. At around 7:30PM, he re-quested to call his wife. He was not under arrest so the agents had no choice but to permit it.

Pollard's voice was full of tension when he reached Anne. "Go see our friends," he told her, "take the wedding album, give them our cactus, and send them my love."

He was speaking in code. He and Anne had purchased a cactus the other day, of the green, growing, and photosyn-thetic variety. However, they had also agreed that "give them our cactus" would mean to get rid of the sensitive American documents at their home because he was in trouble. Some of the secret papers had been slipped into their treasured wed-ding album.

After she persuaded some close friends to hold some pa-pers for her and her husband, a very frightened Anne Hender-son-Pollard contacted pilot Avi Sella. They met at a restaurant and Anne told him, "Avi, you've got to help."

Now very nervous himself, Sella left the table to phone Yagur. The latter gave him bad news. LAKAM had not made any escape plans for those involved in this operation! Sella was baffled. Yagur told him to just skip the US as soon as pos-sible.

When Sella returned to Anne, he tried to give her a reas-surance and confidence that he himself did not feel. "Don't worry," he told her. "We'll take care of everything."

As soon as Sella returned to his hotel room, he told his wife they were taking the first possible plane out of the coun-try. The panicky couple took an all-night taxi ride from Washington, D.C. to New York City. There they caught the first available flight to London.

While the Sellas were decamping in Britain, a gray-faced and sick to his stomach Jay Pollard was submitting to more questioning from NIS and FBI agents. This time he admitted that he had been taking secret documents—hundreds of secret documents—out of the building. He confessed that he had even been selling them but not to a foreign power or anyone he knew to be a representative of another country. Pollard was doing his damndest to follow the guidance of his handlers that he must never, ever mention Israel. He sold the papers to a friend of his, Pollard claimed. What did the friend need them for? Pollard said he was not sure. "Maybe he was using them to help the freedom fighters in Afghanistan," he suggested.

In the meantime Yagur and others were having a conference with Eitan concerning the fate of the Pollards. "We've got to save them," Yagur said. Eitan did not think so. He told Yagur and the others that they should get their own hides out of America as soon as possible. The upshot of their meeting was that Jonathan Jay Pollard would be left as the fall guy.

Jay and Anne, of course, did not know of this decision. Jay was convinced that the Israelis would rescue him. Thus, he and Anne bundled into their green Mustang and headed for the Israeli embassy—and were turned away.

### The Spy Sings

Why did Israel fail to rescue their agent? The reason has not been made public. It has been speculated that Israel knew it was in for a big public relations disaster and decided that giving the Pollards refuge would only aggravate it. It has also been said that turning them away was the result of a simple mix-up.

Elliot Goldenberg in *The Hunting Horse* quotes an unnamed source as saying that Pollard would have been taken into the embassy and flown to Israel if Israel's ambassador to the United States, Meir Rosenne, had been present. Unfortunately for the spy, Rosenne was in Paris. Elyakim Rubinstein was in charge that day and he had not been briefed about plans to aid Pollard. After the incident, Rubinstein became Israel's attorney general. He has also become a vocal supporter of clemency for Pollard.

When Pollard was arrested, the Israeli government immediately denied that he was their agent. Prime Minister Shimon Peres and Foreign Minister Yitzhak Shamir both claimed complete ignorance of Israel's mole in America. A committee was formed ostensibly to ferret out the truth of the matter. Blitzer is probably correct that this not so much the investigating body it was officially supposed to be as a "damage control" mechanism. Predictably, it concluded that Pollard's spying was a "rogue operation" unbeknownst to the highest authorities in Israel.

During his time in jail awaiting trial, Jonathan was hopeful that Israel would intercede on his behalf. Instead, Israel cooperated with the US government in its efforts to nail him. They agreed to turn over all the documents that Pollard had given them.

When it became obvious that the Israelis were not going to get Pollard out of his predicament, he decided to spill the details of the operations in which he had been involved to US authorities. However, he always insisted that he was not committing espionage against America but for its ally Israel.

The charges against him were very serious and carried a possible sentence of life. Anne Henderson-Pollard was charged with two counts, one of "conspiring to receive embezzled government property" and another of "unauthorized possession of national defense information."

Each charge carried a possible maximum of five years behind bars. She was especially terrified of continued incarceration because her time in jail had been horrendous. By the time of the trial, the 25 year-old woman had lost 50 pounds and her hair had gone gray. Henderson-Pollard claimed that she had been "locked in a tiny, windowless, roach and rat infested cell for 23 1/2 to 24 hours a day. I was deliberately denied essential medical treatment and prescriptions for my numerous health problems, and almost died as a result of this."

Joseph DiGenova, a volatile and ambitious man with bushy eyebrows and an intense stare, headed the government's prosecutorial team.

Richard Hibey, a respected attorney, defended Jonathan Pollard. Later, both Jonathan Pollard and his father would express grave doubts about whether or not the lawyer truly had his client's best interests at heart.

The judge in the case was an African American named Aubrey Robinson. He had a reputation as a jurist who ran a tight ship in the courtroom but was considered fair.

Pollard's attorneys cut a deal with the prosecution. Their client would plead guilty if the prosecutors would not ask for the maximum sentence. The deal was accepted.

The spy pled guilty. Jay Pollard sat in the courtroom, visibly trembling, as he made the plea.

"Do you know of any reason why I shouldn't accept your plea?" Judge Robinson asked.

"No, sir, I don't," Pollard replied in a sickly-sounding voice.

The judge tried to impress the gravity of the situation upon the spy and make certain he knew that the deal carried no guarantee. "You realize I could still impose life imprisonment?" Robinson continued.

"Yes," Jay said.

Shortly thereafter, in the same court session, Anne Henderson-Pollard, pitifully thin, hunched over in apparent pain, and wearing a dress of funereal black, pled guilty to a single count of "conspiring to receive and possessing stolen documents."

## Day of Reckoning

The sentencing took place nine months later. It was March 4, 1987. The courtroom was packed. Among those sitting toward the back were Jay's sister, Carol, and Anne's father, Bernard Henderson. Dr. Morris Pollard and Mollie Pollard were too upset to come into the courtroom, so they waited for the news in the office of their son's attorney.

That attorney, Richard Hibey, wore a dark suit and a red

tie as he pled for his client. He began by admitting Pollard's wrongdoing. "In the beginning, he did it for nothing," Hibey told the court. "Later, he received money for his efforts. The money corrupted him. His motivation to help Israel was irreparably soiled by the addictive effect of taking money for his work. His conduct violated his trust as a keeper of the nation's secrets, and when he was found out, he lied long enough to allow his handlers to flee the jurisdiction of the United States. Your honor, there is no excuse for his conduct, and we offer none to absolve him of his crimes."

Then Hibey pointed out the factor that so many people felt mitigated Pollard's crime, namely the friendship between America and the country for which he spied. "Israel is not and has never been an enemy of the United States," Hibey rightfully asserted. "Thus, your honor, any claim of damage, we submit, must be understood in terms of its severity. Here, thank God, the damage is simply not severe ... There is room, therefore, your honor, for leniency while at the same time justice will be served. Thank you."

After Richard Hibey summed up for Jay, his brother James Hibey pled for Anne. Hibey said his client, "did not participate in the operational aspects of this affair. She never participated in obtaining, copying or delivering any classified documents or information to anyone." She was "a wife, albeit a knowing wife, who was motivated by love for her husband. She acted out of genuine concern and love for him, not out of any desire for money." He took note of her precarious medical condition and her need for medicine. "While at the jail," he said, "there were occasions on which she did not receive that medication and once, or finally, through the efforts of counsel, when she did receive it, it was frequently not given to her in a timely fashion. Because of her condition, she was unable to eat the jail food."

Jay Pollard spoke to the court on his own behalf. Like his wife, he had lost a great deal of weight during his confinement. However, he did not look as sickly as she did. "Over the past 15 months which I have been held in isolation," he said, "I have had more than enough time to reflect both upon my motives and upon the impact of my actions on behalf of the government of Israel.

"I have come to the inescapable conclusion that while my motives may have been well meaning, they cannot, under any stretch of the imagination, excuse or justify the violation of the law, particularly one that involves the trust of the government, and there is no higher trust than [for] those in the intelligence community."

He spoke about wishing that he had used legal means to seek remedy when he saw Naval Intelligence withholding information from Israel that he believed they should have shared and said he should have resigned when he found his conscience in such deep conflict with the organization he served. He expressed regret for accepting money for spying while emphasizing that personal gain was never his motive.

Finally, he spoke most movingly and poignantly of the harm he had caused Anne Henderson-Pollard. "I violated another trust," he sadly told the court, "and that was the trust of my wife. Usually when a man and woman decide to get married, it is with the assumption that each will safeguard the interests of the other … I sacrificed her … on the altar … of political ideology. There is nothing virtuous in that …

"So what I did, your honor, was that I violated, in essence, two trusts, one, to the nation—and I say it again, it doesn't matter, ally or otherwise, a law was broken—and I violated another trust, which in some respects, your honor, is a little bit more ancient and perhaps a little bit more sacred, and that is the trust that a wife implicitly has in her husband."

Anne Henderson-Pollard also spoke for herself. Wearing a gray suit and black blouse, clutching her hands over her belly, she was frail and wan. Her voice was terribly weak and many in the courtroom had trouble making out her words. "I pray to God every single day that I will be reunited with my husband," Henderson-Pollard said. "That is all I live for … He is the most wonderful man I have ever laid eyes on or met in my entire life.

"I know that he undertook his actions because he believed

that at the time he was doing good for both the United States and Israel ... My husband and I are vehemently anti-Communist and we would never do anything to harm this country ... We are dedicated and patriotic Americans and we are also loyal to Israel ...

"I love Jay very, very much and when he called to me in his eleventh hour, I responded because I felt that was what a wife should do. I felt that I was, while assisting my husband, not causing any harm to the United States at all. I did not compromise information ... I have never committed espionage in my life, nor would I ever." When Anne sat down, she was weeping. She turned to her husband for comfort.

Assistant US Attorney Charles Leeper summed up for the government. "As I was growing up," he declared in a powerful voice, "I was taught that there are, in fact, two sins that are unforgivable, and they are arrogance and deception. ... it is arrogance and deception which drove this defendant to commit the acts, the criminal acts in this case, and they are also those two character traits, arrogance and deception, typical of the way he has sought to defend and excuse the things that he has done.

"It seems that this defendant believes that if he keeps repeating the words to this court, 'This case does not involve the Soviet Union,' that your honor then will swallow the position that he is taking that he caused no harm to the national security when he sold those thousands of pages of Top Secret and code word documents. Now, in taking that position, this defendant is saying, 'Jonathan Jay Pollard is right but the Secretary of Defense, in his sworn declaration to the court, is wrong when he states that as a result of Jonathan Pollard's activities enormous damage has been wrought to the national security. Jonathan Jay Pollard is right but the President of the United States, when he issued Executive Order 12356, was wrong when he said that the disclosure, the unauthorized disclosure, of Top Secret information to any nation, would cause or could be expected to cause exceptionally grave damage to the national security.'"

Another Assistant US Attorney, David Geneson, followed

Leeper. Geneson is Jewish, a fact that ought to be irrelevant but, alas, is not in this case. "Your honor, something has happened recently which sheds a great deal of light on what is going on in court here today," Geneson said. "I had the opportunity to watch *60 Minutes* this last Sunday night, to watch an interview of the defendant Anne Henderson-Pollard … When she was asked whether she understood what she was getting into, her response was 'Very much so.'" Geneson also quoted Anne as telling the interviewer, Mike Wallace, "I feel my husband and I did what we were expected to do, what our moral obligation was as Jews, what our moral obligation was as human beings. I have no regrets about that."

When the day came for the judge to pronounce sentence, Aubrey said, "I think I should state for the record that during my entire tenure in this court, I have never had more voluminous submissions in connection with the sentencing of a defendant than I have had in this case …

"I have read all of the material once, twice, thrice, if you will, and I have given careful consideration, not only to the submissions but to argument of counsel and I pronounce sentence as follows:

"With respect to the defendant Jonathan Jay Pollard, who is being sentenced for violation of Title XVIII United States Code, Section 794c, I commit the defendant to the custody of the Attorney General or his authorized representative for his life."

People gasped at the harsh sentence. Anne Henderson-Pollard let out screams of grief. "No! No! No!" she cried even as she collapsed in a heap on the floor. Two female bailiffs helped the distraught woman to her feet. She was sobbing as she stood on rubbery legs.

"I am required by law to impose a $50 assessment," Judge Aubrey continued. "There will be no fine.

"With respect to the defendant Anne Henderson-Pollard, I commit the defendant Anne Henderson-Pollard to the custody of the Attorney General or his authorized representative on the first count of the information to a period of five years. With respect to the second count of the information, I commit the defendant to a period of five years to run concurrent by the counts. And as required by the Comprehensive Crime Control Act, I impose a $50 assessment on each count."

## Why so Harsh?

Many, perhaps most, observers were shocked that Jonathan Jay Pollard received a life sentence. After all, the government had not even asked for one. Following the plea agreement, they only requested a "substantial" term. No one else convicted of spying for an ally has gotten more than 14 years in prison. Of course, it is also true that Pollard stole an extraordinary amount of classified material but the sentence still appeared wildly disproportionate to the offense in the minds of many people.

Several reasons have been suggested for Judge Aubrey Robinson's unexpectedly severe judgement. Among them are writings by Casper Weinberger that the jurist read prior to passing sentence and an inadequate defense by Richard Hibey.

Casper Weinberger was Secretary of Defense at the time of the Pollard sentencing. He wrote a 46-page memorandum about the harm caused by the defendant for Judge Robinson. He also wrote a letter delivered by courier to the judge just the day before sentencing. The memorandum was later released to the public with many sections blacked out for reasons of national security. The letter has never been made public.

Exactly why the memorandum was submitted is in dispute. Observers first assumed that it was written and given to the judge at the request of the prosecutor, Joseph DiGenova. Later, DiGenova claimed it had been written at the invitation of Judge Robinson.

Weinberger's memorandum wrote of Pollard's actions in the most damning terms. Among many other things, it said, "It is difficult for me ... to conceive of a greater harm to national security than that caused by the defendant in view of the breadth, the critical importance to the United States and the high sensitivity of the information he sold to Israel ... I respectfully submit that any US citizen, and in particular a trusted government official, who sells US secrets to any foreign nation should not be punished merely as a common criminal. Rather the punishment imposed should reflect the perfidy of the individual actions, the magnitude of the treason committed, and the needs of national security." The word "any" is underlined in the original, reflecting Weinberger's belief that Pollard should not be given leniency because he spied for a friend.

Many critics have charged that Weinberger overreacted to the case for reasons both personal and political. Although Weinberger is part Jewish, a fact he has never hid since he has a Jewish name that he has not changed, he has been accused of harboring anti-Semitic sentiments (negative feelings about Jews by Jewish people are by no means unknown). Weinberger once worked as general counsel to the Bechtel Corporation, a company that built a chemical plant in Iraq.

Moreover, Weinberger's integrity has been seriously questioned. He was involved in the infamous Iran-Contra scandal of the Reagan administration. Indeed, Weinberger was indicted on five criminal charges in connection with Iran-Contra. The counts included obstruction of justice and perjury. He was saved from a trial because newly elected President George Bush pardoned Weinberger.

Richard Hibey is generally considered a very competent attorney. However, his family comes from Lebanon—a country that was at war with Israel. It is quite understandable that a person of Arabic background would be uncomfortable with a Jewish client who had spied on behalf of Israel. Thus, a question lingers as to whether or not it was even ethical for Hibey to accept Jay Pollard's case.

In at least one instance, Hibey showed a peculiar insensitivity toward his client's feelings. Anne was in court, clearly in pain and weeping. Judge Robinson noticed this and asked Hibey if a recess was needed. He replied that it was not. Jay Pollard shouted, "No!" Then his attorney asked for a break.

On the day of sentencing, Hibey asked and received permission to read the letter Weinberger had just sent to Judge

Robinson. However, after reading it, he did not request a continuance so that he might be able to deal with whatever points it made, something that Jay's father, Dr. Pollard, found distressing.

Dr. Pollard has alleged that Hibey deliberately acted against his client's interests, making a weak case so that Jay would receive that harsh sentence that he did. The elder Pollard claims that, "When we finally argued about what he had done, he said to me, 'Well, look what your people did to my people in Lebanon.' I fired him the next day."

Richard Hibey has refused to answer questions concerning his conduct in the Pollard case.

Of course, there are also people who believe that Jonathan Jay Pollard received a harsh sentence because his crimes merited it. Among those is journalist Seymour Hersh who published a 1999 essay in The New Yorker called "The Traitor, The Case Against Jonathan Pollard." He wrote that US "officials told me [Pollard] had done far more damage to American national security than was ever made known to the public."

However, there is an important point overlooked by Weinberger, Hersh, and the many others who call Pollard a "traitor." In the United States constitution, treason is defined as "levying war against them (the United States), or in adhering to their Enemies, giving them Aid and Comfort." Pollard never acted on behalf of an enemy of the United States.

## Politics and Pollard

The Jonathan Jay Pollard case remains a political hot potato. The question of anti-Semitism hovers over it. Is Pollard being treated so severely because he is Jewish and spied for the Jewish state? Some well-informed observers believe so.

However, in 1988, the American Jewish Congress investigated the Pollard case and concluded that anti-Semitism was not a factor in it. Said Phil Baum, their executive director, "We made an independent effort and we could not document any charges of anti-Semitism, no evidence that he was treated differently."

Jewish Americans were deeply affected by the Pollard case because it revived the old suspicion of their supposed "dual loyalties." Indeed, anti-Semites, as could be expected, pounced on the case to make scurrilous accusations against Jews as a group.

Anne Henderson-Pollard served three years and four months behind bars before being paroled in March 1990. Jay divorced her later that year. The way she found out about his plan to dissolve the marriage was especially traumatic for she was in the hospital being treated for her stomach ailment. "With tubes and IVs hooked up to my body," she recalled, "a man dressed as a hospital orderly entered my room. To my total disbelief, he dropped divorce papers on my lap."

Some close to Jay Pollard think that his reasons for filing for divorce were benign. Believing his chances for freedom were slim, he wanted Anne to get on with her life.

In 1988, Israel finally acknowledged publicly that Pollard had indeed been their agent. They also granted him citizenship. Top Israeli officials have visited Jonathan in prison. Many Israeli politicians and Jewish groups, both in Israel and in the US, clamor for his release. They are joined by many non-Jews who believe his sentence was unwarranted.

However, the American intelligence community has strongly opposed clemency for him. The data he gave to a foreign power was very sensitive, they say, and the US must discourage others who may be tempted to follow in Pollard's footsteps. Indeed, one of the reasons he may have been given such a severe sentence by Judge Robinson is the feeling that, since so many Americans are also committed Zionists, it is especially important to deter the millions of its citizens who love Israel from spying on its behalf.

Prison life is always rough. However, as Richard Hibey said in arguing for leniency, "There is hard time and there is hard time." Time for Jonathan Jay Pollard has been among the hardest possible. He is in prison as someone commonly called a "traitor." He is a Jew in a prison system in which there are few Jews and many anti-Semites. In an interview with Wolf Blitzer that took place while Pollard was awaiting trial and still in a jail, Jay told the writer that he lived in constant fear since both the Aryan Brotherhood and Black Muslims—two groups usually at each others' throats—have vowed to kill him.

Immediately after his sentencing, Pollard was transferred to the federal prison hospital in Springfield, Missouri. Here Pollard was among inmates who were severely mentally ill. He claimed to have witnessed so many prisoners cutting their own throats that "I actually have developed the ability to distinguish between the ones who are serious about killing themselves and those who are merely bent on a little self-mutilation." He spent a little over a year at the Springfield prison hospital.

Then he was taken to the prison at Marion, Illinois. Marion is considered the ultimate in maximum security and houses the infamous Mafioso John Gotti. At Marion, solitary is the rule and each prisoner must spend at least 23 of every 24 hours locked in his cell.

Pollard got himself a new legal team. Theodore B. Olson, a handsome, blonde-haired man was the head of it. Olson had been the personal attorney for President Ronald Reagan during part of the Iran-Contra affair. He would later become Solicitor General under President George W. Bush.

Olson and his associates argued before the United States Court of Appeals that their client was entitled to a new trial. This court consisted of three jurists: Stephen F. Williams, Laurence Silberman, and Ruth Bader Ginsburg. Ginsburg, of course, would become a household name when she was appointed to the US Supreme Court.

The reasons Pollard was entitled to a new trial, Olson claimed, were several. The government had secured his cooperation by promising leniency for both Pollard and his wife. However, the prosecution had, in effect, gone back on their part of the bargain by delivering such a damning summation. It failed to properly note Pollard's cooperation. Finally, the Weinberger memorandum and letter had unfairly influenced the judge into taking an unreasonably tough stand against the defendant.

The court turned down the appeal, voting two to one

against Pollard. Ironically, the only vote in his favor was that of Williams, who was also the only non-Jew on the panel.

While serving his sentence, Pollard began corresponding with Esther Zeitz, a strong supporter of his. Zeitz was Canadian and an Orthodox Jew. Eventually, the two of them fell in love through the mail. Although lacking a formal marriage, they came to regard themselves as husband and wife and Zeitz began calling herself Esther Zeitz-Pollard.

Supporters of Jay Pollard believed he stood a good chance of securing his freedom when a lame-duck President Bill Clinton began looking into last minute pardons. Their hopes were dashed for, although Clinton pardoned more than 140 people during his last days as President, Pollard was not among them. The pardoned included Whitewater figure Susan McDougal, Clinton's half-brother Roger Clinton, and, most famously, financier Marc Rich who had fled the country to avoid facing an array of charges including many counts of tax evasion and racketeering.

Many years have gone by since Jay Pollard was a free man. He is now housed at the federal penitentiary in Butner, North Carolina. His receding hairline has become a bald dome. The remaining black hairs have so mixed with white as to make his hair look a dull, dusty brown. He wears it in a longish fashion that, together with beard and mustache, give him the look of an antiquated hippie. Whether awake or asleep, he spends much of each day dreaming, as he has for so much of his life but not with such bittersweet urgency, of living in his dear Israel.

## Bibliography

Blitzer, Wolf. *Territory of Lies.* Harper Paperbacks. New York. NY, 1989.

Goldenberg, Elliot. *The Hunting Horse*. Prometheus Books, Amherst, NY, 2000.

Henderson, Bernard. *Pollard: The Spy's Story.* Alpha Books, New York, NY, 1988.

Melman, Yossi, and Raviv, Dan. *Every Spy a Prince.* Houghton Mifflin Company, Boston Massachusetts, 1990.

Shaw, Mark. *Miscarriage of Justice.* Paragon House. St. Paul, MN. 2001.

"Spy Scandal Sizzles in Israel," U. S. News & World Report, Dec. 9, 1985.

Tashian, Carl. Research Paper #1: Jonathan Pollard Spy Case on the internet.

"Widening Spy Scandals," U. S. News & World Report, Dec. 9, 1985.

"Why Israel spied on U.S.," U.S. News & World Report, June 23, 1986.

## Addendum

In July 2015, after Jonathan Pollard had served 30 years in prison, the U. S. Parole Commission granted him parole. "I am looking forward to being reunited with my beloved wife Esther," Pollard said in a statement his attorneys relayed to the public. He added words of gratitude to his supporters: "I would like to thank the many thousands of well-wishers in the United States, in Israel, and throughout the world, who provided grassroots support by attending rallies, sending letters, making phone calls to elected officials, and saying prayers for my welfare. I am deeply appreciative of every gesture, large or small." The Conference of Presidents of Major American Jewish Organizations released a statement noting that the Conference had "long sought this decision" and calling it "long overdue."

Release occurred on November 20, 2015. It was before

dawn and still dark outside, when he left the prison in Butner, North Carolina. The portly old man avoided journalists and cameras to dash to the vehicle waiting for him.

Only hours after Pollard was paroled, his attorneys were in federal court challenging the tight parole restrictions on their client. Those parole restrictions included the requirement that he have an ankle bracelet monitoring his movements and observe a curfew; that any computer he uses, including one used in employment, be subject to government inspection; and a prohibition on his leaving the United states for at least five years without permission.

Israeli Prime Minister Benjamin Netanyahu stated, "After three long and difficult decades, Jonathan has been reunited with his family." He also expressed this hope: "May this Sabbath bring him much joy and peace that will continue in the years and decades ahead."

Five years after Pollard's release, the parole itself was terminated, leaving him free to leave the United States for Israel. The Justice Department explained, "After a review of Mr. Pollard's case, the U.S. Parole Commission has found that there is no evidence to conclude that he is likely to violate the law."

Pollard stepped down in Israel in December 2020. Prime Minister Netanyahu greeted the 66-year-old man and wife Esther at the airport in Tel Aviv. "It is great that you have finally come home," Israel's leader said.

"We are ecstatic to be home at last," Pollard said. Due to the Covid pandemic, the Pollards spent two weeks in quarantine, as is Israel's policy for newcomers. After they holed up in their Jerusalem apartment for the requisite two weeks, the couple moved about the city freely. It can only be imagined what happiness this elderly man feels at residing in the country he has adored since childhood.

## References

Baker, Peter; Rudoren, Jodi. "Jonathan Pollard, American Who Spied for Israel, Released After 30 Years." *The New York Times.* Nov. 20, 2015.

Hoffman, Gil Stern. "Jonathan Pollard on forthcoming release: 'I'm looking forward to being reunited with my wife.'" *The Jerusalem Post.* July 18, 2015.

Magid, Jacob. "US terminates Jonathan Pollard's parole, ex-spy free to travel to Israel." *The Times of Israel.* Nov. 20, 2020.

TOI Staff. "Jonathan Pollard arrives in Israel, 35 years after his arrest for spying." *The Times of Israel.* Dec. 30, 2020.

# CHAPTER NINE

## The Schizophrenic Falsely Convicted
## as the Bike Path Rapist

Short, bald Altemio Sanchez, 48, sat in a booth with his wife, Kathleen, at the Solé restaurant in Buffalo, New York. Three undercover detectives sat at the bar. They had instructed the restaurant's manager not to allow employees to touch items on the table the Sanchezes shared.

The couple left the restaurant, leaving behind a good tip and a water glass and eating utensils Altemio Sanchez had used. Detectives gathered those items. They followed Sanchez to a bookstore at which he drank out of a coffee cup they also took when he left it behind.

DNA results were back the next day conclusively linking Sanchez to several rapes and three murders.

### A Nice Child

Sanchez had been born on January 19, 1958, in Puerto Rico. When he was two, the family moved to the United States mainland, living first in Florida and later in Buffalo. Sanchez never knew his father, who deserted when Sanchez was two, but was raised by his mother and a stepfather. His aunt, Margarita Torres, recalled him as a child as "nice," "serious," and "quiet."

As an adult, he worked steadily as a machinist in a factory for 23 years and enjoyed a longtime marriage with two children. He was known as a friendly, helpful neighbor. As

Kareem Fahim and David Staba report for *The New York Times,* Sanchez would "offer his generator after a storm" and help neighbors install "heated gutters." He had been a Little League coach affectionately called "Uncle Al" by the players.

However, there was a side Sanchez carefully hid from family and friends. Detectives believe that side erupted in 1981 when he raped a woman.

In 1983, he went to work at the factory he would still work at when arrested.

Police believe Sanchez raped a female jogger in 1986. According to Detective Lissa Redmond, the victim was "raped and strangled in such a way almost every blood vessel in her eyes was burst." Miraculously, she survived.

### Rapist to Murderer

It is believed he may have raped several more victims before killing one. Linda Yalem. a State University of Buffalo sophomore, was jogging on a bike path in 1990 when Sanchez raped and strangled her to death.

In 1991, Sanchez had a minor brush with the law. Believing an undercover policewoman was a prostitute, he asked, "Are you looking for some action?" He offered her money for sex. Arrested, he paid a $75 fine. Apparently, Kathleen was forgiving as their marriage continued. She may not have wanted to break up the family since they were raising two young sons. Sanchez attacked Majane Mazur, 32, a prostitute, in 1992, raping and strangling her. He left her corpse beside railroad tracks. The Bike Path Rapist left a victim alive in 1994. Then his crimes appeared to stop.

In 1996, Sanchez ran in the annual Linda Yalem Memorial Run. Perhaps he got a thrill in running in this race that was designed to honor the memory of his victim.

On September 29, 2006, Joan Diver, wife of chemistry professor Steven Diver and mother of four children, went for a jog. Steven Diver learned she had not picked their youngest child up from day care. He called 911 to report this and directed authorities to the bike path by which he had found her car.

Police combed the area around the bike path and examined her SUV.

Steven Diver organized a search party. A volunteer discovered her corpse about 70 or 80 feet from the path. She had been strangled but not raped. Detective Alan Rozansky was troubled by the double ligature marks around her neck—they reminded him of the Bike Path Rapist. Could he have resurfaced after 12 years? Investigators learned that the Diver murder took place on the sixteenth anniversary of the murder of Linda Yalem.

In "On the Trail of the bike path rapist," NBC News correspondent Keith Morrison reports, "Four police departments – the Buffalo police, police from neighboring Amherst, the state police and the county sheriff joined a special task force to find the man now who had been preying on women for more than 20 years." Morrison elaborates, "FBI profilers said that the bike path rapist most likely worked at night." DNA analysis suggested he was Hispanic.

### Freeing the Innocent, Nailing the Guilty

Detectives combing through old case files discovered very similar crimes before the first attack attributed to the Bike Path Rapist. They also learned something deeply unsettling about those earlier, similar rapes: a man, Anthony Capozzi, was imprisoned for them. In 1985, Capozzi, 29, who had schizophrenia, still lived with his parents. When police came to the Capozzi house, he was certain the mistake would soon be cleared up, and said to Mary Capozzi, his mother, "Ma, don't worry. I'll be back."

Unfortunately, Capozzi bore a striking resemblance at the time to Altemio Sanchez. Victims picked Capozzi out of line-ups as their attacker. Although Capozzi stoutly denied having attacked anyone, he readily acknowledge he suffered from a mental illness usually considered the most severe and debilitating of mental illnesses. It is not known if the jury was unduly influenced by the defendant's mental condition but he was convicted of two rapes and sentenced to 11 to 35 years imprisonment.

Capozzi went before the parole board five times. The Associated Press reports, "His refusal to admit to the crimes made it impossible to complete a mandatory sex offender program." His younger brother urged Capozzi to admit guilt and claim remorse to make it more likely he would be paroled. Capozzi refused to falsely confess.

Investigators interviewed Capozzi at Attica Prison. Those conversations left them convinced he was innocent. Morrison writes, "Their job was to catch a rapist and killer – Joan Diver's killer—not to fret about old resolved cases. Still, they put together what they'd learned about Capozzi and took it to the district attorney." District Attorney Frank Clark said "hard evidence" was necessary to overturn a conviction.

Detective Lissa Redmond commented, "We have our serial killer rapist out there and an innocent man in jail. ... we found ourselves in the middle of two investigations." Detectives requested rape kits and evidence slides from the Capozzi cases. They were told there were none. Detective Dennis Delano said this caused a "sickening" feeling.

Then detectives found a clue in the Capozzi file. It was about a 1981 rape in which Capozzi had been suspected but not charged. The victim in that attack had spotted the man she believed was her attacker driving a car a few days afterward. She took down the license plate number. However, the owner of the vehicle had an alibi. Investigators re-interviewed him. The man asked, "Is this about something that happened many years ago?" A detective said it was.

"My nephew, Altemio Sanchez, was driving the vehicle," the man informed the police.

The investigators arranged to follow Sanchez and retrieved telltale DNA from the restaurant and bookshop.

When detectives first interrogated Sanchez, he calmly maintained his innocence.

Detectives concerned about the injustice suffered by Capozzi soon received welcome news: rape kits and evidence slides from the Capozzi case were found. DNA tests proved that the rapist was not Capozzi but Sanchez. After 22 years of imprisonment, Capozzi was released. Still schizophrenic and now 50 years old, the exonerated mentally ill man went into a psychiatric center. His attorneys filed a lawsuit against New York for wrongful imprisonment that was settled in 2010 for $4.25 million. His sister Pam Guenther remarked, "This money can never make up for what this has cost Anthony and our family but it will allow us to ensure that Anthony will be well cared for the rest of his life."

On May 17, 2007, Sanchez, hobbled by ankle chains, walked slowly into the New York State Supreme Court. He pled guilty to three counts of murder. He was not charged with the rapes because the statute of limitations had expired.

Deputy District Attorney Frank A. Sedita III stated in court that Sanchez's DNA had been found on Yalem and Mazur. It had also been found in Diver's car and authorities could prove he purchased the ligatures that strangled her.

According to Sanchez's attorney, Andrew C. LoTempio, Sanchez rejected the possibility of an insanity defense. "He decided it would be best for his family and the families of the victims to save them from hearing the details of the case," LoTempio stated. "He is saving his wife and children from hearing those dirty details."

Former FBI profiler Gregg McCrary finds the above explanation improbable. "Someone like this, who's done what he's done, has no compassion for the victims," McCrary contends. "He's shown that repeatedly. No one with any compassion or empathy could possibly act like he acted against these victims. So is he doing that to protect them? I'm skeptical of that." McCrary believes Sanchez avoided a trial because "what he would be forced to face in court are his own failures, the fact that they have this airtight evidence. They got him. There's no running room here." LoTempio could not satisfactorily explain the crimes but said their seeds were planted in a troubled childhood. The boy was confused when, after his father left, various male friends began visiting his mother. LoTempio said Sanchez suffered a terrible trauma at age twelve but would not elaborate on what that trauma was. He did say, "When

[Sanchez] talks about his mom, he starts bawling." The attorney said Sanchez recalls experiencing "nasty feelings" when he was about twelve. Such feelings continued into adulthood and were especially strong when he found himself alone.

Whatever the reasons for these heinous crimes, the public can experience relief knowing their perpetrator will be imprisoned for life.

## Bibliography

"After 22 years in prison, man exonerated." *The Associated Press*. CNN.com. April 3, 2007.

Beebe, Michael. "For Bike Path Killer, Tears." *The Buffalo News*. May 19, 2007.

Brown, Scott. "Anthony Capozzi Lawsuit Settled For $4.25 Million." WGRZ.com. July 1, 2010.

Fahim, Kareem and Staba, David. "The Suspect in 3 Murders and 8 Rapes Blended In." *The New York Times*. January 18, 2007.

Morrison, Keith. "On the trail of the bike park rapist." *NBC News*. Sept. 5, 2007.

# CHAPTER TEN

## Gary Dotson, Cathleen Crowell, and the Rape that Never was

It was late July 9, 1977, and Cathleen Crowell, 16, was getting off her shift as a cashier and cook at a Long John Silver's restaurant. She was scared. She and her boyfriend, David Bierne, had engaged in sexual intercourse the previous evening. She feared a pregnancy would lead her foster parents to expel her from the nicest home she had ever lived in.

Years later, she related that her "earliest memory is of my parents fighting." In that memory, her mother was drunk, her father came home, quarrelling began, and her father stormed out of the house. Then her mother started sobbing.

Shortly after this bitter argument, Cathleen's mother entered a mental hospital. A pattern began in which Cathleen's mother regularly entered and exited such institutions. Cathleen and her two older brothers lived with Dad sometimes and with Mom at other times—but never with anyone who provided a truly nurturing environment.

When Cathleen was four, Dad brought the child to stay with an elderly relative whom Cathleen knew as an "aunt." Cathleen recalled this woman as "gruff" and unaffectionate.

At 14, Cathleen was sent to live with foster parents in Homewood, Illinois. Cathleen remembered, "I felt like all this tension was lifted from me because in this house there wasn't a lot of screaming." Unlike all the other homes in which she had lived, this one was welcoming and warm, a place of kindness and encouragement. But it was not an environment of sexual freedom. Cathleen was certain that her foster parents, for all their positive points, would not accept her if they knew she was sexually active.

## Faking Rape

That evening of July 9, 1977, Cathleen faked a rape so her foster parents would not blame her if she was pregnant. She walked into a wooded area where she pinched herself, ripped buttons off her clothes, and made scratch marks on her stomach with broken glass. She knew that she bruised easily so she felt certain that the marks she made from pinching herself could be seen by others as marks an attacker would cause.

Her plan was to tell her foster mom and dad that she had been raped but ask them not to call the police about it. She left the wood—and walked right into the glaring headlights of a police car.

Seeing a bruised teen girl with ripped clothes, the officer drove her to the station. The teenager burst into tears. Earlier she had been terrified her foster parents would kick her out for getting pregnant; now she feared they would expel her from their home for lying! She realized she had painted herself into a corner. But she could not summon the courage to tell anyone—police or foster parents—the truth. So she told authorities a story inspired by a rape scene in a popular romance she recently read, *Sweet Savage Love* by Rosemary Rogers. In that historical novel, a woman was kidnapped by three men in a carriage and raped by one of them. Cathleen updated it to a car.

She was shown mugshots and pretended to examine them. She told officers she did not see any of her attackers among the mugshots. To a police sketch artist, she gave an invented description.

## The Devastating Identification

Within days a cop saw that sketch and thought it resembled high school dropout Gary Dotson. In 1975, Gary was convicted of possession of a stolen TV and placed on a year's probation. The photograph from that arrest, along with several others, was taken to Cathleen at her foster family's house.

She looked through the photographs and handed them back, saying her attacker was not among them. The officers asked her to take a second look.

As she did, she realized that one photograph was strikingly similar to what the sketch artist had drawn. The frightened high school student thought, "If I don't identify him, they're going to know I'm lying."

She pointed to Gary's picture, saying he raped her. As she did so, she thought, "I hope this guy has a good alibi for where he was."

On July 15, 1977, Gary, 20, had finished working as a landscaper when two detectives arrived to arrest him for rape. "You gotta be kidding!" the shocked youth exclaimed. Incredulity soon turned to terror. Gary called his mother, Barbara, from the police station. "Mom, they got me on rape but I didn't rape anyone," he choked out between sobs.

It took almost two years for the case to come to trial. When it did, Cathleen testified convincingly, saying, "I can never forget that face."

State Police forensic scientist Timothy Dixon testified he had found type B blood antigens in a stain found on Cathleen's underpants that were worn the night of the alleged attack. Dixon testified that Dotson was a B secretor and B secretors are only 10% of white males. This appeared to undermine the defense that asserted Dotson was a victim of mistaken identity. Northwestern Law observes, "Because Crowell was a B secretor, only A and AB secretors could be eliminated as sources of the semen … the seminal content of the stain could have come from two out of three men in the white population—rather than the one in ten, as Dixon swore under oath."

Gary testified he had partied that night. Three friends testified he had been with them. Peter Carlson reports in *People*, "Defense attorney Paul Foxglover also stressed the inconsistencies in the prosecution's case. Crowell said her attacker was clean-shaven; Dotson had a moustache." Indeed, it was shown that, only five days after Cathleen was supposedly attacked by a clean-shaven rapist, Dotson had been sporting a thick mustache – which he could not possibly have grown in such a short time period.

The jury convicted Gary. He sobbed as he told the judge, "I didn't do it."

The judge sentenced him to 25-50 years imprisonment.

Barbara Dotson used her social security checks and factory wages to hire attorneys to appeal. When a 1981 appeal was rejected, the depressed Dotson asked friends to stop writing him. "I stopped thinking about the outside," he recalled.

While Gary endured the squalor and deprivations of prison, Cathleen finished high school and attended a junior college for a year. Then she went to New Hampshire where one of her brothers resided. She returned to Illinois to marry her high school boyfriend. The couple settled in New Hampshire. Cathleen became a Christian.

## Cathleen Comes Clean

Cathleen informed her minister's wife about the man who was unjustly imprisoned because of her lies. The wife told her husband. Cathleen told her own husband who said, "Cathy, you have to do the right thing." She told attorney John J. McLario to represent her as she came forward to clear Gary.

Gary was released on bail. On April 11, 1985, Judge Richard Samuels, who had presided at the original trial, refused to overturn the conviction and ordered Gary returned to prison. As Gary was taken, Cathleen screamed, "He's innocent!"

Judge Samuels said, "The jury and I found her [1979] testimony to be credible. I observed her demeanor in court. It was the demeanor consistent with someone who had been raped." Commenting on her 1985 testimony, he said, "She had an inability to recall certain items and she was impeached on certain items."

He also commented, "Recanting testimony is regarded as

very unreliable." As journalist Michael S. Serrill observed in *Time*, "The courts have always regarded recanted testimony with suspicion in part because there are too many bad reasons for witnesses to change their minds: intimidation, bribery, misplaced sympathy for an imprisoned or condemned offender."

70,000 Illinois citizens petitioned Governor James Thompson to free Gary. He convened a special clemency hearing in which he grilled Cathleen. At the end of it, he said he believed Gary guilty but thought six years was adequate imprisonment. Gary was paroled.

## Free Under a Cloud

Cathleen and Gary appeared on several talk shows. Hostess Phyllis George suggested the pair shake hands. They complied—weakly. She then said, "How about a hug?"

Neither of them wanted to hug the other.

Gary found freedom marred by having strangers recognize him on the street—and ask him if he was really a rapist. In November 1985, the 30-year-old parolee married bartender Camille Dardanes, 21.

Cathleen gave Gary $17,500 from Cathleen's book, *Forgive Me*. He spent it on a honeymoon and furniture. Efforts to find a job were fruitless.

In *People*, Montgomery Bower reports, "A problem drinker since the age of 15, Dotson now began to rack up various alcohol-related traffic violations." Gary recalled, "I was always so worried about doing something wrong and being sent back to prison that the pressure made me drink. And the more I drank, the more I screwed up." In August 1985, Camille swore out a complaint that Gary had assaulted her and threatened their baby. She tried to withdraw it but the parole board voted to return him to prison.

The governor released him on Christmas Eve. Again free, he learned Camille had filed for divorce.

Two days later, cops arrested Gary. Zig Zag Tavern cook

Mary Slaughter, 67, said Gary assaulted her. Brower relates, "Witnesses dispute Slaughter's claim that Dotson assaulted her, and some regulars suspect that Dotson is being blamed to keep the violence-prone bar from losing its license."

Gary's mother Barbara said, "He's never been able to shake the label of rapist." She continued, "I only hope the day will come when they can prove he was innocent of the crime."

Luckily for Gary Dotson and all who cared about him, that time came.

Attorney Thomas Breen petitioned the court to allow Cathleen's semen-stained underwear to be DNA tested. It was. The results eliminated Gary Dotson. DNA had previously been used to implicate suspects but he was the first individual ever exonerated through it.

In August 1989, Judge Thomas R. Fitzgerald told Gary, "You, sir, are discharged."

"It's over," Gary said. "It's really over." The cloud of suspicion was scientifically expunged.

The vindicated Gary Dotson was able to get a job as a construction worker. He also started college. "Now that I'm cleared, no one else can dictate my life," he noted with relief. "I won't always have to be looking over my shoulder."

Cathleen died of cancer in 2008 when she was 46. Gary made no public comment. Rob Warden, Executive Director of the Center on Wrongful Convictions at Northwestern University Law School, said, "He really wants to stay under the radar now."


## Bibliography

Brower, Montgomery. "Jailed for a Rape That Never Happened, Gary Dotson Has His Name Cleared at Last." *People*. 8/28/1989.

Brower, Montgomery. "Once Wrongly Imprisoned Gary Dotson Can't Stay Free." *People*. 1/18/1988.

Carlson, Peter. "Freedom Beckons Jailed 'rapist' Gary Dotson When Conscience Moves His 'victim' to Confess." *People*. 4/22/1985.

"Gary Dotson: The rape that wasn't—the nation's first DNA exoneration." *Northwestern Law.*

Serrill, Michael S. "Law: Why It's Tough to Take It Back." *Time*. Apr. 12, 2005.

Webb, Cathleen Crowell. "'Trying to Make It Right.'" *People*. April 29, 1985.

Webb, Cathleen. "Cathleen Webb." *People*. 12/23/1985.

"Woman who lied about rape dies." abc7chicago.com. May 20, 2008.

www.ingramcontent.com/pod-product-compliance
Lightning Source LLC
Chambersburg PA
CBHW072125270326
41931CB00010B/1674